CONCISE GUIDE TO

Psychiatry and Law
for Clinicians

Third Edition

CONCISE GUIDES

Robert E. Hales, M.D.
Series Editor

CONCISE GUIDE TO
Psychiatry and Law
for Clinicians

Third Edition

Robert I. Simon, M.D.

Clinical Professor of Psychiatry
Director, Program in Psychiatry and Law
Georgetown University School of Medicine
Washington, DC

Washington, DC
London, England

Note: The authors have worked to ensure that all information in this book concerning drug dosages, schedules, and routes of administration is accurate as of the time of publication and consistent with standards set by the U.S. Food and Drug Administration and the general medical community. As medical research and practice advance, however, therapeutic standards may change. For this reason and because human and mechanical errors sometimes occur, we recommend that readers follow the advice of a physician who is directly involved in their care or the care of a member of their family. A product's current package insert should be consulted for full prescribing and safety information.

Books published by American Psychiatric Publishing, Inc., represent the views and opinions of the individual authors and do not necessarily represent the policies and opinions of APPI or the American Psychiatric Association.

Manufactured in the United States of America on acid-free paper
04   03   02   4   3   2
Third Edition

American Psychiatric Publishing, Inc.
1400 K Street, N.W.
Washington, DC   20005
www.appi.org

Library of Congress Cataloging-in-Publication Data

Simon, Robert I.
   Concise guide to psychiatry and law for clinicians / Robert I. Simon.—3rd ed.
      p. ; cm. — (Concise guides)
   Includes bibliographical references and index.
   ISBN 1-58562-024-6 (alk. paper)
      1. Psychiatrists—Legal status, laws, etc.—United States.   2. Psychiatrists—Malpractice—
   United States.   I. Title: Psychiatry and law for clinicians.   II. Title.   III. Concise guides
   (American Psychiatric Press)

   KF2910.P75 S4 2001
   344.73′041—dc21

                                                                              00-047538

British Library Cataloguing in Publication Data

A CIP record is available from the British Library.

Dedicated to the memory of
William Anthony Nixon, M.D.,
friend, colleague, gifted psychoanalyst.

CONTENTS

3 CONFIDENTIALITY AND TESTIMONIAL PRIVILEGE 41

4 INFORMED CONSENT AND THE RIGHT TO REFUSE TREATMENT 63

LIST OF TABLES

List of Figures

INTRODUCTION

to the Concise Guides Series

The Concise Guides Series from American Psychiatric Publishing, Inc., provides, in an accessible format, practical information for psychiatrists, psychiatry residents, and medical students working in a variety of treatment settings, such as inpatient psychiatry units, outpatient clinics, consultation-liaison services, and private office settings. The Concise Guides are meant to complement the more detailed information to be found in lengthier psychiatry texts.

The Concise Guides address topics of special concern to psychiatrists in clinical practice The books in this series contain a detailed table of contents, along with an index, tables, figures, and other charts for easy access. The books are designed to fit into a lab coat pocket or jacket pocket, which makes them a convenient source of information. References have been limited to those most relevant to the material presented.

Robert E. Hales, M.D., M.B.A.
Series Editor, Concise Guides

PREFACE TO THE THIRD EDITION

> As to diseases make a habit of two things—
> to help, or at least, to do no harm.
>
> —Hippocrates, *Epidemics,* bk 1, ch 11

> Life is short, the art long, opportunity fleeting,
> experiment treacherous, judgment difficult.
>
> —Hippocrates, *Aphorisms,* sec 1,1

The practice of medicine is an honor and a privilege. It should be enjoyed. Psychiatrists, who in the past were rarely sued, are now feeling the chilling effect of increased malpractice liability. Psychiatrists complain about a new joylessness in treating patients, particularly with the advent of managed care. Some psychiatrists have left practice altogether. For other clinicians, defensive psychiatry has been raised to the level of an art form, creating an illusion of security. Although certain defensive practices are necessary in the real world and may even be incidentally helpful to patients, such practices are more often destructive to good clinical care. Nonetheless, some of the best traditions in medical practice that place the patient's welfare first are essentially defensive; for instance, the time-honored dictum to "first do no harm." Unfortunately, most of the defensive practices currently used are directed at limiting the physician's liability rather than ensuring quality care for the patient.

Ignorance of the law makes the law seem menacing. But a clinically useful knowledge of the law enhances the enjoyment of practice by making the law a working partner. Although clinicians do not need to be lawyers, they are required to practice within the law. Thus, psychiatrists should attempt to incorporate legal issues into their management of patients, turning the law to clinical account for the benefit of the patient whenever possible.

The psychiatrist has a professional and ethical duty to provide care to the patient that transcends standards imposed by the law and regulatory agencies. Psychiatrists do not take the position of being above the law's moral authority and the legal requirements governing medical practice. Whereas legal standards are fixed at a minimum level by necessity, a psychiatrist's professional and ethical duty to the patient is set at a maximum level. The difference represents the gulf that exists between the human condition and the human spirit. This book is dedicated to maintaining that spirit as embodied in the noblest traditions of medicine.

Acknowledgments.   I want to thank Robert E. Hales, M.D., M.B.A., editor of the Concise Guides Series, for asking me to update this book for a new edition. I am indebted to the legal consultants who have assisted me since the first edition of this book was published in 1988. Special thanks go to my loyal assistant, Ms. Polly Brody, whose competence and expertise made this book possible. To my patient wife, who has graciously and unflinchingly supported my clinical writing, I express my loving appreciation.

CLINICAL PSYCHIATRY AND THE LAW

■ OVERVIEW OF THE LAW

The law's influence on medicine can be described as regulatory in nature. The law provides a means of settling disputes between patient and provider (individual or institution). Court decisions, legislative statutes, and administrative guidelines all play roles in determining the rules and regulations by which psychiatrists conduct their clinical practices.

The most common example of the interjection of the law into medicine occurs when patients sue their physicians for malpractice. A malpractice suit is defined as a tort action. A tort is a civil wrong—a noncriminal or non-contract-related wrong—committed by one individual (defendant) who has caused some injury to a second individual (plaintiff) (1).[1] A lawsuit or action in tort is a request for compensation for the damages that have occurred. Malpractice is a tort committed as a result of negligence by physicians or other health care professionals that leads to patient injury.

Psychiatric malpractice is a growing area of tort law. This growth reflects both the progress made in psychiatric care and the psychological sophistication of the public and the judiciary. As society in-

---

[1] For legal definitions, see Appendix B: Glossary of Legal Terms.

creases its use of psychiatric services, it manifests a greater willingness to hold psychiatrists accountable for the care they provide.

Malpractice Claims in the Managed Care Era

Malpractice claims are often brought because bad outcomes combine with bad feelings (2). A good doctor-patient relationship is the most effective natural defense against being sued. Ideally, managed care organizations (MCOs) are designed to provide quality medical care in a cost-effective manner. However, good clinical care may be undermined by negative incentives and other managed care cost-cutting policies that generate role conflicts for physicians between being patient advocates and being guardians of society's resources (3). Psychiatrists are often placed in a conflicting position because of these competing interests, which can jeopardize the doctor-patient relationship and lead to the provision of substandard care.

Managed care has transformed the relationship between psychiatrist and patient. Psychiatrists are now treating chronically, severely ill patients for shorter lengths of time. Much less time is available to develop a therapeutic alliance with the patient. Split treatments in which psychiatrists prescribe medications while nonmedical therapists conduct psychotherapy are common. The psychiatrist usually shares the liability burden in a split-treatment situation if a malpractice claim is brought.

Other factors can heighten liability risks. Psychiatrists who have high-volume practices or who practice at a number of locations are at increased risk of being sued. The psychiatrist who sees more than 25 patients in a day is at a disproportionately increased risk of being sued. Although the psychiatrist with a high-volume practice has a greater chance of encountering a patient who begins litigation, increased liability exposure appears to be more a function of the decreased time spent with the patient than the nature of the patient. Supervision of other professionals also raises psychiatrists' risk of being sued. Psychiatrists are increasingly providing primary care, managing patients with a variety of acute medical illnesses as well as chronic conditions such as hypertension or diabetes. Psychiatrists are also specializing in geriatric pharmacology, adolescent addiction medicine, pain management, treatment of dissociative identity disorder, and treatment of adult children of alcoholics (4). Suits alleging that therapists have implanted false memories of childhood sexual abuse are burgeoning. Such specialization increases the risk of malpractice suits, particularly if psychiatrists practice outside their areas of training or expertise. All of these factors, combined with failed tort reform legislation, have created a risky litigation environment for psychiatrists.

The changing health care marketplace leaves psychiatrists more vulnerable to suits while simultaneously undermining their relationships with patients. The potential occasions for bad feelings and bad outcomes are many (e.g., poor communication, a perceived lack of caring or interest, unavailability during critical events, a perceived unresponsiveness to the patient's particular treatment needs) (5).

When a patient has borderline personality disorder, there are numerous clinical challenges and associated liability risks in the managed care setting. Suicide, violence toward others, the capacity to induce therapist boundary violations, alcohol and drug abuse, impulsive actions, comorbidity, and an unstable transference contribute to a tenuous therapeutic alliance. The result is an increased risk of a bad outcome and bad feelings in both the psychiatrist and the patient. Patients presenting with such challenges usually cannot be treated effectively under current MCO restrictions of health care coverage. These patients should be informed of the need for more intensive care than is available under most managed care plans. The psychiatrist may contract to treat the patient outside the plan (if permitted by the MCO) or make an appropriate referral.

Most MCOs and their peer reviewers are relatively immune from legal liability by state and federal law (6). The risk of suits against managed care companies for the negligent performance of utilization review has been suppressed by the Employee Retirement Income Security Act of 1974 (ERISA) (7). ERISA preempts state laws and prohibits negligence claims in cases involving employer-sponsored health plans. Recently, a number of court cases have held that the intent of ERISA was not to abolish the right of individuals to sue for negligence.

Managed care contracts that contain *hold harmless* and indemnification clauses are a source of potential trouble for psychiatrists. These clauses attempt to insulate MCOs from malpractice judgments against psychiatrists while also placing them in the position of acting as insurers for third-party payers. Psychiatrists should consider obtaining legal counsel before signing any contract that contains such clauses.

Malpractice and Psychiatry: Incidence

There has been a steady rise in malpractice litigation against psychiatrists and other mental health professionals since the early 1970s. In 1975, the annual incidence of claims against psychiatrists was about 1 in 45, or approximately 2.25% (8). In the 1980s, a psychiatrist's chance of being sued in any single year was 1 in 25 (4%) (9). Thus, the rate of occurrence nearly doubled. Through 1995, however, the odds increased to approximately 1 out of every 12 psychiatrists (4). In some states, psychiatrists were sued at the rate of 1 in 6 every year.

The incidence of claims against psychiatrists still remains much lower than that of claims against other medical specialists. Although the potential for malpractice suits remains high for psychiatrists who treat suicidal and violent patients, the plaintiff success rate of these and other malpractice actions is only 2 or 3 out of every 10 claims that are litigated. The rising incidence of malpractice claims against psychiatrists is expected to maintain its current pace. The creative expansion of legal theories of liability against psychiatrists on which relief may be granted will likely continue well into the twenty-first century.

Malpractice Litigation: The Basics

Negligence

The fundamental concept underlying a malpractice action is that of *negligence*. Negligence can be defined as the psychiatrist doing something that he or she should not have done (i.e., commission) or omitting to do something that he or she should have done (i.e., omission).

When health care professionals commit an act of negligence that results in injury to a patient under their care, they may be held liable for malpractice or some other civil action. Civil suits or tort actions against psychiatrists, occasionally referred to as psychiatric malpractice actions, are based on the same legal principles that underlie traditional medical malpractice claims.

Breach of Contract and Other Legal Actions

Although civil claims typically arise because of negligence, they may also result from a breach of contract or from an intentional tort. A *breach of contract* can occur if a patient undertakes treatment based on an agreement in which the psychiatrist promises some result but then fails to produce it. An *intentional tort is* any act willfully committed that the law has declared as wrong (e.g., treating patients without their consent). A fourth type of claim may be based on violations of a patient's civil rights pursuant to federal and state law (e.g., discriminatory treatment practices against institutionalized patients).

Standard of Reasonable Care

Even though a psychiatrist's act is not willful, if because of ignorance or carelessness the act injures a patient, liability is not excused. The law presumes and holds all physicians, including psychiatrists, to a standard of reasonable care when dealing with their patients. This standard of reasonableness has been described as follows:

> In the absence of a special contract, a physician or surgeon is not required to exercise extraordinary skill and care or the highest degree of skill and care possible; but as a general rule he [or she] is only required to possess and exercise the degree of skill and learning ordinarily possessed and exercised, under similar circumstances, by the members of his [or her] profession in good standing, and to use ordinary and reasonable care and

diligence, and his [or her] best judgment, in the application of his [or her] skill to the case. (10)

This standard of care is a legal duty owed by all physicians to their patients once a doctor-patient relationship has been established. The standard of care is the same for residents as it is for attending physicians. If a psychiatrist acts or fails to act, and the resulting care provided to the patient is below this standard, then the duty of care is said to be breached. If a patient is injured as a proximate (direct) result of that breach of care, then an action for malpractice may be available.

Respected Minority Rule

Innovation is critically important to new diagnostic and treatment developments in psychiatry (11). American psychiatry has welcomed credible treatments that have held promise for the alleviation of mental suffering. The causes of most mental disorders are unknown. A professional climate that encourages innovation in research and treatment offers the most productive opportunities for progress. Two legal issues that are applied to the use of innovative therapy are the doctrine of informed consent and whether the innovative therapy represents a departure from standard and accepted practice.

The legal measure of liability relies on standards that determine what is customary. A treatment that is found not to be customary does not necessarily indicate liability. Proving that a treatment is customary usually precludes liability if the treatment was not negligently rendered. Customary treatment does not mean that a majority of therapists use it. Although customary practice is important in determining the standard of care, the judge or jury ultimately decides what society expects of the parties.

In some jurisdictions, it is sufficient to show that a therapy is supported by a *respectable minority* of therapists (12). Unless egregious, even those forms of psychotherapy that would not be employed by most therapists probably fall within the *respected minority rule*. This rule states that a therapist is free to choose from any of the available schools of therapy, even ones that most physicians would not use, if a respected minority of therapists would employ the same therapies under the same circumstances (13).

Causation

When a psychiatrist deviates from a standard of care in the diagnosis and treatment of a patient and the patient alleges damage, a malpractice action will not succeed unless the damage was actually caused by the deviation from the standard of care.

The law divides causation into two categories: cause-in-fact and legal, or proximate, cause. Cause-in-fact is expressed by the *but for rule* and asks the question: but for the conduct of the psychiatrist, would the patient have suffered the injury? If the injury would have occurred without the psychiatrist's conduct, no causation exists. If there is more than one cause of injury, the but-for test might deny recovery in multiple causation.

In addition to the cause-in-fact, the defendant's act or omission must be the proximate cause of the injury. Proximate, or legal, cause exists when an uninterrupted chain of events occurs from the time of the defendant's negligent conduct to the time of the plaintiff's injury. Proximate cause is a legal term of art, not a scientific construct. Intervening causes may occur after the time of the negligent act but combine with the negligent act to cause injury to the plaintiff. In short, the defendant is liable for harm caused by foreseeable intervening forces. For example, a psychiatrist who is initially negligent by harming a patient is also usually liable for aggravation of the patient's condition by the negligent conduct of a subsequent treating physician.

Causation of emotional and mental illness is imperfectly understood. To distinguish emotional harm allegedly caused by the psychiatrist's negligent act or omission from the natural course of the disorder or from other causes in the patient's life can be very difficult.

Compensatory, Nominal, and Punitive Damages

If a patient is successful in suing a psychiatrist, the damages awarded are commensurate with the extent of the injury sustained.

The injury may be physical, psychological, or both. There are generally three types of damages: compensatory, nominal, and punitive. In a successful malpractice action, compensatory damages normally are awarded. This type of award represents the amount of compensation to replace and restore the loss or injury to the plaintiff. Wrongdoers are legally responsible for all natural and direct consequences of their acts. In some extreme situations, punitive damages may be awarded. In a malpractice action, punitive damages are awarded only when the defendant's conduct is considered willful, wanton, malicious, or reckless. The purpose of punitive damages is to punish the wrongdoer rather than to compensate the victim. Mere negligence is insufficient to merit an award of punitive damages. Nominal damages are awarded when plaintiffs suffer no actual harm or loss but only a technical injury to their legal rights. Nominal damages are rarely awarded in malpractice suits.

Major Areas of Liability

Table 1–1 shows the recent allegations of malpractice experienced by the Psychiatrist's Purchasing Group (14), the liability insurer of members of the American Psychiatric Association. As in all mal-

TABLE 1–1. **Frequency of primary allegations for claims filed between 1984 and 1999**

Primary allegation	Frequency of claims (%)
Incorrect treatment	24.3
Incorrect diagnosis	14.7
Suicide	12.3
Drug reaction	7.4
Improper supervision	4.8
Unnecessary commitment	4.2
Undue familiarity	3.3
Breach of confidentiality	2.2
Risk management/other	26.7

practice cases, proof of the standard of care and of any alleged deviation is usually established by expert testimony. Typically, the psychiatric expert testifies about what a reasonably qualified psychiatrist would have done in a similar situation. In cases where the alleged substandard conduct is so outrageous as to constitute gross negligence, the courts have held that no expert testimony is required. The essential elements or "four Ds" of a malpractice claim are listed in Table 1–2.

Courts recognize the imperfections of psychiatric medicine and, accordingly, do not hold clinicians liable for mere mistakes or failing to produce a "cure." Careful documentation that reasonable care was provided in the diagnosis and treatment of the patient provides a powerful defense against a malpractice claim, even if the patient is harmed. The law does not require perfect treatment.

With more than 450 types of therapy identified and innovation a common requisite to treating patients with difficult illnesses, courts have been restrained in declaring a psychiatrist negligent simply because his or her treatment methods differ from those of mainstream psychiatrists. Policies and standards established by the various national organizations, such as the American Psychiatric Association, by the professional literature, and by the acceptance of the different methods of at least a respected minority of professionals will protect the innovative psychiatrist (11). Finally, common sense goes a long way in distinguishing between an innovative treatment approach and a deviation in the requisite standard of care.

TABLE 1–2.   **The four Ds of a malpractice claim**

A doctor-patient relationship must be present, creating the following:
- DUTY of care.
- DEVIATION from the standard of care must have occurred.
- DAMAGE to the patient must have occurred.
- The damage must have occurred DIRECTLY as a result of the deviation from the standard of care.

Defenses

Although each legal defense is case specific, two of the more common defenses deserve mention. First, all civil lawsuits have a statute of limitations that requires that legal action be commenced within a prescribed period of time following the discovery or occurrence of the allegedly negligent act. If no lawsuit is filed within the requisite time period, the suit is barred unless a recognized exception exists that suspends the statute of limitation (15). The time within which a lawsuit can be brought is governed by the laws of the state where the suit is being brought (16).

Second, the use of reasonable professional judgment is a *mainstay defense* (17). The credibility of this defense depends on the physician's compliance with the standard of care as documented by his or her own records. As stated above, the law does not require psychiatrists and other physicians to provide perfect care. For example, in *Centeno v. New York* (18), the court ruled that the decision to release a patient from the hospital and to place the patient on convalescent outpatient status prior to the patient's suicide was not a negligent act but was based on reasonable medical judgment.

■ CLINICAL MANAGEMENT OF LEGAL ISSUES

Standard of Care in Managed Care Settings

It is important for psychiatrists to distinguish between *standard of care* and *quality of care*. Psychiatrists must practice according to acceptable standards of care. The standard of care is a duty owed by psychiatrists to their patients. Quality of care refers to the adequacy of the total care the patient receives from psychiatrists, the treatment team, other mental health providers, reviewers, coordinators of care, and payers. Quality of care is also substantially influenced by patients' health care decisions and the allocation and availability of psychiatric services. The quality of care provided patients may fall below, equal, or even exceed the standard of care. For example, a short hospital stay might be sufficient to treat a patient who is in a transitory suicidal crisis, but a similar stay would likely represent substandard care for a patient with schizophrenia and command hallucinations dictating violence toward others. Short hospitalizations are not appropriate for every patient. Quality care for one patient is not quality care for all patients.

When the quality of care that patients receive under managed care falls below the professional standard of care that psychiatrists are required to uphold, conflict results. Psychiatrists must nonetheless provide competent diagnosis, treatment, and patient management. Although MCOs can establish quality-of-care policies and decide what level of care they will financially support, the standard of care is determined by how the average psychiatrist practices under the same or similar circumstances (19). Psychiatrists are worried that courts will not take into account resource limitations imposed by managed care but will continue to apply the more expansive standards of care established under the traditional insurance system (20).

The standard of care in psychiatry has always been diverse and in flux. This is entirely appropriate, given that the causes of many mental illnesses are unknown and therapeutic innovation offers the hope of finding new and effective treatments (11). Such a view is therapeutically ambitious and humanistic. On the other hand, MCO treatment policies are cost-driven and therapeutically restrictive according to criteria of medical necessity. The meaning of the term *medically necessary* is elusive; it is a proprietary term that governs payment decisions under various private and public medical coverage systems (21). Psychiatrists who are in doubt about the quality of care provided under managed care policies must look to the patient's best interests, uphold their professional and ethical responsibilities to patients, and take the economic consequences if necessary (22). Most physicians support cost containment, efficiency, and accountability measures provided that these measures do not interfere with the doctor-patient relationship and the provision of good clinical care (23).

The practice of medicine is a calling, not a business. Psychiatrists must not forget their professional duties to patients whom they must serve. Managed care policies have influenced and will continue to influence the quality and, in some instances, the standard of care in psychiatry. In the future, professional practice standards may be largely determined by managed care initiatives that reflect the evolving social, economic, and political policies of our society. If this happens, medicine will have lost much of its professional and moral authority.

Clinical Risk Management

Clinical risk management is defined as the combining of professional expertise and knowledge of the patient with a clinically useful understanding of the legal issues governing psychiatric practice. The purpose of clinical risk management is to provide optimal care for the patient, and only secondarily to reduce the risk of legal liability. A clinically useful understanding of the legal requirements governing the practice of psychiatry is essential because it helps guard against unduly defensive practices that can keep the clinician from utilizing the full spectrum of effective treatments.

Given the current litigation climate, only the most naive physician would not consider taking some defensive measures when treating patients with certain problems. For instance, failure to carefully and contemporaneously document risk assessments made in the course of treating a patient who is suicidal or violent may leave the psychiatrist vulnerable in any subsequent litigation. Moreover, careful record keeping is important to the provision of good clinical care. The key is to know when and how to apply defensive measures and, at the very least, to be certain that patients are not harmed by such practices (24).

Some defensive practices are rooted in the best conservative traditions of medicine and are not necessarily reactions to litigation fears. The fundamental principle "first do no harm" is quintessentially defensive, although it originates from the physician's basic concern for the patient's welfare. The use of careful documentation and appropriate consultation represents good clinical practice on behalf of the patient while also providing a shield against litigation. The unduly defensive psychiatrist, however, puts his or her own welfare first in the course of treating the patient. Clinical risk management is a means for practitioners to achieve greater freedom from destructive fears of litigation.

Positive and Negative Defensive Psychiatry

In general, *defensive psychiatry* refers to any act or omission by a psychiatrist that is performed not for the benefit of the patient but solely to avoid malpractice liability or to provide a legal defense against a malpractice claim. Defensive psychiatry comes in two forms—positive and negative—with some psychiatrists practicing both. *Positive* and *negative* do not refer to a value judgment but rather to acts of commission and omission. The positive defensive psychiatrist orders procedures and treatments to prevent or limit liability. These actions may or may not accord with good clinical practice. The negative defensive psychiatrist avoids procedures or treatments out of fear of being sued even though the patient might benefit from these interventions. This latter course is particularly unconscionable and potentially catastrophic. Defensive practices do not automatically shield the psychiatrist against malpractice claims. On the contrary, substandard treatment may result. Thus, the unduly defensive psychiatrist is paradoxically more exposed to a lawsuit.

Destructive Defensive Practices: Some Examples

Examples of defensive psychiatry gone astray are legion. For example, the patient with a serious refractory depression that is unresponsive to drugs may be deprived of electroconvulsive therapy because of unfounded fears of increased liability. The patient experiencing suicidal ruminations who could be treated safely as an outpatient but instead is hospitalized for purely defensive reasons is poorly served. The psychiatrist who prescribes homeopathic doses of medication in the vain hope of helping the patient without risking any harm abrogates his or her professional and legal duty to provide good clinical care to the patient. The patient is unnecessarily exposed to side effects from the drug without the possibility of receiving any benefit. As a result, the patient may continue to suffer and remain impaired. Dissatisfaction with professional services is frequently an unintended consequence of such practices.

In another example, duty-to-warn immunity statutes in some states permit discharge of this duty by warning an endangered third party and calling the police. More clinically appropriate interventions such as starting or changing medications, scheduling more frequent appointments, or pursuing hospitalization may be overlooked by the clinician who reflexively seeks shelter from legal liability under these statutes.

Beyond Legal Requirements

Effective psychiatric treatment must address the tension between clinical practice and legal requirements. The clinician needs a clear working knowledge of the relevant legal requirements governing professional practice. For example, some courts have concluded that what is not documented has not been done. Maintaining an adequate clinical record can be crucial in the defense of a malpractice suit. This bit of legal knowledge can go a long way toward easing the anxieties of therapists who fear being second-guessed by plaintiffs' experts in a court of law. Yet it is disconcerting to discover how often mental health professionals do not keep even minimally acceptable records.

Whenever a legal issue arises in clinical practice, every opportunity should be taken to turn it to therapeutic account for the patient. For example, the doctrine of informed consent is a legal requirement. Before administration of a neuroleptic medication, the patient should be informed about the reasonable risks and benefits that can be expected. Disclosing information in a clinically supportive manner can enhance the therapeutic alliance with the patient.

Psychiatrists have a professional and ethical obligation to provide care to their patients that transcends legal and regulatory standards. Legal standards are minimalist by necessity. They must accord with the human condition. The law measures the physician's provision of care according to the average-clinician, reasonable care standard. Physicians, on the other hand, assume professional and ethical obligations to treat patients to the best of their abilities and according to the highest Hippocratic tradition of the medical profession. For example, the traditional rule of tort law states that a person has no duty to come to the aid of another in distress. A distinct exception to this rule has been created by a number of court decisions and some state statutes that impose a duty on therapists (usually psychiatrists and psychologists) to protect endangered persons from the violent acts of their patients. The no-duty rule is unacceptable for most psychiatrists. The psychiatrist does not act in situations where third parties are endangered by patients strictly from an obligation to meet the law's requirements. Before these legal duties were imposed, psychiatrists protected others who were endangered by their patients by various clinical means and, when all else failed, sought involuntary treatment for violent patients. Similarly, most practitioners maintain a level of confidentiality that far exceeds the current requirements of confidentiality statutes.

■ REFERENCES

1. Keeton WP, Dobb DB, Keeton RE, et al: Prosser and Keeton on Torts, 5th Edition. St Paul, MN, West Publishing, 1984, p 7
2. Appelbaum PS, Gutheil TG: Clinical Handbook of Psychiatry and the Law, 2nd Edition. Baltimore, MD, Williams and Wilkins, 1991, pp 173–174
3. Pellegrino ED: Rationing health care: the ethics of medical gatekeeping. J Contemp Health Law Policy 2:23–45, 1986
4. Benefacts: a message from the APA-sponsored Professional Liability Insurance Program. Psychiatric News 31 (suppl 8):26, April 1996
5. Levinson W: Physician-patient communication: a key to malpractice prevention. JAMA 272:1619–1620, 1994
6. Stone AA: Paradigms, pre-emption, and stages: understanding the transformation of American psychiatry by managed care. Int J Law Psychiatry 18:353–387, 1995

7. Employee Retirement Income Security Act of 1974 (ERISA), 1991. 29 U.S.C.A. §§1001–1461 (1988 and Supp. 1991)

8. American Medical Association: Malpractice in Focus. Chicago, IL, American Medical Association, 1975

9. Perr I: Psychiatric malpractice issues, in Legal Encroachment in Psychiatric Practice. Edited by Rachlin S. San Francisco, CA, Jossey-Bass, 1983, pp 47–59

10. 70 CJS Physicians and Surgeons §41 (1967)

11. Simon RI: Innovative psychiatric therapies and legal uncertainty: a survival guide for clinicians. Psychiatric Annals 23:473–479, 1993

12. Reisner R, Slobogin C: Law and the Mental Health System, 2nd Edition. St Paul, MN, West Publishing, 1990, p 75

13. Malcolm JG: Treatment Choices and Informed Consent: Current Controversies in Psychiatric Malpractice Litigation. Springfield, IL, Charles C Thomas, 1988, pp 49–50

14. Program Participants Report: 1998–1999. Arlington, VA, Psychiatrists' Publishing Group

15. For example, Bolen v United States, 727 F Supp 1346 (D Idaho 1989)

16. See generally King JF: The Law of Medical Malpractice in a Nutshell. St Paul, MN, West Publishing, 1986, p 267

17. Simon RI: Clinical risk management of suicidal patients: assessing the unpredictable, in American Psychiatric Press Review of Clinical Psychiatry and the Law, Vol 3. Edited by Simon RI. Washington, DC, American Psychiatric Press, 1992, pp 3–63

18. Centeno v New York, 48 AD 2d 812, 369 NYS 2d 710 (1975), aff'd 40 NY 2d 932, 389 NYS 2d, 837, 358 NE 2d 520 (1976)

19. Simon RI: Discharging sicker, potentially violent psychiatric inpatients in the managed care era: standard of care and risk management. Psychiatric Annals 27:726–733, 1997

20. Hoge SK: APA resource document, 1: the professional responsibilities of psychiatrists in evolving health care systems. Bulletin of the American Academy of Psychiatry Law 24:393–406, 1996

21. Kuder AU, Kuntz MBF: Who decides what is medically necessary? in Controversies in Managed Mental Health Care. Edited by Lazarus A. Washington, DC, American Psychiatric Press, 1996, pp 159–177
22. Simon RI: Psychiatrists' duties in discharging sicker and potentially violent inpatients in the managed care era. Psychiatr Serv 49:62–67, 1998
23. Abrams FR: The doctor with two heads: the patient versus the costs. N Engl J Med 328:975–976, 1993
24. Simon RI: A clinical philosophy for the (unduly) defensive psychiatrist. Psychiatric Annals 17:197–200, 1987

2

THE DOCTOR-PATIENT RELATIONSHIP

■ OVERVIEW OF THE LAW

The establishment of the doctor-patient relationship creates the professional duty of care owed to a patient. In any lawsuit for medical malpractice, the duty of care is a primary issue. As a general rule, a psychiatrist in private practice may choose whomever he or she wishes to treat (1). Similarly, psychiatrists have no legal obligation to provide emergency medical care absent any contractual or statutory obligation. Once a psychiatrist has agreed (explicitly or implicitly) to accept a patient, ethical and legal obligations are created to provide continuous care until appropriate termination.

The Legal Foundation for the Doctor-Patient Relationship

The legal foundation for recognizing the doctor-patient relationship is based on contract law. The expressed or implied acceptance by a psychiatrist to treat a patient in exchange for something of value (e.g., a fee) serves to create a recognizable relationship with corresponding duties and rights for both parties. The duty of care is not predicated on the payment of a fee. It derives from the "agreement" by the physician to render services. Thus, the contract or agreement created is based upon a *fiduciary,* not a financial, relationship. Initiating the professional relationship does not create any guarantee of specific results, but rather implies a promise that the psychiatrist will exercise reasonable care (2).

When a psychiatrist is performing an evaluation rather than treatment, a doctor-patient relationship is generally not created. If the benefit of the examination inures to a third party such as an employer, insurance company, or the courts, usually no doctor-patient relationship is found. If, however, some benefit is deemed to accrue to the examinee through even a hint of advice or treatment, then a doctor-patient relationship may be established.

Psychiatrists who employ others or supervise other professionals may be held liable for their negligence despite having no direct contact with the patient. Under the doctrine of *respondeat superior,* a supervising or employing psychiatrist is considered to be the *master* (legally speaking) of those under his or her direction, and is *vicariously liable* for their acts. Vicarious liability occurs when the professional had the right or ability to control the subordinate (e.g., supervisee or employee), and the subordinate's negligence occurred within the scope of his or her employment or supervision.

Fiduciary Role: Avoiding Double Agentry

A psychiatrist must always act with good faith, trust, and strict confidence when dealing with a patient. This obligation is implicit within the contractual arrangement and inherent in all psychiatrist-patient relationships as an ethical and fiduciary duty. Persons acting as a fiduciary are not permitted to use the professional relationship for their personal benefit. Psychiatrists must be particularly careful not to exploit transference. Double-agent roles frequently arise when psychiatrists attempt to serve simultaneously the patient and an agency, institution, or society. These conflicts are examined in greater detail as they arise in the clinical management section of each chapter.

Termination and Abandonment

Once a professional relationship has been created, a psychiatrist is legally required to provide treatment until the relationship is properly terminated. The failure to adhere to this rule by abruptly or negligently terminating treatment leaves the psychiatrist susceptible to a suit for abandonment, if any harm to the patient results from the abandonment. Generally, the psychiatrist-patient relationship is terminated in one of the following ways:

- A unilateral act of the patient that indicates a withdrawal from treatment
- Mutual agreement that services are no longer needed or useful
- A unilateral act of the psychiatrist that terminates treatment

Even though a psychiatrist does not have a legal right to discharge a patient at will, a duty of care does not exist forever. If there is no emergency or threatened crisis (e.g., threatened suicide or danger to the public), generally a psychiatrist can safely terminate treatment by following certain procedures (Table 2–1).

Abandonment may be either overt or implied (failure to attend, monitor, or observe the patient). In negligence cases, expert testimony is required to establish the standard of care. When the abandonment is egregious, no expert may be necessary. Many courts have widened the concept of abandonment to include situations in which delay and inattention in providing care caused the patient injury, termed *constructive abandonment* (i.e., as if actual abandonment had occurred) (3).

Finally, psychiatrists risk suit for abandonment if they make themselves inaccessible to patients, particularly if a crisis is occurring or is foreseeable. The following have all been construed by the courts as abandonment:

- Failure to provide patients with a way to contact the psychiatrist between sessions

---

TABLE 2–1. **Proper termination of patient treatment**

The patient is given reasonable notice.
The patient is assisted in finding another therapist.
Appropriate records and information are provided to the new therapist as requested by the patient.

- Failure to maintain reasonable contact with a hospitalized patient
- Failure to provide adequate clinical coverage when away on vacation

■ CLINICAL MANAGEMENT OF LEGAL ISSUES

Creation of the Doctor-Patient Relationship

No professional duty of care is owed a patient unless a psychiatrist-patient relationship exists. Once that relationship is established, however, duties attach, and the psychiatrist can be held liable for damages that are proximately caused by any breach of duty. Whether a psychiatrist-patient relationship legally exists is a factual determination. If the existence of such a relationship is disputed, the courts determine whether the patient entrusted care to the psychiatrist and whether the psychiatrist indicated acceptance of that care. Most often, a psychiatrist-patient relationship is established knowingly and voluntarily by both parties. Occasionally, however, a professional relationship is created with a patient unwittingly.

Although the law imposes no duty on physicians to take a prospective patient, courts have been quick to establish a doctor-patient relationship. Several examples are instructive. Giving advice, making interpretations, or prescribing medication during the course of an independent medical evaluation may create a doctor-patient relationship (4). When an unexamined person has been provided care over the telephone, if that person has the expectation that he or she is accepted for treatment, a doctor-patient relationship may be created (5). Similarly, certain acts by a physician, such as offering to prescribe medication over the telephone, have been construed to constitute a continuation of treatment for purposes of determining the date of accrual of a medical malpractice claim (6) (Table 2–2). When a prospective patient who has phoned for an appointment requires emergency psychiatric care before the date of the initial visit, he or she should be seen as soon as possible. If for valid reasons this is not possible, the person should be referred immediately to another psychiatrist or emergency facility.

TABLE 2–2.	**Actions by therapists that may create a doctor-patient relationship**

Giving advice to prospective patients, friends, and neighbors
Making psychological interpretations during an independent evaluation
Writing a prescription or providing sample medications
Supervising treatment by a nonmedical therapist
Having a lengthy phone conversation with a prospective patient
Treating an unseen person by mail
Giving a prospective patient an appointment
Telling walk-in prospective patients that they will be seen
Acting as a substitute therapist
Providing treatment during an evaluation

Judicial decisions holding therapists liable to nonpatient third persons have increased in recent years. As a result, family members peripherally involved in the therapy of the "basic patient" sometimes try to assert a relationship with the therapist or claim an expanded duty owed to them as nonpatient third parties. This issue is separate from the therapist-patient relationship established with all members in formal family or group therapy. A number of "recovered memory" suits have been brought by families against psychiatrists and other mental health professionals based on the reasoning that the clinician's support for the validity of the memories creates a new duty to the family. Unless a formal part of the patient's therapy, families are usually not considered parties to the case (7). Family members who are brought into the patient's treatment in a brief, adjunctive role must be clearly informed that they are not being seen as patients. If therapy for other family members is indicated, they should be referred elsewhere for treatment.

Psychiatrists are often asked by friends, family members, neighbors, or colleagues for clinical advice or medications. These quasi-medical relationships are fraught with serious problems (8). Psychiatrists who wish to provide such services in these situations must understand they may be creating a doctor-patient relationship with an attendant duty of care. As the psychiatrist would do with any other patient, medical records should be maintained documenting that the standard of care was met in evaluation, diagnosis, and indications for treatment.

Ordinarily, physicians who perform pre-employment or insurance examinations do not establish a sufficient duty to the patient to incur malpractice liability. However, psychiatrists can be sued for performing negligent examinations or for defamation if untrue, damaging statements are made about the examinee. Therapists who examine litigants at the request of the court are typically immune from liability even if they are negligent. Psychiatrists appointed by the court in civil commitment cases are generally protected from liability as well. However, if the psychiatrist medically certifies her or his own patient, liability claims may arise if the commitment was negligently initiated. (This issue is examined further in Chapter 7, Involuntary Hospitalization.)

"Curbside consultations" with colleagues do not usually create a duty of care to the patient. Informal advice given in response to a colleague's question does not usually create liability exposure. If, however, a psychiatrist agrees to provide a consultation to the patient or reviews a patient's chart and renders an opinion, a legal duty of care may be created. Consultants such as pathologists or radiologists may not actually see the patient but are considered to be rendering treatment.

Patient Evaluation

When seeing a prospective patient for the first time, psychiatrists may want to assume a strict evaluation stance for the first few sessions. In actual clinical practice, this may not always be possible. The psychiatrist usually does not know the extent of the prospective patient's disturbance prior to seeing the patient for the first time. Some individuals show floridly psychotic symptoms during the initial visit and may be a danger to themselves or others. The psychiatrist may decide to therapeutically intervene and forgo the initial evaluation period.

What should psychiatrists do if they do not want to accept the patient for treatment? Psychiatrists often feel helpless and trapped when confronted with a new patient in a crisis who requires immediate attention. Psychiatrists who do not want to accept the patient for treatment should attempt to find immediate competent help. In some instances, this may require accompanying the patient to a hospital or emergency room. Professional ethics and concern for the patient who is in a crisis dictate that the patient be assisted in obtaining immediate care (9).

Psychiatrists may find malpractice concerns to be an additional incentive to see prospective patients for a number of evaluation sessions. Psychiatrists have become increasingly vulnerable to suits by patients seen for a short period of time, even less than 30 days. Eight out of every 10 persons who commit suicide pay a visit to a physician within 6 months of their attempt. Fifty percent of individuals who commit suicide have seen a physician within 1 month of death. The psychiatrist should perform a complete suicide risk assessment at the initial evaluation, even if the patient does not appear suicidal.

The Right to Accept or Reject New Patients

The no-duty rule states that a psychiatrist who is self-employed and not required by the policies of others to accept patients owes no duty to enter into a professional relationship with a patient.

When first seeing the patient, the psychiatrist may wish to undertake a brief period of evaluation before deciding whether to accept the patient, making it clear that no treatment will be rendered. Upon completion of the evaluation, a decision by both the psychiatrist and the patient can be made about whether to begin treatment. The psychiatrist must scrupulously avoid rendering advice, interpretations, or any other intervention that might be construed as treatment during the evaluation period.

Psychiatrists have no legal obligation to provide emergency medical care. Nevertheless, the American Medical Association advises, "The physician should, however, respond to the best of his [or her] ability in cases of emergency where first aid treatment is essential" (10). If a psychiatrist undertakes to render assistance to the person "at the wayside," Good Samaritan statutes enacted by every state usually protect against suits for damages arising out of any professional act or omission performed in "good faith" and not amounting to gross negligence (e.g., beginning assistance and then abandoning the victim or rendering care while intoxicated). Good Samaritan laws cover the physician who is not licensed in the state where the emergency care takes place.

Duty of Neutrality and the Fiduciary Role

The *duty of neutrality* is an independent legal formulation that roughly approximates the clinical principle of abstinence. The duty of neutrality and the derivative abstinence principle state that psychiatrists must refrain from gratifying themselves at the expense of their patients. A corollary of both principles is that the psychiatrist's main source of gratification should arise from conducting the treatment process. The only material satisfaction for the psychiatrist is derived from receiving payment for his or her services. The duty of neutrality is based on the legal concept of the fiduciary relationship, requiring all mental health professionals to act in the best interests of their patients by maintaining a position of personal neutrality. Psychiatrists practicing in small communities and rural settings may have to make unavoidable adjustments in treatment boundaries to avoid disruption of the integrity of the doctor-patient relationship (11).

Double Agentry

The practice of psychiatry bristles with moral dilemmas. Double agentry often occurs when mental health professionals have conflicts of interest that interfere with their fiduciary responsibility to act solely in the best interest of the patient.

Traditionally, double agentry has been defined as a conflict between serving the patient and serving some external agency (12). Double-agent roles hold a high potential for disturbing psychiatrists' position of neutrality and fiduciary duty. For example, psychiatrists working in mental institutions must manage the conflict between serving their patients and advancing the goals of the institution and society. Following emergence of the *Tarasoff* doctrine—the psychiatrist's duty to warn and protect endangered third parties—psychiatrists were placed in the conflicting position of preserving patient confidentiality while also serving society's need to be protected from harm. Psychiatrists who work in prisons, in schools, or in the military face potentially serious double-agent conflicts.

Psychiatrists have a professional, ethical, and legal duty to provide competent medical care to their patients. Because psychiatrists do not practice in isolation, they must exercise this duty within the decisions and directives of legal, legislative, and nongovernmental administrative guidelines. Psychiatrists and other mental health professionals must be able to clinically manage conflicting pressures on the duty of care that inevitably arise from these different sectors.

In this book, the term *double agentry* is broadened to include any conflict of interest that interferes with solely serving the patient. Therapists who sexually exploit their patients egregiously violate their fiduciary responsibilities. Double agentry may also occur when patients who have been sexually abused are referred to a new therapist for much-needed treatment. The new therapist, because of forensic interests or moral outrage, may try to convert the treatment relationship into a forensic case. The therapist may encourage a suit and help initiate ethical and licensure proceedings against the former therapist. The therapist should not confound treatment with advocacy. The roles of treater and expert witness must be kept separate to avoid serious conflicts of interest (13). Advocacy should not be misrepresented to the patient as treatment.

The practice of psychotherapy can be a lonely experience. The therapist may feel increasingly isolated and alone, seeking out the friendship and companionship of present or past patients. Although overtly nonsexual, a psychiatrist's personal intrusion into the patient's current treatment or the residual transferences of a former patient can be confusing, upsetting, and even gratifying to the patient. Nevertheless, such boundary violations represent a blatant departure from a position of clinical neutrality. Similarly, psychiatrists who are involved in business dealings with their patients become double agents. "Once a patient, always a patient" is a sound principle that allows patients to go about their lives free from the presence and influence of their therapists.

Supervisor-Supervisee Relationships and Liability

Under the doctrine of *respondeat superior,* or vicarious liability, an institution and its staff (e.g., supervising psychiatrist) may become responsible for the acts and omissions of other mental health professionals. A distinction should be made, however, between medical and nonmedical psychotherapists. In the American Psychiatric Association's *Guidelines for Psychiatrists in Consultative, Supervisory, or Collaborative Relationships With Nonmedical Therapists,* it is stated that the psychiatrist is responsible for the patient's diagnosis and treatment plan, and for the supervision of the nonmedical therapist to ensure that the treatment plan is properly administered with suitable adjustments for the patient's condition (14). The guidelines do not specify the frequency of supervisory contacts. When supervising nonmedical therapists, psychiatrists are responsible for the patients as if the patients are their own.

Direct and Vicarious Liability

When a psychiatrist supervises a psychiatric resident or intern who is treating the psychiatrist's patient, the resident or intern may be considered a *borrowed servant*. As a result, the psychiatrist is vicariously responsible for any negligence of the resident or intern that leads to harm. Interns and residents treating their own patients but supervised by a psychiatrist may incur liability directly for negligence, while the supervisor and the institution may be vicariously liable if supervisory control has been exercised. Psychiatrists supervising other graduate psychiatrists may be viewed as independent contractors who would not likely be liable for acts of negligence of the supervised psychiatrist. While not strictly consultative, the supervisory relationship with graduate psychiatrists appears to be closer to the consultative model, even though it occurs on a continuing basis.

When a psychiatric resident's patient or the patient's family brings suit, the resident is usually named. Residents are held to the same standard of care as attending psychiatrists when they represent themselves to the public as treaters of mental illness. If irreconcilable differences arise between the resident and the attending psychiatrist concerning management of the patient, the resident should seek help from the director of residency training. In addition, the resident's reasoning in managing the patient should be duly noted in the patient's chart. The attending psychiatrist can protect his or her position with a similar notation. Every effort should be made to resolve differences as soon as possible for the benefit of the patient.

The psychiatric treatment team concept has gained considerable popularity in the managed care era. The team usually contains a psychiatrist, a psychologist, a social worker, and other mental health professionals. All team members may be held liable for the negligence of an individual team member. Psychiatrists also may be held liable under the doctrine of joint and several liability for the negligent acts of partners, even though they have not seen the patient. Finally, vicarious liability may be imposed on psychiatrists for the negligent acts of employees committed within the scope of their employment.

Collaborative Relationships: Split Treatment

In a collaborative relationship, responsibility for the patient's care is shared according to the qualifications and limitations of each discipline (14). The responsibilities of each discipline do not diminish those of the other discipline. Split treatment is an example of a collaborative relationship.

The psychiatrist-psychotherapist team must overcome some formidable hurdles to facilitate their collaboration (15, 16). The patient's clinical illness cannot be easily placed into the domain of one clinician or the other. Since neither clinician can rightfully claim to be in charge of the other, there is no established clinical hierarchy. Neither is there a pre-existing agreement by which clinicians convey information about the patient nor is there one about what information needs to be conveyed. Many clinicians are concerned about their legal exposure not only for their own professional conduct, but also for their colleague's.

A greater number of patients who are sicker are being treated in split treatment arrangements. Shrinking of available mental health dollars and increased administrative pressure from third-party payers, particularly MCOs, is the driving force behind the increasing utilization of split treatment in the clinical management of the severely mentally ill.

Psychiatrists and their nonphysician mental health colleagues should reach agreement about the respective clinical duties of each clinician and establish a high degree of reliability and predictability in their clinical interactions. Psychiatrists must guard against the main clinical and legal dangers of collaborative treatment:

- Failure to initially establish clear lines of communication and clinical responsibility, preferably in writing, between the psychiatrist and the nonmedical therapist (e.g., coverage for emergencies, hospitalizations, absences); in split treatment situations, Appelbaum (17) recommends that "all responsibilities should be clearly specified, preferably in a written agreement among the patient, the psychiatrist, and the nonmedical therapist"
- Insufficient clinical knowledge of the patient
- Failure to provide careful monitoring of the patient's clinical condition
- Failure to maintain ongoing communication with the nonmedical therapist regarding the patient's treatment

Patient Billing: Avoiding Double-Agent Roles

Self-serving interventions often occur over billing and fees. Most therapists explain their fees at the beginning of treatment so that patients can either agree, disagree, or enter into negotiations for a mutually agreed on fee. Double-agent roles can arise over billing for times reserved or by discounting or inflating bills.

Discounting of bills occurs when the patient has insurance but is unable to pay the full portion of the bill. The therapist may accept either no payment or a lower payment from the patient. When the psychiatrist accepts the insurance reimbursement as payment in full, the insurer is actually paying 100% of the bill. Insurance carriers look on this practice as fraudulent because the participating psychiatrist is pocketing their "overpayment." Psychiatrists who inflate bills to insurance carriers may also be vulnerable to charges of fraud and misrepresentation.

Inflating of bills refers to charging the insurance carrier a higher fee than the therapist is actually charging the patient. When this happens, the difference is pocketed or applied to the patient's portion. Therapists are not agents of the insurance company, nor should they be agents of the patient against the carrier. Exaggerating the severity of a patient's mental disorder to obtain coverage under managed care is a related deceptive practice. A position of neutrality on insurance matters maintains the psychiatrist's integrity. Double-agent roles often create distrust, vitiating treatment. The credibility of the psychiatrist is also severely undermined in court if she or he becomes entangled with the patient in litigation.

Therapists should bill at a reasonable rate for the services they provide. Billing for missed appointments is appropriate if the patient is advised from the beginning of this practice and freely consents. Charges for missed sessions should not be represented as treatment sessions to third-party payers. This practice could be interpreted as misrepresentation and fraud. Some psychiatrists do not want to act as policeman or to be the patient's conscience on billing matters. Thus, they merely note on the billing form that there is a charge for missed appointments, leaving it up to the patient to report missed appointments to their third-party payer. For patients who pay the psychiatrist directly and then receive reimbursement from their insurance carrier, there may be a disinclination to report missed appointments for obvious financial reasons. This practice may raise questions in the patient's mind about the psychiatrist's integrity, thus having potential consequences. The psychiatrist also may be accused by the insurer of colluding with the patient to defraud it. Psychiatrists who receive direct payment from third-party payers are not paid for appointments reported as missed.

Moreover, under provider contractual agreements, most managed care organizations and other third-party payers prohibit psychiatrists from billing the patient for any unauthorized services including missed appointments. The ethical and prudent course is to note missed appointments on the billing form, even if the psychiatrist must take a financial loss. In some circumstances, an arrangement may be worked out with the patient to pay for missed appointments.

Nonpayment: Clinical Issues

In general, the psychiatrist has no legal duty to treat patients who do not pay. However, the psychiatrist must be careful not to abandon the patient. The patient who runs out of money during the course of extended therapy presents a difficult problem. Terminating the patient's treatment may be very destructive to the unique relationship that develops between psychiatrist and patient. The psychiatrist may decide to treat the patient for a token fee until the patient's financial situation improves, at which time a new fee can be negotiated. However, allowing the patient to pay the money owed at a later date places the psychiatrist in the position of a creditor. This may interfere with the psychiatrist's efforts to maintain a position of neutrality. Similarly, entering into a barter arrangement with a nonpaying patient should be avoided. Patients in need of treatment may not be able to objectively assess the value of their goods. When others assume financial responsibility for the patient, the therapist may wish to formalize the arrangement with a written agreement. As insurance benefits for psychiatric care continue to be cut back by MCO cost-containment policies, treatment of patients needing further care may be improperly terminated.

Abandonment

Once the psychiatrist agrees to treat the patient, a psychiatrist-patient relationship is formed with the duty to provide treatment as long as necessary. When the psychiatrist-patient relationship is unilaterally and prematurely terminated by the psychiatrist without reasonable notice, the psychiatrist may be liable for abandonment if care is still needed by the patient. If an emergency exists, the psychiatrist should see the patient through the current crisis. For patients in perpetual crisis, this is obviously a difficult task. Terminating treatment of a patient who is in serious psychiatric difficulty should be deferred until the immediate crisis is over or until the patient is well enough to be discharged.

Psychiatrists must realize that the following actions by a patient do not automatically terminate the doctor-patient relationship:

- Mere nonpayment of a bill
- Failure to be cooperative in treatment
- Unilateral consultation with another mental health professional
- Failure to keep an appointment

None of these reasons is an appropriate cause for termination if the patient continues to need treatment. These issues should be taken up as treatment matters. If the patient stops coming for regularly scheduled appointments, does the therapist have a duty to contact the patient? The answer to this question depends on whether the patient's absence is a direct function of mental illness. The more severe the illness, the more the psychiatrist should assume responsibility for contacting the patient. When it is not clear whether the patient has terminated treatment, the psychiatrist should attempt to clarify the patient's intentions concerning further treatment. If a patient stops coming for treatment without further explanation, the psychiatrist should send a certified letter (return receipt requested) indicating that treatment has been terminated by the patient.

All of the following actions may constitute abandonment of the patient:

- Failure to instruct the patient concerning side effects of medication
- Failure to stay abreast of the patient's condition
- Failure to admit the patient to a hospital when warranted
- Premature discharge of the patient from the hospital
- Improper referral of the patient

- Sexual relations with a patient or termination of therapy in contemplation of a sexual relationship
- Failure to attend the patient during hospitalization
- Termination of a patient requiring treatment solely on the basis of MCO denial of benefits

Psychiatrists who request other psychiatrists to hospitalize their patients should stay in contact with the admitting psychiatrist and shift temporarily into a consultative role. Unless the patient is being permanently transferred to the care of the hospitalizing psychiatrist, the referring psychiatrist should continue to stay abreast of clinical developments with his or her patient.

Finally, abandonment may be alleged when therapists do not list a phone number in the telephone directory or with directory assistance. Being inaccessible to patients measurably increases their anxiety and causes some patients to go to extraordinary lengths to find their therapists. Ready availability of the psychiatrist appears to diminish patients' anxiety and results in fewer calls. In addition, if an emergency should arise, claims of abandonment are pre-empted when the psychiatrist can be easily contacted.

Substitute Therapists

When a psychiatrist obtains clinical coverage for absences from his or her practice, a psychiatrist of similar experience and training should be substituted. Clinical information about patients who may be considered at suicide risk or vulnerable to regression should be provided to the covering psychiatrist. Patients need to be informed of the substitution as well as the length of the treating psychiatrist's absence. A psychiatrist who uses a substitute is not generally liable for the substitute's negligence unless the substitute psychiatrist is acting as an agent of the psychiatrist or due care is not exercised in selecting the substitute psychiatrist. If a fixed stipend is paid to the covering psychiatrist from fees collected, an agent (employee) relationship is likely established. If the patient is billed and the proceeds are shared with the covering psychiatrist after expenses, then a partnership is created. To avoid possible legal entanglements, the covering psychiatrist should bill independently for services rendered.

Termination

The psychiatrist has the right to withdraw from a case as long as proper notice is given so that the patient may find a suitable substitute. The psychiatrist who concludes that good care can no longer be provided because of the patient's lack of cooperation is not legally obligated to continue to treat the patient, so long as proper arrangements are made to withdraw from the case. The psychiatrist is not required to provide useless treatment.

Unilateral Terminations

The most common reason for unilateral termination of a patient's treatment is likely to be managed care limitations of insurance benefits. The liability exposure for terminating treatment of a patient who is in crisis because of managed care restrictions is high. Termination of treatment of the patient in crisis should be deferred until her or his situation is reasonably stabilized. Before termination, the psychiatrist should give the patient sufficient notice to make other treatment arrangements. The psychiatrist should also review with the patient the current diagnosis, the importance of continuing to take prescribed medications, and the need for additional treatment. A note in the patient's chart and a brief letter sent to the patient should summarize the psychiatrist's treatment recommendations. The psychiatrist may decide to continue to treat a patient after managed care benefits end. Managed care contracts should be checked for any clause that prohibits treatment of managed care patients under a private fee-for-service arrangement.

The patient has the right to leave treatment at any time and without notice. In some instances, the patient may terminate by simply not showing up for scheduled appointments. A patient who is mentally ill and poses a substantial danger to self or others may decide to terminate. In such instances, the psychiatrist's ethical and professional duties to care for the patient continue and require that the psychiatrist consider a variety of clinical interventions.

A malpractice action brought by the patient against the psychiatrist affords the psychiatrist an opportunity to serve notice of termination. Although this course of action is not absolutely protected and legal opinion should be sought on the specific issue of abandonment, termination of the patient's treatment is appropriate to protect the interests of the psychiatrist. Clinically, it is most unlikely that a psychiatrist would want to or could effectively continue to treat a patient who is suing, because of the subsequent impossible transference and countertransference dilemmas that would result. Furthermore, it is also inconceivable that a patient who is suing the psychiatrist for negligence and monetary damages would want to continue treatment with that psychiatrist. Any therapeutic alliance under these circumstances would almost certainly cease to exist.

All therapists' difficulties with patients are not necessarily due to countertransference issues. Some patients are genuinely difficult and demanding in their own right, presenting unique problems that some psychiatrists can handle better than others. Psychiatrists must realize their limitations and not hold grandiose notions that they can treat every patient. If treatment becomes an intolerable ordeal for the psychiatrist, the patient should be referred. Psychiatrists may not terminate patients for capricious reasons and must provide time for the patients to work through the termination.

Professional and ethical duty demands that the psychiatrist not treat patients beyond the point of benefit. Patients can become mired in therapeutic stalemates extending over years. This situation tends to occur when an Axis I clinical syndrome is successfully treated, but the remaining Axis II personality disorder goes undiagnosed or is intractable to treatment. Even though the patient may strenuously resist, it is not an abandonment if such a patient is referred to another therapist who may be able to treat the patient more effectively once the previous treatment is appropriately terminated.

Method of Termination

Termination and the issues surrounding it should be openly discussed with the patient and a notation of the discussion placed in the patient's record. A certified letter notifying the patient of termination should be sent and a return receipt requested, even though courts presume first class mail to be delivered. There is no legal obligation to send a certified or registered letter to the patient. If the therapist wants to be absolutely sure that the patient receives the letter, then the letter should be sent restricted registered, return receipt requested. If the terminated patient is seen again after the letter is issued and termination is still intended, the entire termination process must be reinstituted (Table 2–3).

How much time should be provided to the patient to find another therapist? The time allowed should be based on the severity of the patient's condition and the availability of alternative care. Patients who present complex, severe mental illnesses may find it more difficult to find a psychiatrist willing to treat them. Sufficient notice

---

TABLE 2–3. **Suggested guidelines for termination of patient treatment**

1. Thoroughly discuss treatment termination with patient.
2. Indicate the following in a letter of termination:
   a. Fact of discussion of termination
   b. Reason for termination
   c. Termination date
   d. Availability for emergencies only until date of termination
   e. Willingness to provide names of other appropriate therapists
   f. Willingness to provide medical records to subsequent therapist
   g. A statement of the need for additional treatment, if appropriate
3. Allow the patient reasonable time to find another therapist (length of time depends on availability of other therapists).
4. Provide the patient's records to the new therapist upon proper authorization by the patient.
5. If the patient requires further treatment, provide the names of other psychiatrists or refer the patient to a local or state psychiatric society for further assistance.
6. If the need for further treatment is recommended, a statement about the potential consequences of not obtaining further treatment should be provided.
7. Send the termination letter certified or restricted registered mail, return receipt requested.

also depends on the locality. The availability of psychiatrists in rural settings may be limited. The patient may need more time to find a psychiatrist than would be necessary in a cosmopolitan area. The courts have used such normative words as *ample, sufficient,* and *reasonable* when referring to the time given the patient to find a substitute.

Managed Care and the Discharge of Hospitalized Patients

Doctors, not hospitals or MCOs, are responsible for the discharge of patients (18). Hospitalized psychiatric patients should not be summarily discharged if insurance coverage for recommended continued hospitalization is denied. Provisions for continuing adequate care should be made before the patient is discharged. If a hospital puts pressure on a psychiatrist to discharge a patient who presents a high risk of danger to self or others, both the psychiatrist and the hospital will be at increased risk of liability if the patient or a third party is actually harmed. Psychiatrists must not allow managed care considerations to override their treatment and discharge decisions. The premature discharge of psychiatric inpatients who are at increased risk of committing violence toward themselves or others is likely to become an increasingly important area of litigation in the managed care era (19).

MCO cost-containment policies often restrict physicians' therapeutic discretion while their professional and legal responsibilities to patients continue unchanged. For example, hospital stays are greatly abbreviated, often inappropriately so for psychiatric patients with serious disorders. When managed care guidelines conflict with the psychiatrist's duty to provide appropriate clinical care, the psychiatrist must be prepared to vigorously appeal managed care decisions that abridge necessary treatments. If advocacy efforts fail, patients should be informed of their right to appeal MCO denial of services that the psychiatrist has documented as medically necessary. Once a treatment plan is recommended to the patient, the psychiatrist has a duty to complete the treatment or arrange for a suitable treatment alternative (20). MCOs generally limit or deny *payment* for services but not the actual services themselves. The physician is ultimately responsible for decisions involving patient care and disposition (21).

■ REFERENCES

1. Current Opinions: The Council on Ethical and Judicial Affairs of the American Medical Association. Chicago, IL, American Medical Association, 1989, Section 6.03
2. Brown v Koulizakis, 229 Va 524, 331 SE 2d 440 (1985)
3. Mains J: Medical abandonment. Medical Trial Technique Quarterly 31:306–328, 1985
4. Newman A, Newman K: Physician's duty in independent medical evaluations. Legal Aspects of Medical Practice 17: 8–9, 1989
5. O'Neill v Montefiore Hospital, 11 AD 2d 132, 202 NYS 2d 436 (NY App Div 1960)
6. Shane v Mouw, 116 Mich App 737, 323 NW 2d 537 (Mich Ct App 1982); superseded by statute, as stated in Morgan v Taylor, 434 Mich 180 (1990 Mich Lexis 268 [1990])
7. Gutheil TG, Simon RI: Risk management principles in recovered memory cases: the importance of the clinical foundation. Psychiatr Serv 48:1403–1407, 1997
8. LaPuma J, Priest ER: Is there a doctor in the house? an analysis of the practice of physicians treating their own families. JAMA 267:1810–1812, 1992
9. Simon RI: Clinical Psychiatry and the Law, 2nd Edition. Washington, DC, American Psychiatric Press, 1992
10. The Council on Ethical and Judicial Affairs of the American Medical Association: Current Opinions. Chicago, IL, American Medical Association, 1989, Section 8.10
11. Simon RI, Williams I: Maintaining treatment boundaries in small communities and rural areas. Psychiatr Serv 50:1440–1446, 1999

12. The Hastings Center: In the Service of the State: The Psychiatrist as Double Agent (special supplement). Hastings-on-Hudson, NY, The Hastings Center, 1978

13. Strasburger LH, Gutheil TG, Brodsky A: On wearing two hats: role conflict in serving as both psychotherapist and expert witness. Am J Psychiatry 154:448–456, 1997

14. Official actions: guidelines for psychiatrists in consultative, supervisory, or collaborative relationships with nonmedical therapists. Am J Psychiatry 137:1489–1491, 1980

15. Meyer D, Simon RI: Split treatment: clarity between psychiatrists and psychotherapists, Part I. Psychiatric Annals 29:241–245, 1999

16. Meyer D, Simon RI: Split treatment: clarity between psychiatrists and psychotherapists, Part II. Psychiatric Annals 29:327–332, 1999

17. Appelbaum PS: General guidelines for psychiatrists who prescribe medication for patients treated by nonmedical therapists. Hospital and Community Psychiatry 42:281–282, 1991

18. Simon RI: Discharging sicker, potentially violent psychiatric inpatients in the managed care era: standard of care and risk management. Psychiatric Annals 27:726–733, 1997

19. Simon RI: Psychiatrists' duties in discharging sicker and potentially violent inpatients in the managed care era. Psychiatr Serv 49:62–67, 1998

20. Siebert SW, Silver SB: Managed health care and the evolution of psychiatric practice, in American Psychiatric Press Review of Clinical Psychiatry and the Law, Vol 2. Edited by Simon RI. Washington, DC, American Psychiatric Press, 1991, pp 259–270

21. Wickline v California, 183 Cal App 3d 1175, 228 Cal Rptr 661 (Cal Ct App 1986); see also Wilson v Blue Cross of Southern California et al., 222 Cal App 3d 660 (1990) (Both MCO and physician may be held liable if negligence is "substantial factor" in harming patient.)

3

CONFIDENTIALITY AND TESTIMONIAL PRIVILEGE

■ OVERVIEW OF THE LAW

Confidentiality refers to the right of a patient to have communications spoken or written in confidence not be disclosed to outside parties without implied or expressed authorization. Testimonial privilege is a statutory rule of evidence that permits the holder of the privilege (e.g., patient) the right to prevent the person to whom confidential information was given (e.g., psychiatrist) from disclosing it in a judicial proceeding.

Confidentiality: Clinical-Legal Foundation

The basis for recognizing and safeguarding patient confidences is derived from four general sources. States have acknowledged this right of protection by including confidentiality provisions either in professional licensure laws or in confidentiality and privilege statutes. A second source, and probably the most traditional, is the ethical codes of the various mental health professions. Third, the common law always recognized an attorney-client privilege, but developing case law has also carved out this source of protection for physicians and psychotherapists. In *Jaffee v. Redmond,* 1966, the United States Supreme Court ruled that communications between psychotherapist and patient are confidential and need not be disclosed in federal trials (1). The decision does not apply in state court cases, where most psychotherapist-patient privilege issues arise. Fourth, the right of confidentiality may be subsumed under the right of privacy. Although there is no explicit constitutional right of privacy, such a right has been synthesized from various constitutional guarantees.

Breaching Confidentiality

Once the doctor-patient relationship has been created, the professional assumes an automatic duty to safeguard a patient's disclosures. This duty is not absolute, and there are circumstances where breaching confidentiality is both ethical and legal.

Patients waive confidentiality in a variety of situations. Medical records are regularly sent to potential employers or to insurance companies and managed care organizations (MCOs) for benefits claims. Confidentiality is usually absent when individuals submit to psychiatric evaluations conducted at the request of third parties (e.g., for disability, litigation). Patients' records must be provided by physicians undergoing Medicare or Medicaid fraud investigations. A limited waiver of confidentiality ordinarily exists when a patient participates in group therapy. Legally, whether one group member can be compelled in court to disclose information shared by another group member during group therapy is still unsettled. Many state statutes mandate disclosure by the psychiatrist in one or more situations (see Table 3–1).

Patients' access to their own records is normally controlled by statutes. These statutory provisions are found under the heading of *medical records* or the much broader term *privilege*.

TABLE 3–1.   **Examples of statutory disclosure requirements**

Evidence of child abuse

Initiation of involuntary hospitalization

"Duty to warn" endangered third parties or law enforcement agencies

Commission of a past treasonous act

Intention to commit a future crime

Human immunodeficiency virus (HIV) infection[a]

---

[a]Some states require that the patient's name be reported.

If a patient gives the psychiatrist good reason to believe that a warning should be issued to an endangered third party, the confidentiality of the communication that gave rise to the warning may be lost. For example, the warning of endangered third parties has resulted in psychiatrists being compelled to testify in criminal cases (2).

Testimonial Privilege Defined

The patient—not the psychiatrist—is the holder of the privilege that controls the release of confidential information. Because the privilege applies only to the judicial setting, it is called testimonial privilege. Privilege statutes represent the most common recognition by the state of the importance of protecting information provided by a patient to a psychotherapist. This recognition moves away from the essential purpose of the American system of justice (e.g., "truth finding") by insulating certain information from disclosure in court. This protection is justified on the basis that the special need for privacy in the doctor-patient relationship outweighs the unbridled quest for an accurate outcome in court.

Privilege statutes usually are drafted in one of four ways, depending on the type of practitioner:

1. General physician–patient
2. Psychiatrist-patient
3. Psychologist-patient
4. Psychotherapist-patient

In some cases, the broader physician-patient category has been applied to the psychotherapist when an applicable statute did not exist.

Exceptions to Testimonial Privilege

Privilege statutes also specify exceptions to testimonial privilege. Although exceptions vary, the most common include the following:

- Child abuse reporting
- Involuntary hospitalization

- Court-ordered evaluations
- Cases in which a patient places his or her mental state in question as a part of litigation

This last exception, known as the patient-litigant exception, is commonly applied in will contests, workers' compensation cases, child custody disputes, personal injury actions, and malpractice actions in which a therapist is sued by a patient. If only the opposing side in litigation places a patient's mental state in question, the patient-litigant exception will not usually apply.

Liability

An unauthorized or unwarranted breach of confidentiality can cause a patient great emotional harm. As a result, a psychiatrist can be held liable for such a breach based on at least four theories:

1. Malpractice (breach of confidentiality)
2. Breach of statutory duty
3. Invasion of privacy
4. Breach of (implied) contract

■ CLINICAL MANAGEMENT OF LEGAL ISSUES

Confidentiality and Testimonial Privilege: Distinction

Psychiatrists sometimes confuse confidentiality with testimonial privilege. Arising out of the physician-patient relationship, confidentiality refers to the ethical duty of the psychiatrist not to disclose information obtained in the course of evaluating or treating the patient to any other individual or party without the patient's express permission. The duty of confidentiality is also protected by case law.

Testimonial privilege is established by state statute and belongs to the patient. It provides that when a physician lacks the consent of the patient, he or she cannot be examined in certain legal proceedings about confidential information obtained during the course of treatment.

Ethical and Legal Obligations

Physicians have had an ethical duty to maintain the confidentiality of their patients since the time of Hippocrates. Exceptions exist, however. *The Principles of Medical Ethics With Annotations Especially Applicable to Psychiatry* states, "When in the clinical judgment of the treating psychiatrist the risk of danger is deemed to be significant, the psychiatrist may reveal confidential information disclosed by the patient" (3, Section 4, Annotation 8). Examples of scenarios in which common sense and good judgment can lead to a decision to breach patient confidentiality include the following:

1. A patient is at significant risk of committing violence, and the act can be stopped only by the psychiatrist's intervention.
2. A patient is at significant risk of committing suicide, and the act can be stopped only by the psychiatrist's intervention.
3. A patient who is responsible for the lives of others or to the public, such as an airline pilot, bus driver, or police officer, shows marked impairment of judgment.

Aside from statutory disclosure requirements and judicial compulsion, no legal obligation exists to provide information, even to law enforcement officials. Any limitation on the maintenance of confidentiality should be explained to patients from the beginning of an evaluation or treatment. Statutes in a number of states provide patients with the right of access to their records. Therapeutic discretion to withhold information from the patient usually exists when the psychiatrist can establish that disclosure would be detrimental to the patient. Psychiatrists should have a working familiarity with the relevant statutes in their states that govern confidentiality and disclosure.

Minors

The general rule is that confidentiality follows the legal ability to consent to treatment. Mental health confidentiality statutes usually provide a definition of young minors. With young minors, the parents or guardians are the legal decision makers. Thus, parents have a right to know about the course of treatment as well as the diagnosis and prognosis. Confidential information must be revealed cautiously so that damage is not done to the treatment or to the child's relationship with caregivers.

All states, including the District of Columbia and other federal jurisdictions, require health care providers and other mandated reporters to report child abuse. Child abuse laws generally require reporting of any physical injuries suspected of being inflicted on a child by other than accidental means, or in any situation in which a child is believed to have been injured by a parent (4). The typical statutory language requires reporting if there is "reason to believe" or "reason to suspect" child abuse. Child abuse reporting laws apply to physical abuse, sexual abuse, emotional maltreatment, and physical neglect.

One parent's consent is generally sufficient for therapists to release medical records or testify about treatment. If the child's parents are divorced, the custodial parent generally has the right of consent. In cases in which there is disagreement between the parents regarding waiver, the therapist should seek guidance from either the applicable statute or the courts.

In states where minors are legally able to consent to treatment, they are usually able to authorize the disclosure of medical information. From age 14 to 15, minors may be considered emancipated when not living at home or if they are self-supporting. Minors may be judged to be mature minors by physicians when they possess sufficient maturity to understand and consent to treatment. Consent of a parent generally is not required in a genuine emergency.

Whether or not the minor patient has consent rights, every effort should be made to preserve confidentiality for the sake of the treatment. The conflicting interests of the minor's independent right to confidentiality and the parents' need to have information for making reasonable treatment decisions are always present. In *The Principles of Medical Ethics With Annotations Especially Applicable to Psychiatry,* recognition is given to these conflicting interests: "careful judgment must be exercised by the psychiatrist in order to include, when appropriate, the parents or guardian in the treatment of a minor. At the same time, the psychiatrist must assure the minor proper confidentiality" (3, Section 4, Annotation 7). Whenever information about an adolescent is to be released to a third party, the psychiatrist should obtain the written authorizations of both the parent and the patient.

Economic reality rather than legal theory may determine the right to confidential information. Therapists or hospitals are often unwilling to treat a minor patient without the consent and signature of a financially responsible person. When the parent receives an itemized bill or statement from a therapist or insurance provider, privacy can no longer be maintained. Parents have a right to inquire about the professional services provided to their child for which they are being billed. If parents do not consent to nonemergency treatment of a minor, they are not responsible for payment of care. Some state statutes make this explicit (5).

Valid Authorization

A valid, informed authorization for the release of information protects a psychiatrist ethically and legally. State law and mental health confidentiality statutes generally specify the requirements for a valid authorization.

Consent should be obtained in written form as a permanent record. Blanket consents should be avoided. Instead, consent should be given for a specific release of information. A sample consent form that preserves patient self-determination is shown in Figure 3–1.

Waiver of Confidentiality

Psychiatrists should satisfy themselves that the patient waiving confidentiality understands the kind of information requested and the nature of the information in the record. When clinically appropriate, the patient may be allowed to see all information to be released to others. If the patient does not want to know the content of the disclosure, the psychiatrist should assess whether that decision is competent and record the fact of the patient's choice in the medical record. Psychiatrists should take extreme care not to in-

---

Date:

I hereby authorize Dr. _____ to release the circled information for the following purposes:

_____

_____

[Specify any limitations.]

- Psychiatric and medical history, including diagnoses
- Records of outpatient treatment
- Records of psychiatric hospitalization and treatment
- Limited psychiatric information as follows:

I understand that I have a right to inspect and copy any information authorized for release by me. I also have the right to revoke consent at any time. This is a □ one-time consent or □ continuing consent [please check one]. I have been apprised of the possible problems of waiving the privilege of privacy. Please send this information to the following individual and address:

_____

_____

Signature: _____

Address: _____

_____

FIGURE 3–1. **Authorization for release of medical information.**

---

advertently disclose confidential information in their daily work, professional correspondence, or social exchanges.

All states require that acquired immunodeficiency syndrome (AIDS) cases be reported to public health authorities. Some states also require reporting of the patient's name. A number of states require the reporting of cases or names of individuals who test positive for human immunodeficiency virus (HIV). Confidentiality and disclosure issues with HIV-positive individuals are discussed in an official American Psychiatric Association policy statement (6).

The situation is entirely different when an evaluation is being performed for a third party, such as court evaluations, pre-employment interviews, or disability evaluations. Unless a treatment relationship has been established between the psychiatrist and patient, a duty of confidentiality does not arise. The individual should be told at the outset that the information obtained is not governed by the ethics or laws governing confidentiality. Moreover, the individual should understand that she or he will not be given a report by the psychiatrist. The report instead will be sent directly to the interested third party. Consent is implied when the individual proceeds with the evaluation.

Confidentiality and Crime Revelations

The law generally does not require the psychiatrist to report past criminal offenses disclosed by a patient (7). Certain psychiatric patients confess to crimes that they have never committed. Unless the therapist is certain that the patient has recently committed a heinous crime that may be repeated or that the patient may be a serial killer, the mere revealing of the crime should be handled initially as a treatment issue. If a patient confesses to having committed a serious crime in the past, the therapist's response should be that the revelation is grist for the therapeutic mill. The psychiatrist is not a prosecutor and should not confuse treatment with forensic roles. If the conflict for the patient is whether to go to the authorities, the optimal approach would be to attempt to resolve this issue in therapy.

Future crimes are another matter. In a number of states, therapists are required to reveal a patient's intent to commit a future crime or harmful act (8). In addition, the duty to disclose knowledge of impending harm has been imposed by courts adopting a *Tarasoff*-type duty to warn endangered third persons. Child abuse statutes in every state require that patient disclosures of present or intended future child abuse be reported. Suspected child abuse overrides confidentiality. The types of future crimes subject to unauthorized disclosure are typically stipulated by statute. In the absence of such guidance, it is clinically appropriate to manage the threat of a future crime as a treatment issue, while maintaining close scrutiny of the patient's potential for acting out.

Writing About Patients

Psychiatrists, unlike nonpsychiatric physicians, are obliged to disguise their clinical data, even to the detriment of its scientific value, in order to safeguard the privacy of their patients (9). If a patient's identity cannot be adequately disguised, consent of the patient is required for publication. If the psychiatrist does not obtain the patient's consent, he or she may be subject to legal liability and ethical charges if the subject of the writing is recognized.

If the patient gives consent without having reviewed the book or article, the requirement for informed consent may not be met. Consultation with another psychiatrist after the patient has had an opportunity to read the work should be considered in order to evaluate the patient's capacity to consent.

Delinquent Bills

There are no ethical principles that forbid therapists from using collection agencies or the courts to collect bills. Nonetheless, ethical and legal obligations to protect the patient's confidentiality continue even though the patient breaches the treatment contract by not paying the bill. Patients may not want therapists to reveal their status as patients. They may sue for breach of confidentiality when disclosure of such information is made to a collection agency or in a court proceeding.

Whenever possible, therapists should try to recover fees by means other than collection agencies or the courts. If the patient is unresponsive, the therapist may decide to bring suit or employ a collection agency. The patient should be informed that such actions will take place if the bill is not paid within a specified period of time. When using a collection agency or suing, the therapist is ethically and legally obligated to reveal only essential information that is necessary for the purpose of fee collection. Essential information includes the patient's name and the amount owed. Itemized bills should be general, indicating "office visits" rather than the type of therapy. Any applicable statutes should be consulted regarding the procedure for collection and any limits placed on the type of patient information that can be legally disclosed.

Therapists may not harass patients by threatening criminal prosecution, disclosing false information to ruin their credit reputation, contacting the debtor's employer before obtaining a judgment, making unjustified disclosures of information about the debt, using abusive language, or other tactics. Similarly, they should not hire anyone who resorts to these types of tactics. Therapists must not withhold services that they are ethically and legally required to provide in order to put pressure on patients for payment.

Confidentiality After Death

Unless there is a specific court decision or statute providing for the release of patient records after death, the duty to maintain confidentiality that existed in life follows the patient in death.

The *Opinions of the Ethics Committee on the Principles of Medical Ethics* (10) addresses this issue:

Question: Can I give confidential information about a recently deceased mother to her grieving daughter?

Answer: No. Ethically, her confidences survive her death.

Legally, this is an issue varying from one jurisdiction to another. Further, there is a risk of the information being used to seek an advantage in the contesting of a will or in competition with other surviving family members.

If a deceased patient's family requests the medical record, written authority from the executor or administrator of the patient's estate should be obtained before releasing it. When the estate has been settled, an executor or administrator no longer exists; therefore, the courts may need to be consulted for guidance. Laws concerning the release of privileged records vary from state to state. If ethical obligations to preserve confidentiality and legal requirements for disclosure conflict, consultation with an attorney is advisable.

If the psychiatrist feels compelled to reveal confidential information after the patient's death, legal risks may be minimized by providing just enough information for the task at hand. Details of the patient's therapy are rarely, if ever, required. Relevancy is the guiding rule. The controversy raised by the disclosures of the treating psychiatrist following the death of a major American poet, Anne Sexton, underscores many of the complex legal and ethical issues surrounding after-death release of confidential information (11).

The APA *Guidelines on Confidentiality* (12) are explicit concerning disclosure of information by a psychiatrist after the death of a patient:

> Psychiatrists should remember that their ethical and legal responsibilities regarding confidentiality continue after their patients' deaths. In cases in which the release of information would be injurious to the deceased patient's interests or reputation, care must be exercised to limit the released data to that which is necessary for the purpose stated in the request for information.

Comments about third parties are rarely necessary for the purposes of record keeping (i.e., facilitating ongoing treatment, future availability for other physicians, research, or legal purposes). The potential for legal liability exists when words contained in a medical record independently reflect on and defame those still living. The dead or their survivors cannot sue for defamation or invasion of privacy because these are personal rights that die with the individual (9). Privilege, however, does not expire on the death of the patient. Privilege continues after death and may be claimed by the deceased patient's next of kin or legal representative. Privilege seeks to protect the patient from embarrassment, which could extend to family members after the patient dies.

Testimonial Privilege

Although testimonial privilege belongs to the patient and prevents disclosure of information in court obtained during the course of treatment, so many exceptions exist that it is often considered to be almost illusory.

Exceptions to Testimonial Privilege

Every state has enacted physician-patient or psychotherapist-patient privilege statutes. The information that is usually privileged includes not only the patient's direct communications but also information gained through examination and treatment, and the physician's diagnosis and conclusions.

For the treating psychiatrist, the law on testimonial privilege applies equally to criminal and civil proceedings unless a statute creating the privilege limits its application. For instance, criminal prosecutions and workers' compensation proceedings frequently are excluded from privilege. Many of the medical privilege statutes are inapplicable to a homicide prosecution when disclosure relates to the homicide or its immediate circumstances. Furthermore, testimonial privilege covers only the content of communications, not the existence of a treatment relationship. As a result, under a discovery demand, the identity of the treating psychiatrist may be divulged.

Testimonial privilege prevents a physician from being compelled to testify about confidential communications unless consent is obtained from the patient. The statutes are not uniform, varying from state to state. Some statutes protect all communications between doctor and patient, whereas others take a narrow view of privilege, protecting only treatment communications. Testimonial privilege may not exist for personal relationships, court-ordered examinations, or employment and insurance examinations. Typical exceptions to testimonial privilege are listed in Table 3–2.

The psychotherapist-patient privilege usually applies only when a therapist-patient relationship exists. Only communications of a professional nature are protected. Third parties present during the communication between the therapist and the patient may be compelled to testify and are not barred by privilege.

A legally competent adult may execute a valid waiver of testimonial privilege. If the patient has been adjudicated incompetent, the legal guardian possesses the right of waiver. Parents or guardians have the right to waiver for a minor child, although older adolescents may possess the right under certain circumstances.

Subpoenas

Physician-patient or psychotherapist-patient privilege statutes allow patients to prevent a treating psychiatrist from disclosing in court information obtained during the course of treatment. Two basic exceptions to this statutory privilege are the patient's competent consent and a court order. *The Principles of Medical Ethics* states: "A psychiatrist may release confidential information only with the authorization of the patient or under proper legal compulsion" (3, Section 4, Annotation 2). The psychiatrist should explain to the patient the possible impact of testimony and disclosure of the psychiatric record on the treatment.

Attorneys involved in active litigation have an absolute right to obtain a subpoena by merely attesting to a belief that certain individuals have information that is relevant to the lawsuit. A subpoena does not have the legal force of a court order. A court order judicially commands someone to do or not do something.

TABLE 3–2.	**Typical exceptions to testimonial privilege**
	Valid patient consent
	Court order
	Civil commitment proceedings
	Criminal proceedings
	Child custody disputes
	Court-ordered report
	Patient-litigant exception
	Child abuse proceedings

A subpoena by itself is not "proper legal compulsion." The subpoena merely compels the psychiatrist to appear, not to testify. There are two basic types of subpoenas:

- The *subpoena duces tecum,* which requires the psychiatrist to bring medical records
- The *subpoena ad testificandum,* which requires the attendance of the psychiatrist, usually for testimony

Attempting to avoid being served a subpoena is both unrealistic and unethical (13).

When receiving a subpoena, the psychiatrist must still regard all information obtained during the course of therapy as privileged from testimonial disclosure until reviewed and properly resolved by legal authority or accompanied by a signed consent from the competent patient. If compelled to testify, the psychiatrist is ethically obligated to provide only information that is relevant to the specific issue before the court. A request to testify about information that is irrelevant or that appears to exceed the scope of the court order should be questioned directly by the testifying psychiatrist. An appeal to the judge by either the patient's attorney or the psychiatrist may be necessary to clarify the relevancy of the requested information. In deposition or administrative hearings, irrelevant, sensitive information should not be provided without a court order or specific consent by the competent patient.

When no consent accompanies the subpoena, the psychiatrist should ascertain from the patient or the patient's attorney whether consent is forthcoming. In the absence of competent consent from the patient, the patient's attorney or the psychiatrist may file a motion to quash the subpoena on the basis of protection under physician-patient privilege and the duty to maintain confidentiality. The court will rule on the motion, settling the question of whether the psychiatrist must testify or turn over records.

Psychiatrists who believe that certain disclosures would be unethical and damaging to the patient may decide to resist disclosure within the full limits of the law. If this fails, psychiatrists may still refuse to divulge information as a matter of conscience. In this

situation, however, psychiatrists may risk a contempt-of-court ci-
tation and its legal consequences (14).

Record Keeping

Clinically, keeping a record during the course of the patient's treatment serves a number of purposes. Review of the record between
sessions helps summarize treatment response and permits a better
understanding of the patient and the treatment process. If the patient
interrupts or terminates treatment but later decides to resume therapy, the prior record will prove helpful in refreshing the therapist's
memory. Accurate record keeping will also help resolve disputes
over billing. Additionally, pressure for record keeping is increasing
because of the need to maintain quality for accreditation, for financial reimbursement, and for legal purposes. The growing use of
electronic recording and transmission of personal medical information by fax, Internet, and computers raises major concerns about
the maintenance of confidentiality.

Some courts have concluded that what is not recorded was not
done (15, 16). Generally, in the absence of corroborating records,
an assertion in court that certain actions were taken is a question
for the fact finders who must consider the issue of proof. When an
adequate record exists, the possibility of proving that an action
(e.g., treatment or procedure) was taken is significantly enhanced.
Experienced lawyers observe that worse than having no record at
all is a patient's record that carefully documents negligent treatment. The essential characteristics that form the basis for writing
good medical records are listed in Table 3–3.

TABLE 3–3. **Essential characteristics of good medical records**

Clear
Concise
Complete
Careful
Contemporaneous

TABLE 3–4. **Major management and treatment decisions to be documented**

Amount of medication prescribed
Instructions for the taking of medication
Warnings issued to the patient about risks and side effects of medications
Risk-benefit assessments
Informed consent
Any waivers of confidentiality
Noncompliance with treatment
Significant phone conversations
The reasoning behind treatment interventions and noninterventions

---

The record should document major management and treatment decisions (see Table 3–4). Usually, no useful purpose is served by noting the patient's or the therapist's fantasies, derogatory opinions toward others, or any other information not directly relevant to documenting treatment decisions. Treatment process notes documenting intimate details may be necessary for supervision of student psychotherapists and psychoanalysts. However, these records probably should not be kept after their educational or research function is served. A consistent policy of destroying treatment process records should be considered. The destruction of records can be certified and the certificate kept permanently. State laws usually forbid destruction of records if the intent is to prevent disclosure at a judicial proceeding. If the psychiatrist discloses at a judicial hearing that treatment process records are routinely destroyed, the presence of a consistent policy will tend to negate questions about credibility.

Psychiatrists must also realize that the psychiatric record can become an iatrogenic factor in exacerbating a patient's condition, particularly if it contains damaging, or frightening information. Many states allow patients access to their records. The physical record maintained by the psychiatrist is the property of the psychiatrist. The information contained in the record belongs to the patient. The original record should never be relinquished to the patient. Only a copy of the record should be provided. The psychiatrist should be present whenever patients wish to inspect their records in order to answer questions.

Psychiatrists sometimes keep two separate sets of records: one set for diagnosis, prognosis, and treatment decisions; the other for speculations of the psychiatrist and the fantasies and intimate details of the patient's life. Although Illinois and the District of Columbia permit dual records, such a distinction is not normally accepted by the courts. The work-product privilege that protects attorneys' records has not been applied to medical practice. Concealing records is a violation of the law. Instead of using illegal means, the psychiatrist should exercise extreme caution when writing in the patient's record, entering only information that is pertinent to the diagnosis and treatment plan of the patient. Medical records should never be altered, particularly in anticipation of or following notice of a lawsuit. Perfectly defensible cases are lost when it is discovered that the medical record has been altered. If the psychiatrist needs to make additional notations in the record, the notes should occur in proper sequence and be accurately dated.

State laws and administrative regulations in a number of states require that a patient record be kept. Some state regulations and statutes specify the number of years that medical and hospital records must be held. Records should be kept until the relevant statute of limitations has lapsed. Statutes of limitations usually require that a suit be brought within 2 or 3 years from the time of the last treatment or from the time of discovery of the injury caused by the treatment. Psychiatrists who retire should keep their records at least until the statute of limitations runs out. The statute of limitations usually extends longer for minors and incompetent patients. Some statutes spell out the nature, content, and style of record keeping to be maintained, who may receive records, and under what conditions. Psychiatrists need to be aware of these requirements and conduct their record keeping accordingly.

Professional organizations do not provide specific guidelines for record keeping. However, the American Psychiatric Association has published resource documents that provide guidance on maintaining confidentiality in the era of information technology (17).

State licensing and certification laws may contain record-keeping requirements. Violation of these legal requirements may lead to suspension or loss of the practitioner's license. No time limit exists for ethical charges filed by patients to professional organizations. Licensing authorities are not constrained by the same time limitations established for legal actions. Patients may bring complaints after civil and criminal statutes of limitation have expired.

Confidentiality in Managed Care Settings

The psychiatrist should obtain the patient's or an appropriate substitute decision-maker's consent to provide information to the MCO. Unless the patient is a minor, the subscriber's consent should not be automatically relied on. Even if the patient has signed the insurer's blanket authorization form, the subscriber's consent may be insufficient if she or he no longer possesses decision-making capacity. If the patient is not the subscriber, then a file signature may not have been obtained, and no prior consent exists to release information to the MCO. Unknown callers who state they are utilization reviewers requesting information about a patient should be independently verified. The caller's name and telephone number should be obtained and that person's employment and position with the MCO checked.

A conservative approach that provides just enough information for utilization review purposes is sufficient (18). Violent fantasies and impulses, whether directed at oneself or others, represent highly personal, sensitive information that must be handled with professional tact and discretion. The temptation to exploit such information by emphasizing (if not exaggerating) it is enormous, because doing so may be seen as the only way of obtaining necessary care for the patient. Moreover, if insurance benefits are denied, the psychiatrist cannot readily discharge a patient who is diagnosed as severely psychiatrically ill. Limitations on confidentiality created by mandatory reporting, particularly the duty to warn and protect endangered third parties or to inform the police, should also be disclosed to patients who are making threats against identifiable persons or who were threatening or violent to others just prior to evaluation. In *Jaffee,* the decision reminds therapists that, in addition to the more common disclosures that may arise in treatment, a discussion should also occur about ethically and legally mandated disclosures (19).

■ REFERENCES

1. Jaffe v Redmond, 116 S.Ct. 1923 (1996)
2. Leong GB, Eth S, Silva JA: The psychotherapist as witness for the prosecution: the criminalization of Tarasoff. Am J Psychiatry 149:1011–1051, 1992
3. American Psychiatric Association: The Principles of Medical Ethics With Annotations Especially Applicable to Psychiatry. Washington, DC, American Psychiatric Association, 1998
4. Kaplan SJ: Physical abuse of children and adolescents, in Family Violence: A Clinical and Legal Guide. Edited by Kaplan SJ. Washington, DC, American Psychiatric Press, 1996, pp 21–22
5. Holder AR: Minors' rights to consent to medical care. JAMA 257:3400–3402, 1987
6. APA Official Actions: AIDS Policy: Position Statement on Confidentiality, Disclosure, and Protection of Others. Am J Psychiatry 150:852, 1993
7. Slovenko R: Psychiatry and Confidentiality: Testimonial Privileged Communication, Reporting Duties, and Breach of Confidentiality. Springfield, IL, Charles C. Thomas, 1998, p 158
8. Melton GB, Petrila J, Poythress NG, et al: Psychological Evaluations for the Courts, 2nd Edition. New York, Guilford, 1997, pp 76–77
9. Slovenko R: The hazards of writing or disclosing information in psychiatry. Behav Sci Law 1:109–127, 1983
10. American Psychiatric Association: Opinions of the Ethics Committee on the Principles of Medical Ethics With Annotations Especially Applicable to Psychiatry. Washington, DC, American Psychiatric Association, 1998, Section 4-K

11. Goldstein RL: Psychiatric poetic license? postmortem disclosures of confidential information in the Anne Sexton case. Psychiatric Annals 22:341–348, 1992

12. American Psychiatric Association Committee on Confidentiality: Guidelines on confidentiality. Am J Psychiatry 144:1522–1526, 1987

13. Simon RI: Clinical Psychiatry and the Law, 2nd Edition. Washington, DC, American Psychiatric Press, 1992, p 65

14. In re Lifschutz, 2 Cal 3d 415, 467 P2d 557, 85 Cal Rptl 829 (1970); see also Caesar v Mountanos, 542 F2d 1064 (9th Cir 1976), cert denied, 430 U.S. 954 (1977)

15. Whitree v State, 56 Misc 2d 693, 290 NYS 2d 486, 489–499 (1968)

16. Abille v United States, 482 F Supp 703, 708 (ND Cal 1980)

17. American Psychiatric Association Resource Document on Preserving Patient Confidentiality in the Era of Information Technology. Washington, DC, American Psychiatric Association, 1996; see also American Psychiatric Association Resource Document on Computerized Records: A Guide to Security. Washington, DC, American Psychiatric Association, 1996

18. Corcoran K, Winslade WJ: Eavesdropping on the 50-minute hour: managed mental health care and confidentiality. Behav Sci Law 12:351–365, 1994

19. Shuman DW, Foote W: Jaffee v Redmond's impact: life after the Supreme Court's recognition of a psychotherapist-patient privilege. Professional Psychology: Research and Practice 30:479–487, 1999

4

INFORMED CONSENT AND THE RIGHT TO REFUSE TREATMENT

■ OVERVIEW OF THE LAW

Informed consent is a legal theory in medical malpractice that provides a patient with a cause of action for not being adequately informed, before giving consent, about the nature and consequences of a particular medical procedure or treatment. The theory of informed consent is founded on two distinct legal principles. The first is the right of every patient to determine what will or will not be done to his or her body, often referred to as the right of self-determination (1). The second principle emanates from the fiduciary nature of the doctor-patient relationship. Inherent in a physician's duty of fiduciary care is the responsibility to disclose honestly and in good faith all requisite facts concerning a patient's condition. Included among factors to be disclosed are any treatment benefits, risks, alternatives, and consequences. The primary purpose of the doctrine of informed consent is to promote individual autonomy, and secondarily to foster rational decision making (2).

There are three essential elements to the doctrine of informed consent:

- Competency
- Information
- Voluntariness

Usually, clinicians provide the first level of screening in identifying the patient's health care decision-making capacity and in deciding whether to accept a patient's treatment decision. Competent informed consent also requires that the patient should be told about the risks, benefits, and prognosis both with and without treatment, and about alternative treatments and their risks and benefits. Finally, the patient should voluntarily consent or refuse the proposed treatment or procedure, with a reasonable level of competency.

Competency

Legally, only competent persons may give an informed consent. An adult patient will be considered legally competent unless adjudicated incompetent or temporarily incapacitated due to a medical emergency. Incapacity to make health care decisions does not prevent treatment. It merely requires the clinician to obtain substitute consent. Legal competence is very narrowly defined in terms of cognitive capacity. This definition derives largely from the laws governing transactions. Clinical conditions that produce affective incompetence or denial of illness are not usually recognized by the law unless they significantly diminish a patient's cognitive capacity. Patients with mental disorders may understand information provided about their condition but lack insight and be unable to appreciate the information's significance.

In *In the Guardianship of John Roe* (3), the Massachusetts Supreme Judicial Court recognized that denial of illness can render a patient incompetent to make treatment decisions. Moreover, patients with mood disorders may feel too good (omnipotent) or too bad (hopeless) to consider taking recommended medications. Schizophrenic patients often fear that a drug will do serious harm. They lack a balanced consideration of both the risks and the benefits of a proposed medication. One study, which used three different assessment instruments to measure subjects' competency to make treatment decisions, found that patients with schizophrenia or major depression demonstrated poorer understanding of treatment disclosures, poorer reasoning in decision making regarding treatment, and a greater likelihood of failing to appreciate the severity of their illness or the potential treatment benefits than did comparison subjects (4).

Competency is not a scientifically determinable state; it is situation specific. Although there are no hard-and-fast definitions, legally germane to determining competency is the patient's ability to

- understand the particular treatment option being proposed,
- make a treatment choice, and
- verbally or nonverbally communicate that choice.

The problem with this three-pronged definition is that it obtains a *simple* consent from the patient rather than an *informed* consent, because risk-benefit analysis and alternative treatment choices are not provided or considered. A review of case law and scholarly literature reveals four basic standards for determining competency in decision making (2). Following are these standards, in order of levels of mental capacity required:

- Communication of choice
- Understanding of relevant information provided
- Appreciation of available options and consequences
- Rational decision making

Psychiatrists generally feel most comfortable using a rational decision-making standard in determining incompetency. Most courts, however, prefer the first two standards. A truly informed consent reflecting the patient's autonomy, personal needs, and values requires the application of rational decision making to the risks and benefits of appropriate treatment options provided by the clinician.

A valid consent can be either *express* (oral or in writing) or *implied* from the patient's actions. The competency issue is particularly sensitive when dealing with minors or persons with mental disabilities who lack the requisite cognitive capacity. In both cases, it is generally recognized in the law that an authorized representative or guardian (e.g., a parent) may consent for the patient.

Information

The standard for exercising a legally sufficient disclosure varies from state to state. Traditionally, the duty to disclose has been measured by a professional standard: either what a reasonable physician would disclose under the circumstances or the customary disclosure practices of physicians in a particular community. In the landmark case *Canterbury v. Spence* (5), a patient-oriented standard was applied. This standard focused on the "material" information a reasonable person in the patient's position would want to know in order to make an adequately informed decision. An increasing number of courts have applied this standard, and some have expanded "material risks" to include information regarding the consequences of not consenting to the treatment or procedure (6).

A *material risk* is defined as one that a physician knows (or should know) would be considered significant by a reasonable person in the patient's position. Even in patient-oriented jurisdictions, there is no duty to disclose every possible risk. The issue of how much information a patient must comprehend in order to provide a valid consent is normally resolved by requiring a doctor to convey all appropriate information in terms that the "average patient" would understand (see Table 4–1).

Voluntariness

For a consent to legally be considered voluntary, it must be given freely by the patient and without the presence of any form of co-

---

TABLE 4–1. **Informed consent: reasonable information to be disclosed**

Although there exists no consistently accepted set of information to be disclosed for any given medical or psychiatric situation, as a rule of thumb, five areas of information are generally provided:

1. Diagnosis: description of the condition or problem
2. Treatment: nature and purpose of proposed treatment
3. Consequences: risks and benefits of the proposed treatment
4. Alternatives: viable alternatives to the proposed treatment, including risks and benefits
5. Prognosis: projected outcome with and without treatment

---

ercion, fraud, or duress impinging on the patient's decision-making process. In evaluating whether a consent is truly voluntary, the courts will typically examine all of the relevant circumstances, including the psychiatrist's manner, the environmental conditions, and the patient's mental state.

Exceptions and Liability

There are four basic exceptions to the requirement of informed consent (see Table 4–2).

In situations where immediate treatment is necessary to save a life or prevent imminent serious harm, and it is impossible to obtain either the patient's consent or that of someone authorized to provide consent for the patient, the law will typically "presume" that the consent would have been granted. Two distinctions must be understood when applying this exception. First, the emergency must be serious and imminent, and second, the patient's condition—and not the surrounding circumstances (e.g., adverse environmental conditions)—determines the existence of an emergency.

A second exception is applied when a patient lacks sufficient mental capacity to give competent consent or is found to be legally *incompetent,* that is, someone who is incapable of providing informed consent. Under these circumstances, consent must be obtained from a substitute decision maker.

The third exception, therapeutic privilege, is the most difficult to apply. Courts differ in their standards for invoking therapeutic privilege. Informed consent may not be required if the psychiatrist determines that a complete disclosure of possible risks and alternatives might be injurious to the patient's health and welfare. How-

TABLE 4–2.	**Basic exceptions to obtaining informed consent**
	Emergencies
	Incompetency
	Therapeutic privilege
	Waiver

ever, failure to obtain informed consent from a patient because the psychiatrist fears that the patient will refuse medication is not an appropriate exercise of therapeutic privilege. Therapeutic privilege should not be used as a means of circumventing the requirement to obtain a patient's informed consent for recommended treatment or procedures.

Finally, a physician need not disclose risks of treatment when the patient has competently, knowingly, and voluntarily waived his or her right to be informed (e.g., when the patient does not want to be informed of drug side effects).

Absent a situation allowing one of these four exceptions, a psychiatrist who treats a patient without first obtaining informed consent is subject to legal liability. In some jurisdictions, a lack-of-informed-consent action may be defeated if case law or statute provides that a reasonable person under the given circumstances would have consented to treatment. As a rule of thumb, treatment without any consent or against a patient's wishes may constitute a battery (an intentional tort), whereas treatment commenced with an inadequate consent will be treated as an act of medical negligence.

Right to Refuse Treatment

An institutionalized mentally disabled person has a right to refuse treatment. Buttressed by constitutionally derived rights to privacy and freedom from cruel and unusual punishment, the common law tort of battery, and the doctrine of informed consent, persons with mental disability are now afforded protections traditionally reserved for the legally competent. This "new freedom" often runs directly counter to the dictates of clinical judgment (i.e., to treat and protect). As a result of this conflict, the courts vary considerably regarding the parameters of this right and the procedures to be followed.

Two landmark cases illustrate this point. In *Rennie v. Klein* (7), the Third Circuit Court of Appeals recognized a qualified right to refuse neuroleptic medications for involuntarily hospitalized patients in state institutions. The court, after extended litigation, found that this right could be overridden and antipsychotic drugs administered "whenever, in the exercise of professional judgment, such an action is deemed necessary to prevent the patient from endangering himself or others." In the second case, *Rogers v. Okin* (later *Mills v. Rogers*) (8), the court decided that in the absence of an emergency (e.g., serious threat of extreme violence or personal injury), any person who has not been adjudicated incompetent has a right to refuse antipsychotic medication. Incompetent persons have a similar right, but it must be exercised through a "substituted judgment treatment plan" that has been reviewed and approved by the court.

These two decisions are often viewed as legal bookends to the right to refuse treatment. The *Rennie* case became the model for subsequent legal decisions that adopted a treatment-driven rationale for the right to refuse treatment. *Rogers* became the basis for rights-driven approaches taken by other courts in litigating the right to refuse treatment.

Numerous state and federal decisions have tackled some aspect of this issue. Nearly all states recognize an involuntarily hospitalized patient's right to refuse medication in the absence of an emergency. Case law determinations of emergencies range from a risk of imminent harm to self or others to a deterioration in the patient's mental condition if treatment is halted. Until either more states enact legislation or the United States Supreme Court squarely rules on this issue, jurisdictions will continue to vary regarding the substance of the right to refuse treatment and the procedures by which this right can be implemented.

■ CLINICAL MANAGEMENT OF LEGAL ISSUES

Informed Consent

The legal doctrine of informed consent is consistent with the provision of good clinical care. The informed-consent doctrine allows patients to become partners in making treatment determinations that accord with their own needs and values. In the past, physicians operated under the medical principle of *primum non nocere*—"first do no harm." Today, psychiatrists are required to practice within the legal model of informed consent and patient autonomy. Most psychiatrists find increased patient autonomy desirable in fostering development of the therapeutic alliance that is so essential to treatment. Patient independence is the goal of most psychiatric treatments.

Competency

Competence can be a confusing term because it may be used to mean legal competence, or it may have a broad variety of subjective clinical definitions. Mishkin (9) recommends distinguishing the terms *incompetence* and *incapacity*. Incompetence refers to a court adjudication, whereas incapacity indicates a functional inability as determined by a clinician. An operational definition of competence is the mental capacity to make a decision in accordance with the patient's goals, concerns, and values. Clinicians use various terms, such as decision-making capacity, medical-psychological capacity, clinical competence, or functional capacity, in defining the mental capacity to consent to treatment.

The criteria used to define or measure legal competency are heavily weighted in favor of cognitive functioning. Cognitive functioning may be reasonably intact but unusable if behavioral control is under the influence of a mood disorder. Thus, patients with such conditions may be considered affectively incompetent. For instance, severely depressed patients may fully understand the nature of their disorder but may nonetheless reject treatment because of their pervasive feelings of hopelessness, helplessness, and worthlessness. Manic patients tend to emphasize the risks of medications while denying their mental illness.

Clinical Evaluation

When therapists evaluate a patient's competency, they do so from a clinical perspective. No matter what test of competency is used, the following may influence the evaluation of competency:

- Clinical factors such as the patient's psychodynamics
- Therapist's psychodynamics

- Accuracy of the historical data provided by the patient
- Accuracy of information provided to the patient
- Stability of the patient's mental state
- Effect of the setting where the consent is obtained

The mental capacity to give consent is typically influenced by a number of psychological and physical factors. The determination of health care decision-making capacity in psychiatric practice is not a single event but a continuous process.

Competency is a here-and-now, contextual matter. The competence of a patient is determined by reference to a particular issue at hand. Rarely is a patient so incompetent as to be unable to make at least some decision about medical care. Even patients adjudicated incompetent by a court of law may retain at least some capacity to make medical care decisions. Moreover, the law requires only *minimal* mental capacity to understand the nature of a particular choice. At a minimum, in assessing decision-making capacity, the patient should be able to understand the particular treatment choice proposed, to make a treatment choice, and to be able to communicate that decision. When such capacity to provide a simple consent is clearly lacking, medical decision making is frequently referred to a substitute decision maker concerning the extent to which treatment may or may not be provided. When a patient appears to be competent, a decision by that patient that seems irrational is not by itself a basis for determination of the patient's incompetence. Legal advice may be needed if the competency issue cannot be resolved by additional medical and psychiatric consultation.

Minors

Traditionally, minors have been considered by the law to be incompetent for most purposes, including the right to make treatment decisions. Normally, the mental health professional must obtain the consent of the parent or legal guardian. There are, however, statutory and judicial exceptions to this rule. An exception is permitted for emergencies; in most states, this exception is an extension of that provided for adults. In some states, an exception is allowed that permits treatment if the delay in obtaining parental consent would, in the physician's judgment, endanger the health of the minor. An exception also exists for the emancipated minor who is no longer under parental control. Marriage or military service always emancipates a minor. Age, residence, financial independence, property ownership, pregnancy, and parenthood also will be considered by the court in determining a minor's appropriate status.

The mature-minor exception allows a physician to treat a minor based on the patient's consent if the minor demonstrates sufficient capacity to appreciate the nature, extent, and consequences of medical treatment. Although every state has not adopted the mature-minor exception, there are no reports of physicians being held liable for treating minors over age 15 on their own consent.

In cases involving divorced parents, decision-making authority regarding health matters, education, and religious training of minor children belongs to the custodial parent. Under appropriate circumstances, psychiatrists may obtain a history from the noncustodial parent and, if full evaluation seems indicated, provide an affidavit or testify for the noncustodial parent who is requesting the court to order or permit such an evaluation. However, it is considered unethical for a psychiatrist to evaluate a child and to testify in court against the expressed wishes of a custodial parent. Court decisions, as well as statutory interpretations of "parent," have limited the use of that word to the parent who has been awarded custody under a divorce decree (10).

Regarding the involuntary hospitalization of minors, the U.S. Supreme Court in *Parham v. J.R.* (11) held that in addition to prescribed state law procedures, the federal due-process clause requires review of a parental decision to commit a minor child by an independent and neutral physician. The court rejected the claim that the due-process clause necessitates more rigorous procedural safeguards.

Standards for Disclosure

As already mentioned, the psychiatrist is not required to inform the patient of every conceivable risk. When a necessary treatment presents minimal risks, the duty to disclose is not as rigorous as when a treatment presents a higher risk, is dangerous, or is intrusive. When less dangerous but equally effective alternative treatments are available, the duty to disclose alternative treatments is heightened accordingly. For instance, if neuroleptic medication is prescribed for a patient with anxiety symptoms when a benzodiazepine would be equally effective, the increased risk of serious side effects from the neuroleptic medication as well as the availability of potentially less risky treatments will require disclosure.

Most psychiatrists would consider selective serotonin reuptake inhibitors (SSRIs) to be the first-line treatment for major depression. In the past, heated controversy existed on the issue of psychotherapy versus medication for major depression (12, 13). Today, patients with major depression should be informed of the availability of a wide variety of antidepressant drugs in combination with psychotherapies that have proven to be effective treatments.

The type of information generally disclosed is outlined in Table 4–1. Typical risks include the probability of death, problems of recuperation, disability, and the chances of disfigurement. For example, tardive dyskinesia could result in disfigurement. Also, patients should be given an adequate opportunity to have all of their questions answered.

Exceptions to Disclosure

As noted, the most common exceptions to disclosure are incompetency, emergency, therapeutic privilege, and waiver.

Incompetency

Patients may lack the mental capacity to give a competent informed consent to a proposed treatment or procedure. Patients who are incompetent are defined by the law as incapable of giving an informed consent. If consent is required, the psychiatrist must obtain it from a substitute decision maker (e.g., next of kin, treatment review panel, court).

Emergency

The law also implies consent under the circumstances of an acute, life-threatening crisis requiring immediate medical attention and treatment. The law assumes that every rational person under these circumstances would consent to treatment. Often, clear definitions of psychiatric emergencies do not exist in state law. Clinicians should document their definition of the emergency, preferably in the language of the governing statute, if such a statute exists.

Therapeutic Privilege

Therapeutic privilege allows a physician to withhold full disclosure of risks in cases when such disclosure might have a serious, detrimental effect on the patient's physical and psychological welfare. Thus, a very disturbed patient who requires treatment interventions that carry greater risks and side effects is more likely not to be informed. Some psychiatrists misunderstand therapeutic privilege to apply if the information provided may cause the patient to reject treatment. This is incorrect. Therapeutic privilege should not be used to circumvent the legal requirement to obtain patient consent. Clinically, therapeutic privilege should be invoked only after it is clear that disclosure could cause the patient to become so alarmed and distraught that significant disruption of the patient's decision-making abilities or serious clinical regression would likely occur. Although the doctrine of therapeutic privilege has been recognized by a number of courts and is codified in some statutes, not all courts have accepted it.

Waiver

On occasion, a patient may request not to be informed about a treatment or procedure. When patients voluntarily and knowingly make this request (i.e., realizing they have a right to this information and are competent), the request may be honored and consent is deemed waived. A record should be made of the patient's waiver in the medical chart, as well as a notation that the implications of such a waiver were discussed as a treatment issue.

Maintaining a Clinical Perspective

The psychiatrist should be the person responsible for discussing treatment with the patient. Sending a nurse or other mental health personnel to obtain consent is usually insufficient. The psychiatrist should be available to answer questions by the patient about the proposed treatment. The information should be presented in a manner intelligible to the patient. False assurances of "no risk" should be distinguished from supportive, hopeful statements about treatment. Risks should be explained to next of kin when exceptions are made to informing the patient directly. Finally, the psychiatrist should always keep a clear record of the consent process undertaken with the patient.

Informed Consent and the Patient With Psychosis

In accordance with the evolving doctrine of informed consent, psychiatrists should obtain consent for all treatments. Even though a patient is psychotic, the psychiatrist is not relieved from attempting to obtain consent for treatment. Psychosis does not necessarily equate with an inability to consent. Some patients with psychosis are quite capable of giving a valid consent to treatment. Obviously, consent to treatment may be given by a patient lacking decision-making capacity. A natural clinical bias in favor of treatment leads some practitioners to assume that if patients consent to treatment, the consent is competently given. For patients lacking the capacity to consent, informed consent should be obtained from a substitute decision maker. Furthermore, consent should be viewed as a continuing educational process rather than a ritualistic act in the service of defensive psychiatry.

Frequently, patients may initially refuse treatment recommendations as a way of dealing with feelings of helplessness or for other important psychological reasons. Nonetheless, the vast majority of patients accept treatment recommendations after first refusing (14). It needs to be established that the consent to treatment is competently given. Consideration should be given to renewing consent more frequently for patients (both inpatients and outpatients) taking high doses of neuroleptics.

For some acutely disturbed hospital patients, a delay in starting drug therapy may be necessary until the therapeutic alliance has had time to develop. Initially, these patients may not be able to provide a valid consent if disclosure of side effects seriously frightens them or when such disclosure contributes to further regression. Furthermore, acutely disturbed patients may not be able to understand the information provided or to weigh risks and benefits of a proposed treatment or procedure. Nonetheless, the clinician must understand that the law requires that informed consent be obtained from the first day of treatment. When patients make an incompetent refusal or acceptance of drug treatment, proxy consent by relatives may be permitted in some jurisdictions. A number of states do not permit consent to treatment by next of kin for patients with mental disorders. Moreover, jurisdictions are increasingly requiring an adjudication of incompetence and the appointment of a guardian to provide consent. In some states, only the substituted consent of a judge is valid. Substitute consent by treatment review panels and other administrative bodies may also be available (15).

Situations in which nonconsenting patients with psychosis represent an acute threat of harm to themselves or others may be treated as emergencies under implied consent. A patient who has been incompetent may quickly regain and maintain competence shortly after hospitalization, even without acute treatment. As soon as the patient regains sufficient mental capacity to give a valid consent to treatment, it should be obtained directly from the patient. Patients who do not indicate a choice by either accepting or refusing treatment should have their competency assessed on other reasonable criteria (e.g., compliance with ward routine, relationships with staff). A thorny problem is presented by patients who do not voice an acceptance or refusal of treatment but give nonverbal assent by following instructions for hospitalization and treatment. These patients may lack the mental capacity to consent to treatment and should be monitored on a continuing basis for their capacity to provide a valid consent.

In some states, patients with psychosis who remain incompetent and refuse treatment but represent no danger to themselves or others may not be treated unless they are first adjudicated incompetent and a surrogate decision maker is appointed. In an increasing number of states, nonjudicial administrative procedures that meet due-process requirements are being used in determining the need for involuntary medication (4).

Under managed care, hospital stays have been greatly reduced, often to less than a week of inpatient care. Only the most disturbed patients who are suicidal, homicidal, or both are admitted. Sufficient time does not usually exist for the psychiatrist and staff to develop a therapeutic alliance with patients who have severe mental disorders. Consequently, these patients may continue to refuse treatment, requiring involuntary hospitalization and transfer to a state institutional facility.

Incompetent Patients: Consent Options

A number of consent options are available for patients lacking the mental capacity to provide or withhold consent to treatment (see Table 4–3).

Proxy consent by next of kin is becoming less available as an option. Relying on the consent of next of kin in treating a patient who is believed to be incompetent may increase the chances of

---

TABLE 4–3. **Common consent and review options for patients lacking mental capacity for health care decisions**

Proxy consent of next of kin[a]

Adjudication of incompetence; appointment of a guardian

Institutional administrators or committees

Treatment review panels

Substituted consent of the court

Advance directives (living will, durable power of attorney, or, in some cases, health-care proxy)

Statutory surrogates (spouse or court-appointed guardian)[a,b]

[a]May be excluded for treatment of mental disorders.
[b]Medical statutory surrogate laws (when treatment wishes of patients are unstated).
Source. Adapted from Simon RI: *Clinical Psychiatry and the Law,* 2nd Edition. Washington, DC, American Psychiatric Press, 1992, p. 109. Used with permission.

liability. If, for example, it is later discovered that the patient was incompetent and that the relative had no authority to consent, the psychiatrist may be held liable for conducting an unauthorized treatment. Moreover, proxy consent by next of kin for treatment of a mental disorder is not available in a number of jurisdictions. It is important to remember that a decision made by the patient that seems irrational is not, by itself, an acceptable basis for the determination of incompetence. Competent persons regularly make irrational or foolish decisions. Competent persons have a right to refuse treatment and must not be treated against their will.

Substitute Decision Makers

The courts are reluctant to impose liability when the psychiatrist acts in good faith and uses reasonable medical judgment in making a medical determination of health care decision-making capacity, particularly if the treatment is needed and the incapacity of the patient is clear. The risk of suit can be avoided by adhering to statutory procedures for the determination of incompetency and in obtaining substituted consent. When a psychiatrist is in doubt regarding a patient's capacity to make a treatment decision, legal advice may be necessary.

When patients lack the mental capacity to give or withhold consent for treatment, substitute consent from a decision maker must be sought. When the psychiatrist suspects patient incompetence and proxy consent is not permitted, a judicial determination of incompetency and permission to treat may be required, either through a court order or through a declaration of incompetence and the appointment of a guardian who will provide treatment consent. In most states, involuntarily hospitalized patients who are thought to lack the mental capacity to refuse treatment cannot be treated against their will without an adjudication of incompetence and the substituted consent of the court. Involuntary hospitalization does not automatically equate with incompetence to consent to or refuse treatment. Moreover, recent court cases have found that prisoners have constitutionally protected interests in not being treated against their will and possess a qualified right to refuse treatment (16).

Consent by Third Parties

The statutes of every state define procedures by which a judicial determination of competency and the establishment of guardianship can be made. A petition may be filed with the appropriate court for a declaration of incompetency and guardianship. Typically, a family member or relative is appointed guardian. Although some courts will appoint a general guardian to make all decisions, often limited guardianship is provided for the purpose of consent to treatment. In some jurisdictions, the judge will be the substitute decision maker. Unless proxy consent by a relative is provided by statute or by a recent judicial opinion, good-faith consents by next of kin should not be relied on in the treatment of a psychiatric patient who is believed to be incompetent (17). Some courts, however, have sanctioned such consents, even in the presence of a statutory provision for incompetency determinations, in situations where the relative providing consent supported the patient.

For the patient who remains incompetent, an increasing number of states provide administrative procedures authorized by statute that permit involuntary treatment of the incompetent, refusing, mentally ill patient who does not meet current standards for involuntary hospitalization. A durable power of attorney provides consent through enacted durable-power-of-attorney statutes. In some instances, this procedure may not meet judicial challenge, or the patient may revoke this arrangement. In order to rectify the sometimes uncertain status of the durable power of attorney as applied to health care decisions, a number of states have passed or are considering passing health care proxy laws. The health care proxy is a legal instrument akin to the durable power of attorney but specifically created for health care decision making (18). Living-will laws permit individuals to explicitly state their wishes concerning life-sustaining treatment. Efforts to fashion a psychiatric living will as an alternative to involuntary treatment have been attempted. The legal sufficiency of such a document remains untested. Right-to-die statutory surrogate laws authorize certain individuals, such as a spouse or a court-appointed guardian, to make treatment decisions when the patient has not expressed his or her wishes in writing.

With the increasing civil libertarian emphasis within legislatures and the courts, psychiatrists who unilaterally decide that a patient refusing treatment is incompetent and institute treatment run the risk of litigation. Because every state specifically defines who may substitute consent and under what circumstances, patients may later refer to these statutes should a lawsuit arise. Thus, statutory provisions will ordinarily protect psychiatrists who adhere to established procedures for competency determination.

Consent Refusal and Patient Management

Despite time and resource restrictions in managed care settings, every effort should be made to develop a working alliance with a nonconsenting patient. Legal options for obtaining consent should not be used unless required by an emergency, by the failure of clinical interventions, or by law.

Initially, the psychiatrist should look upon the patient's refusal as a treatment issue. Concerns expressed by patients based on previous experience with adverse drug effects or observations of other patients undergoing unpleasant or frightening side effects are not uncommon. The following play a major psychological role in drug refusal:

- Transference and countertransference issues
- Idiosyncratic meanings of treatment to the patient
- Staff conflicts
- The influence of family and friends
- Enacting power struggles
- Maintaining a sick role that brings secondary gains
- Not wanting to give up the internal gratifications that disabling symptoms may provide
- Denial of mental illness

The act of taking medications may break down denial, confirming the patient's worst fears about being mentally ill. Whenever possible, the therapist should attempt to maintain a treatment position vis-à-vis treatment refusal.

Voluntary Hospitalization

Voluntary admissions make up approximately 73% of the 1.6 million yearly admissions to psychiatric care facilities (19). Most state statutes have attempted to encourage voluntary admission in the hope of aiding treatment. Individuals who voluntarily admit themselves are presumed to understand the conditions of admission as a matter of law. The issue of competency has been omitted as a requirement except in a few states (20).

Patients are required by hospitals to sign consent forms for admission. Patients should be informed whether the voluntary admission is pure or conditional. Pure, or informal, voluntary admission permits the patient to leave the hospital at any time. Only moral suasion may be used to encourage the patient to stay. Conditional voluntary admission usually contains a provision that permits detaining the patient for a specified period of time after the patient has given written notice of intention to leave. This provision is used when the patient appears to be a danger to self or others.

In the U.S. Supreme Court case *Zinermon v. Burch* (21), a mentally ill patient who was unable to give informed consent for treatment was permitted to go forward with a civil rights action against state officials after he was committed to a state hospital using voluntary commitment procedures. The court held that Florida must have some system of procedures to screen all voluntary patients for competency, excluding incompetent persons from the voluntary admission process. For the few states that require competent consent to voluntary admission, screening procedures must be created to exclude incompetent patients. Although the court did not directly address whether a voluntary patient must be competent to consent to admission, Appelbaum (21) states that "*Zinermon* will likely refocus attention on the often-neglected process of voluntary admissions." The American Psychiatric Association Task Force on Consent to Voluntary Hospitalization (22) provides helpful guidelines for obtaining appropriate consent from patients who are voluntarily hospitalized.

The task force report makes two basic assumptions:

1. Preservation of voluntary admission whenever possible is preferable to admitting large numbers of voluntary patients involuntarily.
2. The primary safeguards for patients who are voluntarily hospitalized are clinical, not legal.

A patient's capacity to consent to a voluntary admission is deemed to be sufficient if the choice communicated by the patient is one of assent. This simple or "weak" consent enables the mentally ill to have ready access to hospitalization. Problematic admissions can be managed through oversight mechanisms (23).

In reality, the distinction between voluntary and involuntary admission is not as clear as stated in statutory law. Patients often are induced or pressured into accepting voluntary admissions. If voluntary admission were to be maintained as truly voluntary, involuntary admissions would likely increase. Strict application of the informed consent doctrine to voluntary patients would discriminate against patients temporarily lacking the mental capacity to provide a knowing consent, or against patients with partial mental incapacity who give a doubtful consent. This discrimination would produce considerable tension between the real needs of patients and the requirements of the law.

Consent Forms

Although an occasional statute may specify that a written consent form be used, no such legal requirement ordinarily exists. The advantages of a written disclosure form signed by the patient are twofold:

- The patient cannot later claim that adequate information was not provided.
- The signed form establishes exactly what was disclosed and that the consent process took place.

When consent forms are used, they should be included as part of the informing process. The form should be considered a memorandum of agreement between the clinician and the patient without adding new information. Thus, the form may be presented after negotiations are complete and the patient has consented to treatment. The consent form is used to document the existing consent rather than to obtain it, and is intended to protect the institution and the psychiatrist, not the patient.

The greatest disadvantage of written consent forms is that a particular treatment hazard or side effect may be omitted. Consent forms are either "all or nothing" concerning the information provided. The best means of protecting oneself against an unjustified claim of lack of informed consent is to write a note in the patient's record (see Table 4–4).

The obtaining of consent should not be delegated to nurses or other personnel. The reasoning for invoking an exception to obtaining consent should be clearly explained.

Informed Consent in Managed Care Settings

As part of the psychiatrist's continuing legal and professional duty to the patient (or the patient's substitute decision maker) to obtain informed consent, full disclosure should be made of all treatment options, even those not covered under the terms of a managed care plan (24). Patients should also be informed about grievance and appeals processes, if insurance coverage for recommended treatments is denied. An increasing number of states are enacting laws making "gag rules" under MCO's contractual provisions illegal.

TABLE 4–4. **Informed consent information to be recorded in the medical chart**

Information imparted to the patient
The mental capacity of the patient to understand such information
Any evidence relied on to indicate that the information was understood
Whether the patient's consent was voluntary

Gag rules limit information about treatment options furnished by physicians to patients or prohibit physicians from revealing restriction of benefits or provider financial incentives. Psychiatrists should not sign managed care contracts that contain limitations on full disclosure to patients.

Gutheil refers to consent obtained under gag rule conditions as "economic informed consent" (25). Anticipated limitations on inpatient treatment imposed by managed care should be discussed with the patient early in the admission process so that alternative treatment plans can be considered and hasty decisions avoided. Disclosures about treatment limitations need to be made in a clinically supportive manner, particularly with potentially violent patients. Patients can become quite disturbed when psychiatrists speak to them about limitations of coverage. The patient may perceive the psychiatrist as working for the insurance company, thus adversely affecting the doctor-patient relationship. (Consent to provide information to MCOs is discussed in Chapter 3, Confidentiality and Testimonial Privilege.)

■ REFERENCES

1. Schloendorff v Society of New York Hospital, 211 NY 125, 105 NE 92 (1914), overruled, Bing v Thunig, 2 NY 2d 656, 143 NE 2d 3, 163 NYS 2d 3 (1957)
2. Appelbaum PS, Lidz CW, Meisel A: Informed Consent: Legal Theory and Clinical Practice. New York, Oxford University Press, 1987, pp 84–87
3. In the Guardianship of John Roe (3) 411 MA 666 (1992)
4. Grisso T, Appelbaum PS: Comparison of standards for assessing patients' capacities to make treatment decisions. Am J Psychiatry 152:1033–1037, 1995
5. Spence v Canterbury, 464 F2d 772 (DC Cir), cert denied, 409 US 1064 (1972)
6. Truman v Thomas, 27 Cal 3d 285, 611 P2d 902, 165 Cal Rptr 308 (1980)

7. 462 F Supp 1131 (D NJ 1978), remanded, 476 F Supp 1294 (D NJ 1979), aff'd in part, modified in part and remanded, 653 F2d 836 (3d Cir 1980), vacated and remanded, 458 US 1119 (1982), 720 F2d 266 (3d Cir 1983)

8. 478 F Supp 1342 (D Mass 1979), aff'd in part, rev'd in part, 634 F2d 650 (1st Cir 1980), vacated and remanded sub nom, Mills v Rogers, 457 US 291 (1982), on remand 738 F2d 1 (1st Cir 1984); see also Rogers v Commissioner of Department of Mental Health, 390 Mass 489, 458 NE 2d 308 (Mass 1983), cert denied, 484 US 1010 (1988)

9. Mishkin B: Determining the capacity for making health care decisions, in Issues in Geriatric Psychiatry. Edited by Billig N, Rabin PV. Adv Psychosom Med 19:151–166, 1989

10. Gary v Gary, 631 SW 2d 781 (Tex Ct App 1982); Texas Fam Code Ann §14.08(c)(1) (Vernon 1985)

11. 442 US 584 (1979)

12. Klerman GL: The psychiatric patient's right to effective treatment: implications of Osheroff v Chestnut Lodge. Am J Psychiatry 147:409–418, 1990

13. Stone AA: Law, science, and psychiatric malpractice: a response to Klerman's indictment of psychoanalytic psychiatry. Am J Psychiatry 147:419–427, 1990

14. Simon RI: Clinical Psychiatry and the Law, 2nd Edition. Washington, DC, American Psychiatric Press, 1992, p 132

15. Zito JM, Lentz SL, Routt WW, et al: The treatment review panel: a solution to treatment refusal? Bulletin of the American Academy for Psychiatry and the Law 12:349–358, 1984

16. United States v Charters, 863 F2d 302 (4th Cir 1988); Charters v U.S., cert denied, 110 S Ct 1317 (1990); Washington v Harper, 494 US 210 (1990); United States v Watson, 893 F2d 970 (8th Cir), cert denied, Watson v US, 110 S Ct 3243 (1990)

17. Klein JI, Onek JN, Macbeth JE: Legal and Risk Management Issues in the Private Practice of Psychiatry. Washington, DC, American Psychiatric Press, 1994, pp 1–27

18. The Health Care Proxy Law: A Guidebook for Health Care

Professionals. Albany, NY, New York State Department of Health, January 1991

19. Appelbaum PS: Voluntary hospitalization and due process: the dilemma of Zinermon v Burch. Hospital and Community Psychiatry 41:1059–1060, 1990

20. Gutheil TG, Appelbaum PS: Clinical Handbook of Psychiatry and the Law, 2nd Edition. New York, McGraw-Hill, 1991, pp 43–44

21. 494 US 113 (1990)

22. American Psychiatric Association: Task Force Report 34: Consent to Voluntary Hospitalization. Washington, DC, American Psychiatric Association, 1993

23. Hoge SK: On being "too crazy" to sign into a mental hospital: the issue of consent to psychiatric hospitalization. Bulletin of the American Academy for Psychiatry and the Law 22:431–450, 1944

24. Simon RI: Psychiatrists' duties in discharging sicker and potentially violent inpatients in the managed care era. Psychiatr Serv 49:62–67, 1998

25. Gutheil TG, personal communication, October 20, 1996

5

PSYCHIATRIC TREATMENT

■ OVERVIEW OF THE LAW

Psychopharmacology: Standard of Care

All physicians are judged by a standard of care. The standard is based on the reasonableness of their acts as compared with what the average or prudent physician would have done in a similar situation. If a patient alleges that he or she was negligently treated, the court will look closely at not only what treatment was chosen but also why it was chosen (e.g., its reasonableness).

Typically, when treating a patient with medication, the exercise of reasonable care involves several factors. The psychiatrist should conduct a thorough clinical evaluation of the patient, including all appropriate laboratory tests, a review of present and past medication use, drug allergies, and a complete background history. Also, the psychiatrist has a duty to advise the patient regarding the use of medication and to provide sufficient information, so that an informed consent may be obtained. If a physical examination is indicated, it may be performed by the psychiatrist or the patient may be referred. It may be prudent to refer the patient for a physical examination to avoid potential troublesome transference and countertransference developments.

Medication and Liability

The law recognizes that psychiatric treatment is inexact, and therefore, only reasonable care is required. In administering psychotropic medication, certain treatment procedures are generally considered standard, and unless an emergency situation arises, they should generally be followed:

- A complete clinical history
- Disclosure of sufficient information to obtain informed consent for procedures and treatments
- Complete documentation of all treatment decisions, particularly when a medication is changed, adjusted, or reinstated
- Appropriate supervision of a patient's progress
- Monitoring the patient's reaction to the medication

When neuroleptics are prescribed, the patient's potential for developing tardive dyskinesia (TD) is a major concern. Several large judgments have been rendered against psychiatrists for failure to obtain informed consent from or to properly monitor the progress of a patient on neuroleptic medication who subsequently developed TD (1). Psychiatrists administering psychotropic medication should become familiar with the TD management guidelines promulgated by the American Psychiatric Association (APA) (see Table 5–1). The guidelines remain pertinent in the era of atypical antipsychotics, even though current research indicates a significantly lower incidence of TD with these newer agents (2). No official guideline, however, can substitute for sound clinical judgment in the treatment and management of patients.

Electroconvulsive Therapy

Electroconvulsive therapy (ECT) continues to be used by psychiatrists in treating mainly major depressive disorder. The APA Task Force on ECT has made specific nonbinding recommendations for its use and administration (3). Legislative and judicial decisions regarding ECT include numerous indications and contraindications for its use. Provisions often are made for consultation and review, medical procedures required before and during treatment, regulation of the frequency of treatment, and specific record-keeping requirements (4). Furthermore, the Joint Commission on Accreditation of Healthcare Organizations (JCAHO) considers ECT to be a special treatment procedure and requires hospitals to have written

---

TABLE 5–1. **Recommendations for prevention and management of tardive dyskinesia**

---

1. Review indications for neuroleptic drugs; consider alternative treatments when available.
2. Educate the patient and his or her family regarding benefits and risks. Obtain informed consent for long-term treatment, and document it in the medical record.
3. Establish objective evidence of the benefit from neuroleptics, and review it periodically (at least every 3–6 months) to determine ongoing need and benefit.
4. Utilize the minimum effective dosage for chronic treatment.
5. Exercise particular caution with children, the elderly, and patients with affective disorders.
6. Examine the patient regularly for early signs of dyskinesia, and note them in the medical record.
7. If dyskinesia does occur, consider an alternative neurological diagnosis.
8. If presumptive tardive dyskinesia is present, reevaluate the indications for continued neuroleptic treatment and obtain informed consent from the patient regarding continuing or discontinuing neuroleptic treatment.
9. If a neuroleptic is continued, attempt to lower the dosage.
10. If dyskinesia worsens, consider discontinuing the neuroleptic or switching to a new neuroleptic. At present, clozapine may hold some promise in this regard, but it is important to stay alert to new research findings.
11. Many cases of dyskinesia will improve and even remit with neuroleptic discontinuation or dosage reduction. If treatment for tardive dyskinesia is indicated, utilize more benign agents first (e.g., benzodiazepines and tocopherol), but keep abreast of new treatment developments.
12. If movement disorder is severe or disabling, consider obtaining a second opinion.

Source. Reprinted from American Psychiatric Association: *Tardive Dyskinesia: A Task Force Report of the American Psychiatric Association.* Washington, DC, American Psychiatric Association, 1992, pp. 250–251. Used with permission.

policies concerning its use (5). Violation of statutory regulations or of JCAHO and hospital policies governing ECT can provide a basis for the allegation of negligent treatment.

Malpractice liability arising from the use of ECT has generally been confined to five situations:

1. Failure to obtain informed consent
2. Conducting an inadequate pretreatment examination
3. Negligent administration of premedication
4. Negligent administration of ECT, causing fractures or other injuries
5. Failure to provide adequate posttreatment supervision

By far, obtaining inadequate or no informed consent creates the greatest potential for liability in what is now generally considered to be a "tort-free" psychiatric procedure.

Psychotherapy

Psychotherapy is considered by the law to be inexact, evolving, and based on principles difficult to quantify and measure. Currently, more than 450 schools of psychotherapy exist. As a result, malpractice actions for negligent psychotherapy are infrequent and typically unsuccessful (6). As a rule, a particular therapeutic practice or technique need only be considered "reasonable" as judged by an ordinary therapist. This standard is very broad and vague. Certain actions (such as sexually exploiting the patient's transference) and certain intentional and quasi-intentional torts (e.g., "technique" amounting to battery) have been subject to legal action. Moreover, other abuses, such as breach of confidentiality, abandonment, and negligent termination, have all been held to be tortious acts.

On the other hand, an increasing number of malpractice suits are being brought against therapists for treatment-boundary violations under legal theories of negligent psychotherapy and abandonment. Reasonably clear boundaries for the conduct of psychotherapy exist that are accepted by most competent therapists from a wide variety of theoretical orientations (7). Although a number of boundary violations may eventually evolve into therapist-patient sex, many other such violations do not. Nonetheless, patients may be psychologically harmed by boundary violations that do not lead to therapist-patient sex (8). Boundary violations may precede exploitation of the patient for money or a "social relationship." Unchecked boundary violations usually produce serious errors in diagnosis and treatment.

■ CLINICAL MANAGEMENT OF LEGAL ISSUES

Prescribing Medication

Prescribing Medication for Unapproved Uses

Prescribing an approved medication for an unapproved use does not violate federal law. Whenever a psychiatrist prescribes a drug for a use that is not yet approved by the Food and Drug Administration (FDA)—for example, an anticonvulsant for a mood disorder, lithium for violence, medroxyprogesterone acetate for paraphilias, a tricyclic and monoamine oxidase inhibitor combination for refractory depression—the decision should be based on reasonable knowledge of the drug based on a firm scientific rationale and sound medical studies. The psychiatrist should have accessible texts or journal articles to substantiate that the decision to prescribe a drug for a nonapproved use is based on competent psychiatric practice. For instance, the psychiatric literature supports the use of a variety of drugs in patients with rapid-cycling bipolar disorder that do not have FDA approval for the treatment of this often-malignant condition (9). "Off-label" prescribing of medications is at the discretion of the physician once a drug has been approved. The psychiatrist is not restricted by FDA-approved indications and labeling. Restrictions apply only to the manufacturer's representations in advertising.

The standard for informed consent is correspondingly heightened when a drug is prescribed for an unapproved use. The patient or guardian must be informed that he or she will be taking a drug for a use that has not been approved by the FDA and should be warned of all reasonably foreseeable risks. The nature of the disclosure should be recorded in the patient's chart. Once a drug is marketed, its use is the responsibility of physicians, and its prescription is at their sole discretion.

A number of medications used by psychiatrists to treat various psychiatric disorders of children do not have official FDA approval to be used as psychopharmacological agents. Excluding psychostimulants for attention-deficit disorder, only a few psychotropics have FDA approval for use in children, for example, haloperidol (Haldol), thioridazine (Mellaril), chlorpromazine (Thorazine), pimozide (Orap), imipramine (Tofranil), and clomipramine (Anafranil). All other psychotropics, including the frequently used antidepressants desipramine (Norpramin), fluoxetine (Prozac), and lithium, carry a disclaimer, "Not recommended below age 12 since safety and efficacy have not been proven in this age group" (10, p. 40). Furthermore, there are a scant scientific knowledge base in the psychiatric literature and little data available from controlled clinical trials to support off-label prescribing for children. Until more studies become available, clinicians have found many of these drugs to be useful in treating children, by following clinical hunches, using trial and error, or through just plain serendipity.

Unapproved Drugs

The prescription of an unapproved drug technically violates the law. Under 21 U.S.C. §355, to "introduce or deliver for introduction into interstate commerce" an unapproved drug is a violation of the law. For example, this issue arose with clomipramine, which had been approved for use in the treatment of obsessive-compulsive disorder (OCD) in Canada and other countries before it was officially approved in the United States. The psychiatric literature supported the treatment of OCD with clomipramine. Its side-effect profile was similar to that of other tricyclic antidepressants.

Generally, the FDA's policy is not to prosecute physicians who prescribe legitimate drugs approved in other jurisdictions. In limited circumstances, access to unapproved drugs may be available under regulations established under the authority of the FDA (11). The risk of malpractice is increased, however, if a patient is harmed by a drug that is not approved as effective and safe by the FDA.

Physicians' Desk Reference or Drug Insert

The *Physicians' Desk Reference* (PDR) is published privately by a commercial firm. The publisher compiles, organizes, and distributes product descriptions prepared by the manufacturers' medical department and consultants. The FDA requires that products that have official package inserts be reported in the PDR in the identical language appearing on the circular.

A drug's package insert lists almost all of the side effects ever reported in drug trials, even if not produced by the drug under consideration; that is, side effects found in similar drugs are also reported. The side effects reported in the package insert may not be weighted in terms of probability of occurrence in the course of clinical usage. The legal significance of the package insert or PDR listing varies with each jurisdiction.

Courts generally follow the reasoning in *Ramon v. Farr* (12), which held that drug inserts do not by themselves set the standard of care. Rather, such inserts are only one factor to be considered among others, such as the scientific literature, approvals in other countries, expert testimony, and other pertinent factors. The existence of a substantial scientific literature that justifies the clinician's treatment is vastly more persuasive than FDA approval.

Although the PDR is frequently used by lawyers in court, it would be a serious error for clinicians to regard the PDR as a primary standard-of-care reference and a constraint on their clinical judgment. Psychiatrists are responsible for making informed decisions, taking into account their own clinical training and experience and the relevant psychiatric literature. The PDR is not a comprehensive clinical text. Patient care may be compromised if psychiatrists rely on the PDR rather than the professional literature and the usual community standards of practice as their main source of clinical guidance. In essence, the PDR should be considered as only one of several sources of information that a psychiatrist may rely on for making medication decisions. Official guidelines, however, cannot take the place of sound clinical judgment as applied to the special treatment needs of a patient.

Inappropriate Administration of Psychotropic Medications

Inappropriate administration of medication includes the following:

- Failure to perform or obtain an adequate physical examination when indicated
- Failure to obtain a medical history before prescribing psychoactive medication

When psychiatrists decide to prescribe a psychoactive medication for patients, they must familiarize themselves with their patients' medical history and physical condition. In particular, a history of allergic reactions to medications must be noted. If questions exist about a patient's health, consultation with a physician who can conduct a full medical investigation is in order. Psychiatrists are liable for failing to diagnose organic conditions. They have a firm responsibility to search out organic causes of psychological illness, either by their own examination or by referral to competent specialists.

Prescribing neuroleptics for patients who suffer from anxiety may be an example of medicating inappropriately. However, the clinical needs of the patient are the determining factors. Psychoactive medications that are indicated for one type of psychiatric disorder may be empirically useful for a nonindicated disorder in other patients. Informed consent requirements are usually heightened when a drug is prescribed off label.

The use of polypharmacy, or multiple medications, has often been disparaged as a "shotgun" approach to treatment that may significantly increase the possibility of serious side effects. Nevertheless, certain patients may benefit from rational psychopharmacology, where diagnostic clarity exists and response to single-drug regimens has been poor.

An attempt to impose social control on patients with mental illness through "chemical straitjackets" represents an inappropriate indication for psychoactive medication, if the objectionable behavior is not directly the result of a psychiatric disorder. For example, a neuroleptic may be lifesaving for a severely agitated elderly patient with congestive heart failure, dementia, and psychosis. Neuroleptic medications should not be used to suppress objectionable behavior that is a lifelong aspect of the patient's personality rather than symptomatic of a treatable psychiatric disorder. In addition, psychoactive drugs should never be used as a form of punishment. Although "chemical restraints" raise issues concerning deprivation of civil rights, malpractice actions are more likely.

The enactment of statutory regulations establishing medication-prescribing guidelines will influence the standard of care in providing drug therapy. For example, the Omnibus Budget Reconciliation Act of 1987, implemented October 1, 1990, regulates the use of psychotropic drugs in long-term health care facilities receiving funds from Medicare and Medicaid (13). The Health Care Financing Administration guidelines for neuroleptic drugs include documentation of the psychiatric diagnosis or specific condition requiring neuroleptic use, prohibition of as-needed neuroleptic use, and gradual dose reductions of neuroleptics combined with attempts at behavioral programming and environmental modification (14).

Exceeding Recommended Dosages

Some psychiatric patients may require the administration of psychoactive medications that exceed dosage guidelines. The reasons for such a decision must be clearly documented in the patient's record. The patient should be made aware that drug guidelines are being exceeded. If very high levels of medication are required, the patient may need to be hospitalized until a safer maintenance level of the medication can be achieved.

A patient's failure to renew prescriptions may pose a serious danger to his or her care. Thus, prescriptions that require frequent renewal may lead to noncompliance. With neuroleptics, the prescription of what might appear to be a lethal amount to the ordinary patient may be only a single dose for a patient with chronic schizophrenia on long-term maintenance therapy. The psychiatrist should note these differences in the patient's medical record, including the fact that tolerance to the toxic effects of neuroleptic medication develops quickly.

A psychiatrist covering for a treating psychiatrist should prescribe only enough medication to hold the patient over until the treating psychiatrist's return. If the treating psychiatrist will be away for a long period of time, the covering psychiatrist may need to personally evaluate the patient in order to prescribe smaller amounts of medication. Typically, only a brief history, including diagnosis and treatment, is provided, either orally or in writing, to the covering psychiatrist. Therefore, renewal of medications over the telephone must be done with great care. In some instances, renewal of medications may require seeing the patient.

Monitoring Side Effects

Psychiatrists have a duty to use reasonable care in prescribing, dispensing, and administering medication. Monitoring the patient and warning of side effects fall within this duty. As part of the working alliance with patients, the psychiatrist should inform them of possible side effects of medication, encouraging the patient to report any serious side effects that arise. Open communication about potential problems with medications enhances the therapeutic process through the establishment of trust and reduces the problem of noncompliance.

Some basic side effects are sometimes overlooked. Patients must be warned about driving or working around dangerous machinery if the medications that they are taking produce drowsiness or slowed reflexes. Similarly, patients must be warned of the dangers of mixing alcohol with psychoactive drugs. Clinicians need to be aware of drug-induced memory impairment, particularly with certain benzodiazepines. The resulting amnesia can be psychologically and socially disabling.

Monitoring the patient's clinical condition rather than placing exclusive reliance on laboratory test results is imperative. For example, patients undergoing lithium therapy have developed signs and symptoms of toxicity when lithium levels were in the therapeutic range (15).

Prescribing for Unseen Patients

Psychiatrists should avoid prescribing medication for unseen patients. Psychiatrists who work in clinics may be asked to prescribe medications for patients seen only by nonmedical therapists. Reports received from a nonmedical therapist about an unseen patient are not a sufficient basis for prescribing medication. Nonmedical therapists are not trained in psychopharmacology. Their reports should not be relied on when forming a clinical opinion about prescribing psychoactive drugs for the patient. Psychiatrists who prescribe medication are responsible for such treatment even though another provider is primarily responsible for the overall care of the patient. In split treatment arrangements, psychiatrists remain highly vulnerable to malpractice actions stemming from improper supervision of patients who develop serious or fatal reactions to medications.

In large hospitals or institutions, a psychiatrist may not be able to see all of his or her patients. The psychiatrist may be required to write a prescription covering a period of many months for drugs that are dispensed by nurses or mental health aides. The only generally acceptable solution for the psychiatrist is to see the patient each time before a prescription is written. If this cannot be done, the reasons should be carefully documented.

Psychiatrists sometimes authorize a prescription for persons unknown to and unseen by them who live some distance away where medical services are not available. Psychiatrists need to be aware that prescribing for unseen patients will likely be construed as creating a doctor-patient relationship, if an untoward reaction to the medication becomes the basis of a lawsuit.

No stock answer can be given to the question of how frequently a psychiatrist should see a patient. Generally, psychiatrists should schedule return visits with a frequency that accords with the patient's clinical needs. The longer the time between visits, the greater the risk of adverse drug reactions and developments in the patient's condition. The interval between visits should not ordinarily be longer than 6 months. Patients who are being treated should not be allowed to go unsupervised.

The psychological issues surrounding patient compliance and noncompliance with prescribed medications are complex and need to be explored by the psychiatrist with the patient. For this reason, medications should be dispensed in the context of a therapeutic relationship in which the many psychological meanings associated with the taking of medication can be explored (16).

Generic Drugs

Generic drugs that contain the same active ingredients as established brand-name drugs may not possess the same clinical efficacy because of differential absorption, distribution, and elimination rates in the human body. Therapists may become confused when a patient reports no symptom improvement, not realizing that the generic drug lacks the brand-name formulation's therapeutic efficacy. Whether generic or brand-name, the well-selected drug that achieves maximal therapeutic efficacy in the shortest time will likely be cost saving in the long run.

The psychiatrist is responsible for selecting the appropriate medication for the patient. Only when the psychiatrist signs the "generic substitution permissible" line may the pharmacist substitute a less-expensive drug with the same active ingredients. In a number of states, drug product selection laws stipulate that the prescriber must expressly indicate "do not substitute" in some manner when declining generic substitution. To pursue a consistent prescribing and monitoring policy, the psychiatrist should be aware of the legal issues surrounding generic drugs (16).

Finally, prescriptions must be written legibly. Illegible prescriptions are a major source of drug dispensing errors. If the psychiatrist's handwriting tends to be unreadable, the prescription should be printed. In addition, the amount should be written out so that the number of doses cannot be changed by drug-abusing patients. The directions for taking the medication generally should be specific rather than written: "sig: as directed." The pharmacist should be instructed to label all medications. Unlabeled medications may be difficult to identify by emergency room personnel should the patient require emergency care.

Tardive Dyskinesia and Informed Consent

The vast majority of important TD litigation has been in the context of equity rather than malpractice cases (e.g., injunction, mandatory relief such as in the case of *Rennie v. Klein* [17]). Nevertheless, a significant number of malpractice suits have been brought against psychiatrists by patients who developed TD. The allegations of negligence concerning neuroleptic treatment have included improper dosages, excessive length of treatment, failure to monitor, inappropriate indications, and failure to obtain informed consent (warning of the risk of TD) (18). Psychiatrists should not be lulled into complacency by current research findings of relatively low incidence of TD with the newer atypical antipsychotics. More research is required to establish the long-term safety of these medications.

The greater the risk of any treatment, the greater the clinician's obligation to disclose even relatively remote risks. If alternative treatments are available that present lesser risks or a greater probability of success, the duty to disclose increases. For example, if a neuroleptic is given when a benzodiazepine or buspirone might be equally effective (such as in the treatment of an anxiety disorder), then detailed disclosure of the risks of neuroleptic treatment is necessary.

Because the incidence of TD is quite low within the first 6 months of neuroleptic treatment, some clinicians believe that it is not a material risk at the start of treatment and need not be disclosed (19). Nevertheless, plaintiffs' attorneys are fond of pointing out in court that all psychiatrists have been on notice concerning TD since 1973. At that time, psychiatrists were first informed of TD through the FDA *Drug Bulletin,* a publication sent to all physicians who have a drug prescription number. Furthermore, informed consent is required by law from the first day of treatment unless an emergency exists or unless therapeutic privilege can be legitimately asserted.

When TD occurs several years after initiation of neuroleptic treatment, an absence of an early informed consent may cause serious legal problems. For example, many patients with chronic mental illness are transient. They may have been taking neuroleptics that were prescribed by a number of previous physicians. Further, they may not be able to provide the current psychiatrist with an accurate medication history. A delay in obtaining informed consent from such patients extends the period of continuous neuroleptic intake without a valid consent. The patient may develop TD while under the treatment of a subsequent psychiatrist who is merely continuing or adjusting neuroleptic medications. Providing and recording full disclosure to patients is, with certain exceptions, the best policy medically, ethically, and legally.

Because some patients with psychosis may have impaired mental capacity, only basic information about TD should be communicated. The acceptance of treatment by an incompetent patient is often not questioned because it accords with the psychiatrist's therapeutic intent. Consent options for patients who lack health care decision-making capacity are discussed in Chapter 4, Informed Consent and the Right to Refuse Treatment. A patient with psychosis and TD may be able to give a fully informed consent to undertake the risk of continued neuroleptic treatment. In some cases, continued treatment with neuroleptics of a patient with TD may represent good clinical practice consistent with the patient's overall treatment needs, even though a lawsuit may be filed later. For instance, patients with psychosis and TD who are having an acute exacerbation of their symptoms or who require maintenance therapy may need continued neuroleptic treatment. If the mental disorder is severe enough, the psychiatrist and the patient with TD may be willing to sacrifice long-term outcome for important short-term gains from the continued use of neuroleptics. When restarting drugs with patients manifesting TD, informed-consent procedures should be started immediately. If the patient needs to continue neuroleptic therapy in the presence of TD, a confirming second opinion should be obtained.

Electroconvulsive Therapy and Informed Consent

The APA Task Force on ECT recommended that policies and procedures should be developed to ensure proper informed consent. Informed consent should include how, when, and by whom the treatment will be administered as well as the nature and scope of

---

TABLE 5–2. **Recommended information to be provided to patients being considered for electroconvulsive therapy (ECT)**

Who is recommending ECT and for what reason

A description of applicable treatment alternatives

A description of the ECT procedure, including the times when treatments are given and the location where treatments will occur

A discussion of the relative merits and risks of the different stimulus electrode placements and the specific choice that has been made for the patient

The typical range for number of treatments to be administered as well as a statement that reconsent will be obtained if the number of treatments in the index course exceeds a set maximum number (for that facility)

A statement that there is no guarantee that ECT will be effective

A statement concerning the need for continuation treatment

A description of the likelihood and severity (in general terms) of major risks associated with the procedure, including mortality, cardiopulmonary dysfunction, confusion, and acute and persistent memory impairment; in addition, delineation of the common minor side effects of ECT (e.g., headaches and musculoskeletal pain)

A statement that consent for ECT also entails consent for appropriate emergency treatment in the event that this is clinically necessary during the time the patient is not fully conscious

A description of any restrictions on patient behavior likely to be necessary before, during, or after ECT

An offer to answer questions at any time regarding the recommended treatment and the name(s) of the individual(s) who can be contacted with such questions

A statement that consent for ECT is voluntary and can be withdrawn at any time

---

Source. Reprinted from American Psychiatric Association: "Consent for Electroconvulsive Therapy," in *The Practice of Electroconvulsive Therapy: Recommendations for Treatment, Training, and Privileging,* Second Edition (A Task Force Report of the American Psychiatric Association). Washington, DC, American Psychiatric Association, 2000, p. 107. Used with permission.

information provided (3) (see Table 5–2). Policies and procedures should be consistent with JCAHO and hospital policies as well as local and state regulatory requirements, which vary substantially among the various jurisdictions.

Some states may not allow ECT to be used, even under life-threatening circumstances, unless there is full compliance with regulatory procedures. Thus, due-process requirements in some states obviate the implied consent that is normally presumed to exist in genuine emergency situations. As a result, necessary treatment may be delayed. Some states require a court order for the nonconsenting, involuntarily hospitalized patient who needs ECT (16).

Psychotherapy and Informed Consent

Very few therapists warn patients of the risks of a proposed method of psychotherapy, although the potential benefits may be extolled. Nevertheless, untoward transference reactions, regressive dependency states, and worsening clinical conditions occur with some regularity in psychotherapy. Prolonged nontherapeutic stalemates are not unusual. To the extent that psychotherapeutic modalities can produce benefits, they may also cause harm. Accordingly, patients need to be informed of both the benefits and the risks of specific psychotherapies. For example, a lawsuit alleging that therapists negligently created false memories of sexual abuse invariably have, as an element of the claim, the therapist's failure to obtain informed consent from the patient concerning the dangers of the treatment undertaken (20). Any limitations of treatment and confidentiality under managed care contracts should be explained at the beginning of treatment.

An initial period of evaluation allows the patient time to consider the therapist, the therapist's technique, and the interactional process between the therapist and the patient. This time also allows the therapist to make a reasonable diagnostic and treatment assessment of the patient. The nature of the patient's difficulties should be described in plain language using descriptive terms that underlie psychiatric nosology. Also, the following should be discussed with the prospective psychotherapy patient:

- Anticipated benefits
- Potential risks

- A cautious prognostic assessment
- Expected outcome with and without treatment
- Available alternative treatments, including risks and benefits

Alternative therapeutic modalities need to be carefully discussed with patients. The psychiatrist can no longer recommend just one form of treatment. Although therapists may not be proficient in using more than a few treatment approaches, they should be up-to-date in their knowledge of the available treatments used by competent, ethical therapists. At a minimum, therapists should be able to intelligently explain alternative therapies, including risks and benefits, to the patient. If a patient requires another method of treatment for which the therapist lacks proficiency, the patient should be referred to a therapist who can provide such treatment.

In managed care settings, patients requiring long-term psychotherapy will need to be informed of the limitation of treatment. Patients who have recovered or are currently recovering memories of childhood sexual abuse will likely need extended psychotherapy. This is also true of some patients with borderline personality disorder. These patients should be referred to competent therapists outside the managed care plan or treated by the current therapist under a private arrangement. Psychiatrists should refer to their contracts concerning the permissibility of billing patients directly.

In *Osheroff v. Chestnut Lodge* (21), long-term psychotherapy was prescribed for an inpatient with a major depression. After 7 months of psychotherapy, the patient's psychiatric condition had worsened. The plaintiff was transferred to another hospital, where treatment with an antidepressant medication was initiated. Improvement occurred rapidly. After the lawsuit was filed, an arbitration panel found for the plaintiff. Both sides exercised their right to a trial. Before trial, the case was settled for an undisclosed amount.

The treatment of a psychiatric disorder exclusively by psychotherapy when proven, effective biological treatments exist can bring a suit for negligent treatment. An intense debate concerning biological versus psychodynamic treatment of psychiatric disorders grew out of the *Osheroff* case (22, 23).

Recovered Memories of Sexual Abuse

The current clamorous controversy concerning recovered memories of sexual abuse threatens to undermine the credibility of the mental health professions. The debate has generated intense passions that have driven an increasing number of recovered memory cases into the courts. Patients alleging recovered memories of abuse have sued parents and other alleged perpetrators. In a number of instances, the alleged victimizers have sued therapists who, they claim, negligently induced false memories of sexual abuse. In an about-face, some patients have recanted and joined forces with others (usually their parents) to sue the therapists.

The memory debate has polarized most therapists into believers and disbelievers. Strongly held personal biases about recovered memories represent a new occupational hazard for clinicians. Such feelings can undermine the therapists' duty of neutrality to their patients, creating deviant treatment boundaries and the provision of substandard care.

Litigation in recovered memory cases is expected to soar in the coming years. Some predict multimillion dollar verdicts against mental health practitioners. A jury awarded more than $10 million to the plaintiffs in a case alleging that therapists implanted memories of satanic sexual abuse. A fundamental allegation in these cases is that the therapist abandoned a position of neutrality to suggest, persuade, coerce, and implant false memories of childhood sexual abuse. The guiding principle of clinical risk management in recovered memory cases is maintenance of therapist neutrality and establishment of sound treatment boundaries.

Further complicating the matter is the empirical evidence about memory mechanisms, which (as is typical for any emerging science) reveals contradictory findings about how and what persons retain in memory and forget in various settings. Empirical studies often fail to distinguish whether allegedly repressed memories are not retrieved or simply not reported to researchers.

Valid risk management has a solid clinical footing and is secondarily informed by awareness of the legal issues. The following risk management principles should be considered when evaluating or treating a patient in psychotherapy who recovers memories of abuse (20):

- Maintain therapist neutrality; do not suggest abuse
- Stay clinically focused; provide adequate evaluation and treatment for patients presenting problems and symptoms
- Carefully document the memory recovery process
- Manage personal bias and countertransference
- Avoid mixing treater and expert witness roles
- Closely monitor supervisory and collaborative therapy relationships
- Clarify nontreatment roles with family members
- Avoid special techniques (e.g., hypnosis or sodium amytal) unless clearly indicated; obtain consultation first
- Stay within professional competence; do not take cases you cannot handle
- Distinguish between narrative truth and historical truth
- Obtain consultation in problematic cases
- Foster patient autonomy and self-determination; do not suggest lawsuits
- In managed care settings, inform patients with recovered memories that more than brief therapy may be required
- When making public statements, distinguish personal opinions from scientifically established facts
- Stop and refer, if uncomfortable with a patient who is recovering memories of childhood abuse
- Do not be afraid to ask about abuse as part of a competent psychiatric evaluation

Prescribing Medications in Managed Care Settings

In managed care or other treatment settings, the prescribing of medication in the absence of a working doctor-patient relationship does not meet generally accepted standards of good clinical care. Such a practice is a prime example of fragmented care. It diminishes the efficacy of the drug treatment itself and may even lead to the patient's failure to take the prescribed medication. Fragmented care, in which the psychiatrist functions only as a prescriber of medication while remaining uninformed about the patient's overall clinical status, constitutes substandard treatment that may lead to a malpractice action.

Split treatment situations require that the psychiatrist stay fully informed of the patient's clinical status as well as of the nature and quality of treatment the patient is receiving from the nonmedical therapist (24, 25). Split treatment situations are collaborative arrangements (26). In a collaborative relationship, responsibility for the patient's care is shared according to the qualifications and limitations of each discipline. The responsibilities of each discipline do not diminish those of the other disciplines. Patients should be informed of the separate responsibilities of each discipline. Periodic evaluation of the patient's clinical condition and needs by the psychiatrist and the nonmedical therapist is necessary to determine if the collaboration should continue. On termination of the collaborative relationship, the patient should be informed by both the psychiatrist and the nonmedical therapist, either separately or jointly. In split treatment situations, if negligence is claimed on the part of the nonmedical therapist, it is likely that the collaborating psychiatrist will be sued (27).

Psychiatrists who prescribe medications in a split treatment arrangement should be able to hospitalize patients, should that become necessary. If the psychiatrist does not have admitting privileges, then prior arrangements should exist with other psychiatrists who can hospitalize patients in an emergency. Some patients with severe mental disorders are being seen in split treatment arrangements. The psychiatrist should determine whether the patient's condition is appropriate for split treatment. Acutely disturbed patients will likely require that their entire management and follow-up be provided by a psychiatrist. Split treatment is increasingly used by MCOs and represents a potential malpractice minefield.

In managed care settings, psychiatrists increasingly are required to prescribe medications from a restrictive or closed formulary. For example, selective serotonin reuptake inhibitors (SSRIs) are currently considered the first-line treatment for depression. However, some MCOs may allow only the prescribing of tricyclic antidepressants (TCAs). TCAs have a much greater lethality than SSRIs for patients who overdose. Psychiatrists, at their professional discretion, should determine which medications will be prescribed according to the special clinical needs of the patient. Psychiatrists should vigorously resist attempts to restrict their choice of drugs by a restrictive or closed formulary or by therapeutic substitution (i.e., interchanging a different chemical agent from the same therapeutic class; for example, substituting a TCA for an SSRI). The prescribing of specific medications should be determined by the psychiatrist alone based on the clinical needs of the patient. An appeal should be filed if a prescription for a non-formulary-approved drug is denied.

■ REFERENCES

1. See, e.g., Clites v State, 322 NW 2d 917 (Iowa Ct App 1982); Hedin v United States, No 583–3 (D Minn Dec 27th 1984), appeal dsmd, No 2085–5057 MN (8th Cir May 21, 1985); Barclay v Campbell, 704 SW 2d 8 (Tex 1986); Faigenbaum v Oakland Medical Center, 373 NW 2d 161 (Mich Ct App 1985), superseded by statute, as stated in Trotsky v Henry Ford Hospital, 425 NW 2d 531 (Mich App 1988); American Cyanamid v Frankson, 732 SW 2d 648 (Tex Ct App 1987); Snider v Harding Hospital (No 84-CV-06–3582) Franklin Cty Ct Comm Pleas (Columbus, OH, August 1988)

2. Glazer WM: Expected incidence of tardive dyskinesia associated with atypical antipsychotics. J Clin Psychiatry 61 (suppl 4):21–26, 2000

3. American Psychiatric Association: The Practice of Electroconvulsive Therapy: Recommendations for Treatment, Training, and Privileging, 2nd Edition (A Task Force Report of the American Psychiatric Association). Washington, DC, American Psychiatric Association, 2000

4. Winslade WJ, Liston EH, Ross JW, et al: Medical, judicial, and statutory regulation of ECT in the United States. Am J Psychiatry 141:1349–1355, 1984

5. Joint Commission on Accreditation of Healthcare Organizations: Consolidated Standards Manual. Oak Brook Terrace, IL, Joint Commission on Accreditation of Healthcare Organizations, 1999

6. Simon RI: The practice of psychotherapy: legal liabilities of an "impossible" profession, in American Psychiatric Press Review of Clinical Psychiatry and the Law, Vol 2. Edited by Simon RI. Washington, DC, American Psychiatric Press, 1991, pp 3–91

7. Simon RI: Treatment boundary violations: clinical, ethical, and legal considerations. Bulletin of the American Academy for Psychiatry and the Law 20:269–288, 1992

8. Simon RI: Psychological injury caused by boundary violation precursors to therapist-patient sex. Psychiatric Annals 21: 614–619, 1991

9. Simon RI: Clinical risk management of the rapid cycling bipolar patient. Harv Rev Psychiatry 4:245–254, 1997

10. Bender KJ: NIMH seeks improved pharmacotherapy for children. Psychiatric Times 12:40, 1995

11. King SM: Legal and risk management concerns relating to the use of non-FDA approved drugs in the practice of psychiatry. Rx for Risk 6:1–5, 1998

12. Ramon v Farr, 770 P2d 131 (Utah 1989)

13. Hendrickson RM: New federal regulations, psychotropics, and nursing homes. Drug Therapy August (suppl):101–105, 1990

14. Health Care Financing Administration Department of Health and Human Services: Medicare and Medicaid requirements for long-term care facilities. Final rule with request for comments. Federal Register, February 12, 1989, pp 5316–5336

15. Lewis DA: Unrecognized chronic lithium neurotoxic reactions. JAMA 250:2029–2030, 1983

16. Simon RI: Clinical Psychiatry and the Law, 2nd Edition. Washington, DC, American Psychiatric Press, 1992, pp 203–205

17. 462 F Supp 1131 (D NJ 1978), remanded, 476 F Supp 1294 (D NJ 1979), aff'd in part, modified in part and remanded, 653 F2d 836 (3d Cir 1980), vacated and remanded, 458 US 1119 (1982), 720 F2d 266 (3d Cir 1983)

18. Simon RI: Somatic therapies and the law, in American Psychiatric Press Review of Clinical Psychiatry and the Law, Vol 1. Edited by Simon RI. Washington, DC, American Psychiatric Press, 1990, pp 3–82

19. Schatzberg AF, Cole JO: Manual of Clinical Psychopharmacology, 2nd Edition. Washington, DC, American Psychiatric Press, 1991, p 6

20. 62 Md App 519, 490 A2d 720 (MD Ct App), cert denied, Chestnut Lodge v Osheroff, 304 MD 163, 497 A2d 1163 (1985)

21. Gutheil TG, Simon RI: Clinically based risk management principles for recovered memory cases. Psychiatr Serv 48:1403–1407, 1997

22. Klerman GL: The psychiatric patient's right to effective treatment: implications of Osheroff v Chestnut Lodge. Am J Psychiatry 147:409–418, 1990

23. Stone AA: Law, science, and psychiatric malpractice: a response to Klerman's indictment of psychoanalytic psychiatry. Am J Psychiatry 147:419–127, 1990

24. Meyer DJ, Simon RI: Split treatment: clarity between psychiatrists and psychotherapists. Psychiatric Annals 29 Part 1 (5):241–245, 1999

25. Meyer DJ, Simon RI: Split treatment: clarity between psychiatrists and psychotherapists. Psychiatric Annals 29 Part 2 (6):327–332, 1999

26. Sederer LI, Ellison J, Keyes C: Guidelines for prescribing psychiatrists in consultative, collaborative and supervisory relationships. Psychiatr Serv 49:1197–1202, 1998

27. Woodward B, Duckworth K, Gutheil TG: The pharmacotherapist-psychotherapist collaboration, in American Psychiatric Press Review of Psychiatry, Vol 12. Edited by Oldham J. Washington, DC, American Psychiatric Press, 1993, pp 631–649

6

SECLUSION AND RESTRAINT

■ OVERVIEW OF THE LAW

The Federal Government, most states, and the Joint Commission on Accreditation of Healthcare Organizations (JCAHO) now regulate and limit the use of restraints and seclusion. A clinical definition of seclusion is to place and retain an inpatient in order to treat, contain, and control emergency clinical conditions. Seclusion may be further defined by statute according to an objective standard (i.e., locked door) or a subjective standard (i.e., patient believes he or she is restricted to the room). A clinical definition of restraint is to limit the patient's physical movements by the use of mechanical devices to prevent imminent harm to the patient or others. Statutory language may include the use of drugs in the definition of restraint.

Legal challenges to the use of restraints and seclusion have been made on behalf of institutionalized individuals who are mentally ill and mentally retarded. Normally, these lawsuits do not stand alone but are a part of a challenge to a wide range of alleged abuses within a hospital.

Generally, courts' hold or consent decrees provide that restraints and seclusion can be implemented only when a patient presents a risk of harm to self or others and when no less-restrictive alternative is available. Additional considerations include the following:

- Restraint and seclusion can be implemented only by a written order from an appropriate medical official.
- Orders are to be confined to specific, time-limited periods.
- A patient's condition must be regularly reviewed and documented.

- Any extension of an original order must be reviewed and reauthorized.

In addition to these guidelines, some courts and state statutes outline certain due-process procedures that must be followed before a restraint-seclusion order can be implemented. Typical due-process considerations include some form of notice, a hearing, and the involvement of an impartial decision maker. Absent language to the contrary, these procedures may be eased in cases of emergency. Notably, patient due-process protections are required only in cases in which restraint and seclusion are used for disciplinary purposes.

The acceptability of restraint or seclusion for the purposes of training was recognized in the landmark case *Youngberg v. Romeo* (1). *Youngberg* involved a challenge to the "treatment" practices at the Pennhurst State School and Hospital in Pennsylvania. The U.S. Supreme Court held that patients could not be restrained except to ensure their safety or—in certain (undefined) circumstances—"to provide needed training." In *Youngberg,* the Court recognized that the defendant had a liberty interest in safety and freedom from bodily restraint. The Court added that these interests were not absolute and were not in conflict with the need to provide training. The Court also held that decisions made by appropriate professionals regarding restraining the patient would presumptively be considered correct. The Court's decision in *Youngberg* is viewed as the first step in the right direction by advocates for the developmentally disabled. In addition, psychiatrists and other mental health professionals have lauded the decision because the Court recognized that professionals, rather than the courts, are best able to determine the needs of patients, including determining when restraint is appropriate.

The Health Care Financing Administration (HCFA) (2) has issued new rules and guidelines governing the use of restraints. The Omnibus Budget Reconciliation Act of 1987 provides stringent rules for the use of restraint in nursing homes. Most states have enacted statutes regulating the use of restraints, specifying the circumstances in which restraints can be used. Those circumstances arise only when a risk of harm to self or others is imminent. Statutory regulation of the use of seclusion is far less common. Only about one-half of the states have laws relating to seclusion. The majority of states with laws regarding seclusion and restraint require some type of documentation of their usage.

Most litigation involving seclusion and restraint of psychiatric patients is based on constitutional issues (3). However, malpractice cases alleging negligent use of seclusion and restraint have been litigated. In *Fleming v. Prince George's County* (4), a physician was found to have violated the standard of care by placing the plaintiff in restraints without attempting to determine the cause of her "obstinate and stubborn" behavior. The plaintiff was severely injured when she attempted to escape. In *Pisel v. Stamford Hospital* (5), the plaintiff was found unconscious and pulseless, with her head wedged between the bed's steel railing and mattress. The evidence showed that the appropriate standard of care required that "no objects or furniture should be left (in the seclusion room) that could cause the patient harm" (e.g., the steel bed frame). The court awarded $3.6 million in damages.

In other cases, courts have granted a summary judgment in favor of the defendant or ordered dismissal of a case in which the plaintiff failed to introduce sufficient evidence that improper restraint was used (6) or where the defendant's actions were the cause of the injury (7).

The stringent legal and administrative control of seclusion and restraint should not deter the psychiatrist from using these emergency, often lifesaving, modalities. To avoid using appropriate seclusion and restraint because of a fear of legal liability can result in serious harm to patients and members of the hospital staff.

■ CLINICAL MANAGEMENT OF LEGAL ISSUES

Indications

There are three main clinical indications for seclusion and/or restraint (8):

- To prevent clear, imminent harm either to the patient or to others when control by other means is ineffective or inappropriate
- To prevent significant disruption of the treatment program or damage to the physical surroundings
- To assist in treatment as part of ongoing behavior therapy

The legal and clinical appropriateness of using seclusion and restraint for the purpose of behavior-modification treatment is unclear. Such treatment may risk legal liability if used with competent patients. Behavior-therapy methods such as contingent restraint and locked time-out may be used to manage patients who are about to become seriously dangerous. There are two other clinical indications applicable only to seclusion:

- To decrease sensory overstimulation
- To provide seclusion at the patient's voluntary request (see Table 6–1)

Voluntary requests by patients for seclusion may be honored in order to provide support for weakening impulse control, to diminish seriously threatening contact with others, and to lessen the frightening experience of "flashbacks" and overstimulation in patients recovering from toxic reactions. A viable therapeutic alliance with the staff usually exists when a patient can ask for seclusion. Manipulative patients may try to use seclusion to avoid ward activities and treat-

---

TABLE 6–1. **Indications for seclusion and restraint**

To prevent clear, imminent harm to the patient or others

To prevent significant disruption to treatment program or physical surroundings

To assist in treatment as part of ongoing behavior therapy

To decrease sensory overstimulation[a]

To comply with patient's voluntary reasonable request[b]

---

[a]Seclusion only.

[b]First seclusion; then, if necessary, restraints.

ment programs, to test staff resolve, or to attempt to draw the staff into sadomasochistic power struggles. Therefore, the motivation behind requests for seclusion must be carefully evaluated.

In addition to federal regulations, most states have freedom-from-restraint-and-seclusion statutes. Mental health professionals who use these management modalities should be familiar with these regulations and laws. Professional opinions on the clinical use of physical restraints and seclusion vary considerably. Unless precluded by federal or state law or by JCAHO and hospital policies, a variety of uses for seclusion and restraint can be justified on both clinical and legal grounds (9). For example, the American Psychiatric Association Guidelines for Inpatient Psychiatric Units regarding HIV infected patients states, "If a patient engages, or threatens to engage, in behavior that places other individuals at risk for potential HIV infection, the responsible physician should assure the appropriate steps are taken to control the behavior and, if necessary, isolate and/or restrain the patient" (10).

No accurate data are available on how frequently restraints are used in hospitals and long-term care facilities. One poll of 60 nursing units found that the rates of restraint ranged from 0% to 5% (11). Recent news media attention has focused on a number of patient deaths allegedly caused by the use of seclusion and restraint (12). Congress has proposed statutes that would grant certain freedoms from restraint to all patients in facilities receiving federal funds. For example, restraints could be used only to ensure physical safety to patients or others and would, except in an emergency, require a physician's written order.

A new federal rule by HCFA (2) requires that hospital patients be seen face to face by a physician or licensed independent practitioner (LIP) within 1 hour from the time a patient is restrained. An LIP is an individual who is recognized by both state law and hospital policy as having the independent authority to order restraints and seclusion for patients. This requirement is part of expanded policies regulating seclusion and restraint applicable to all hospitals receiving Medicare and Medicaid funds. The 1-hour requirement differs from the corresponding JCAHO mandate because the latter allows nurses to undertake evaluation and management tasks (13). The JCAHO standard also permits the physician or LIP to conduct an in-person evaluation of the patient within 4 hours of the initiation of restraint or seclusion for patients 18 years old or older. For children and adolescents under age 17, the in-person evaluation must be conducted within 2 hours of the initiation of restraint and seclusion. The 1-hour visit requirement by the HCFA is also recommended by the American Psychiatric Association Task Force on the Psychiatric Uses of Seclusion and Restraint (14). Regardless of accreditation status, Medicare- or Medicaid-participating hospitals must meet the standards in the Patient's Rights Condition of Participation (15). The HCFA is working with the JCAHO to assure that the new Medicare requirements are incorporated into JCAHO standards.

The JCAHO has made major revisions to its standards for the use of restraint and seclusion, effective January 2001, that seek to reduce the use of restraint and seclusion to provide greater assurance of safety and protection of patients with psychiatric or substance abuse disorders. The revised standards restrict the uses of restraints and seclusion to emergency situations in which there is imminent risk that the patient may inflict self-harm or harm others. Restraints are to be used only as a last resort. The JCAHO has agreed to work with the HCFA to enforce the 1-hour rule in hospitals receiving Medicare and Medicaid funds.

Contraindications

Patients with medical and psychiatric conditions that are extremely unstable require the close attention of staff. The staff of psychiatric units that have seclusion rooms some distance from the nursing station must carefully consider whom they place in seclusion. Patients with dementia who cannot tolerate decreased stimulation (so-called sundowners among the elderly) or patients who are delirious may represent contraindications to seclusion. Patients with severe drug reactions or overdoses, patients who require close monitoring of their dosages, or extremely self-destructive, overtly suicidal patients should not be placed in seclusion unless close supervision and direct observation can be provided (see Table 6–2).

Using seclusion as a punishment or for the sole convenience of staff is absolutely contraindicated. Secluding a patient to protect others is a clear indication, but the harm must be imminent. The mere expression of rude behavior is not, by itself, a legitimate reason for seclusion. For patients who are well known to the hospital staff, the emergence of obnoxious behavior may be an early warning signal of an impending loss of control and physical violence. As a result, the staff may need to seclude the patient preemptively if it is known that other modes of management have not been effective in the past.

The potential for misuse of seclusion and restraint is always present. Sometimes it is not clear whether the seclusion is motivated by staff anxiety concerning management of the patient, or if it is based on the legitimate clinical needs of the patient. Seclusion may be requested in desperation to gain the psychiatrist's attention when staff members feel that the psychiatrist has been unresponsive to their concerns about the patient. Close supervision by the psychiatrist of the use of restraint and seclusion is necessary. These procedures must be used only when indicated and are never routine. Seclusion and restraint must never be used in place of proper care.

TABLE 6–2.   **Contraindications to seclusion and restraint**

For extremely unstable medical and psychiatric conditions[a]

For patients with delirium or dementia who are unable to tolerate decreased stimulation[a]

For overtly suicidal patients[a]

For patients with severe drug reactions, those with overdoses, or those requiring close monitoring of drug dosages[a]

For punishment of the patient or convenience of staff

---

[a]Unless close supervision and direct observation are provided.

■ IMPLEMENTING SECLUSION AND RESTRAINT

National guidelines for the proper use of seclusion and restraint have been established by the American Psychiatric Association Task Force on the Psychiatric Uses of Seclusion and Restraint (14). The following pertain to the emergency use of seclusion and restraint:

- The physician should visit the patient within 1 hour of seclusion or restraint.
- Secluded patients should be visited at least once a day and the need for continued restraint or seclusion reviewed.
- When a patient is restrained or secluded for more than 72 consecutive hours, the case should be reviewed by the hospital director.
- Restraint techniques should be rehearsed and approved by the facility's staff, and the facility's legal counsel should advise staff whether such techniques are in accord with state and federal statutes governing the use of seclusion and restraint.

The Task Force examined the indications for seclusion and restraint in three critically sensitive areas: treatment of children and adolescents, of the elderly, and of individuals with developmental disabilities. Although the task force report was published in 1985, the guidelines continue to represent good clinical practice that should protect patients from abuse and practitioners from legal liability. Since the task force report was published, a number of the report's recommendations have been adopted or independently formulated as federal, state, JCAHO, and hospital policies and regulations.

Initiation of emergency restraint and seclusion procedures by nursing and other professional staff, in accordance with established hospital policy, requires the psychiatrist's review and order for continuation (16). The psychiatrist should be notified immediately. Emergency implementation of restraint and seclusion generally should not exceed 1 hour without a physician staff member's oral order. In facilities that receive federal funds (Medicare or Medicaid), HCFA requires that restrained hospital patients be seen face to face by a physician or LIP within 1 hour of being restrained (2).

The HCFA has adopted the concept of time-limited orders of the JCAHO's 1999 Hospital Accreditation Standards (13). The intent statement provides that written orders for restraint or seclusion for "behavioral health patients" are limited to 4 hours for adults, 2 hours for children and adolescents ages 9 to 17, or 1 hour for patients under age 9. After the first hour of face-to-face assessment of the restrained patient, the psychiatrist should generally see the patient within 3 hours. The psychiatrist must document his or her visit and describe the patient's condition, the need for restrictiveness, and any plans for further special monitoring or precautions to be taken by the staff.

Subsequent visits by the psychiatrist are a matter of clinical judgment. Although a patient may need to be seen more frequently, a minimum of one visit a day is usually appropriate. The seclusion and restraint orders should be reviewed on each visit and the need for continued restriction documented (16). A risk-benefit analysis should be conducted describing the benefits (e.g., improvement in physical state, mental status, and control of violence) balanced against the adverse physical and emotional consequences of seclusion and restraint. The ability of the staff to handle the patient, with and without restriction, should also be evaluated.

The patient in seclusion or restraint must be observed every 15 minutes by members of the nursing staff. With some very violent patients, observation may be possible only through a window. The patient may need to be observed continuously or to have a staff member in the seclusion room. If a relationship can be established with the acutely disturbed patient, the time in seclusion usually can be significantly reduced, particularly when the relationship permits smooth transition to the open ward. If the door can be left open when the patient is quiet ("open seclusion"), nursing staff may not need to check more than every 30 minutes. The clinical observations made during these checks should be recorded and used in assessing the patient's progress and readiness to leave restraint or seclusion.

Toileting should be done at least every 4 hours. If the patient cannot use an adjoining toilet, then a bedpan will be necessary.

Toileting can be one of the most difficult management problems in seclusion. Lion and Soloff (16) report that assaults by patients are most apt to occur during toileting. This is not surprising, considering that issues of control, humiliation, and invasion of privacy are all intimately involved with toileting.

If possible, patients should not be allowed to eat alone, because meals are important occasions for social interaction. Assaultive patients, however, may use food or utensils as weapons against themselves or others, thus requiring supervision. Adequate administration of fluids is essential because of profuse sweating and the potential for dehydration. This is particularly true of seclusion rooms that tend to have inadequate air conditioning or poor ventilation.

The process of removing a patient from seclusion and restraint is initiated when the initial goals of restriction have been met—that is, when the patient no longer poses a threat to others or self and is no longer disruptive to the therapeutic setting of the ward. Ideally, the psychiatrist should use incremental steps in removing the patient from seclusion and restraint. As each step of a ward transition plan is successfully negotiated, the next step is taken. Introduction to ward routine can be done while the patient is still spending some time in seclusion. It is possible that the patient might suddenly regress or become assaultive. Accordingly, a risk-benefit assessment should be made prior to final separation from seclusion. If the patient can form a reasonably stable relationship with a staff member, chances of successfully negotiating transfer to the open ward are maximized (9).

Finally, the clinician must always recognize that mechanical restraints should be used only as clinical interventions. Tinetti et al. (17) found that the use of mechanical restraints in nursing homes for safety and behavioral management rather than to treat medical conditions is a prevalent practice. These findings confirm earlier data from the HCFA (18). Stringent guidelines for the use of restraints in nursing homes were included in the federal Omnibus Budget Reconciliation Act of 1987. According to guidelines issued by the Department of Health and Human Services, restraints should be limited to treating a resident's medical symptoms. A treatment plan must carefully consider less restrictive alternatives, and specific informed consent must be obtained from the resident, family member, or legal representative (19).

Chemical Restraints

Psychotropic medications, such as neuroleptics or atypical antipsychotics, should not be used solely for the purpose of physically immobilizing a patient. Psychotropic medications are indicated for the treatment of a patient's psychiatric disorder that is the cause of behavior requiring emergency control and containment. "Chemical straitjackets" rarely have a place in the treatment of the mentally ill. Patients in long-term care facilities may present chronic personality and behavioral problems that are difficult for the staff to manage. On occasion, cantankerous, difficult but not mentally ill residents have been placed on long-term psychotropic medications by an exasperated clinical staff. In response to these and other abuses, the Omnibus Budget Reconciliation Act of 1987 regulates the use of psychotropic drugs in long-term care facilities receiving funds from Medicare and Medicaid (20). The HCFA guidelines for neuroleptic drugs (21) include the following:

- Documentation of the psychiatric diagnosis or specific condition requiring neuroleptic (and, presumably, atypical antipsychotics) use
- Prohibition of neuroleptics if certain behaviors alone are the only justification
- Prohibition of as-needed neuroleptic use
- Gradual dose reductions of neuroleptics combined with attempts at behavioral programming and environmental modification

In *Rogers v. Commissioner, Department of Mental Health* (22), a landmark right-to-refuse-treatment case, the Massachusetts Supreme Judicial Court held that where drugs were being given to patients for the purpose of restraint rather than treatment, the state regulatory policy governing restraint was to be employed.

Seclusion and Restraint in Managed Care Settings

The treatment of psychiatric inpatients has changed dramatically in the managed care era. Most psychiatric units, particularly those in general hospitals, have become short-stay, acute care psychiatric facilities. Generally, only suicidal, homicidal, and gravely disabled patients with major psychiatric disorders pass strict precertification review for hospitalization. Approximately half of these patients have comorbid substance-related disorders. The purpose of hospitalization is crisis intervention and management to stabilize patients and to ensure their safety.

Under these circumstances, insufficient time, a severely ill patient population, and rapid turnover do not ordinarily allow therapeutic alliances to develop with psychiatrists and staff that are essential to patient stabilization and management. Thus, there is usually a heavy reliance on medications to curb violent, destructive behaviors. The temptation is great to use chemical straitjackets solely for the purpose of physically immobilizing the out-of-control patient. Furthermore, managed care organizations (MCOs) will not usually pay additional benefits for intensive care such as seclusion and restraint. One-to-one monitoring of patients may be required but is not usually covered by MCOs. The patient's family or the hospital will have to absorb the additional costs of such intensive care. Nevertheless, the use of seclusion and restraint may be required by the emergency clinical needs of the patient, even when insurance coverage is denied by an MCO.

■ REFERENCES

1. 457 US 307 (1982), on remand, Romeo v Youngberg, 687 F2d 33 (3rd Cir 1982)
2. 42 Code of Federal Regulations 482.13 (f)3 (II) (C) 1999
3. Perlin ML: Mental Disability Law: Civil and Criminal, Vol 3. Charlottesville, VA, Michie, 1989, pp 50–51
4. Pisel v Stamford Hospital, 180 Conn 314, 430 A2d 1, 12–14 (1980)

5. Fleming v Prince George's County, 277 Md 655, 358 A2d 892, 895–897(1979)

6. Steward v City of New Orleans, 418 So2d 1389 (La Ct App 1982), cert denied, 423 So2d 1159 (La 1982)

7. Jenkins v United States, 562 F Supp 471 (D.D.C. 1983)

8. Gutheil TG, Tardiff K: Indications and contraindications for seclusion and restraint, in The Psychiatric Uses of Seclusion and Restraint. Edited by Tardiff K. Washington, DC, American Psychiatric Press, 1984, pp 11–17

9. Simon RI: Clinical Psychiatry and the Law, 2nd Edition. Washington, DC, American Psychiatric Press, 1992

10. Guidelines for Inpatient Psychiatric Units. Approved by the APA Board of Trustees, December 15, 1996. Washington, DC, American Psychiatric Association

11. JCAHO Clamps Down on Restraint Use. Hospital Peer Review. December 1996, pp 159–160

12. Appelbaum PS: Seclusion and restraint: congress reacts to reports of abuse. Psychiatr Serv 50:881–882, 885, 1999

13. Joint Commission on Accreditation of Healthcare Organizations: Comprehensive Accreditation Manual for Behavioral Health Care: Restraint and Seclusion Standards for Behavioral Health. Chicago, IL, Joint Commission Accreditation of Healthcare Organizations, 2001, TX 7.1.5, TX 7.1.6

14. American Psychiatric Association: The Psychiatric Uses of Seclusion and Restraint (Task Force Report no 22). Washington, DC, American Psychiatric Association, 1985

15. Department of Health and Human Services: Medicare and Medicaid Programs; Hospital Conditions of Participation: Patient's Rights; Interim Final Rule. Federal Register, July 2, 1999, pp 36069–36089

16. Lion JR, Soloff PH: Implementation of seclusion and restraint, in The Psychiatric Uses of Seclusion and Restraint. Edited by Tardiff K. Washington, DC, American Psychiatric Press, 1984, pp 19–34

17. Tinetti ME, Liv WL, Marottoli R, et al: Mechanical restraint use among residents of skilled nursing facilities. JAMA 265:468, 1991

18. Health Care Financing Administration: Medicare/Medicaid Nursing Home Information, 1987–1988. Washington, DC, U.S. Department of Health and Human Services, 1989

19. Health Care Financing Administration Department of Health and Human Services: Medicare and Medicaid: requirements for long-term care facilities. Final rule with request for comments. Federal Register, February 12, 1989, p 5322

20. Hendrickson RM: New federal regulations, psychotropics, and nursing homes. Drug Therapy August (suppl):101–105, 1990

21. Health Care Financing Administration Department of Health and Human Services: Medicare and Medicaid: requirements for long-term care facilities. Final rule with request for comments. Federal Register, February 12, 1989, pp 5316–5336

22. Rogers v Commissioner, Department of Mental Health, 390 Mass 489, 458 NE 2d 308, 321 (1983)

7

INVOLUNTARY HOSPITALIZATION

■ OVERVIEW OF THE LAW

Involuntary Hospitalization: Rationale

There is a long history of state intervention in the legal detainment of individuals for noncriminal acts that remains unsettled. The civil deprivation of a mentally ill person's freedom is premised on two legal doctrines: police power and *parens patriae*. Police power permits the state to take certain actions necessary to safeguard the welfare of its citizens (e.g., detaining a person who is mentally ill in a psychiatric hospital when that person presents a risk of danger to society). The *parens patriae* doctrine permits the state to act on behalf of those citizens unable to care for themselves because of an infirmity (e.g., mental disability).

Civil Commitment: Usage of the Term

The term *civil commitment* is not used in this book in its strict legal sense, which encompasses both voluntary and involuntary commitment. Psychiatrists do not usually think of a voluntary hospitalization as a commitment, even though patients who undergo conditional voluntary admission may be detained against their will for varying periods of time. When psychiatrists speak of involuntary hospitalization, they usually just say "commitment." In order not to confuse the reader, the terms *voluntary* and *involuntary hospi-*

talization are used whenever possible. Civil commitment is used synonymously with involuntary hospitalization, except when referring to outpatient commitment.

Criteria

A person may be involuntarily hospitalized only if certain statutorily mandated criteria are met. Although state statutes vary, three main substantive criteria—whether found alone or grouped together—serve as the foundation for all commitment requirements (see Table 7–1). Generally, each state spells out which criteria are required and what each means. Unfortunately, terms such as *mentally ill* are often loosely defined. As a result, the responsibility for proper definition passes to the clinical judgment of the petitioner.

In addition to permitting commitment of individuals with mental illness, certain states have enacted legislation that permits the involuntary hospitalization of individuals in three other distinct groups:

TABLE 7–1. **Typical substantive and miscellaneous criteria for civil commitment**

Substantive criteria
  Mentally ill
  Dangerous to self or others
  Unable to provide for basic needs

Miscellaneous criteria (in conjunction with one or more of above criteria)
  Gravely disabled (unable to care for self to the point of likely self-harm)
  Refusing hospitalization
  Patient is in need of hospitalization
  Danger to property
  Lacks capacity to make rational treatment decisions
  Hospitalization represents least-restrictive alternative

Note. Criteria are statutorily determined, varying from state to state.

- Those who are developmentally disabled (mentally retarded)
- Those with substance abuse problems (alcohol, drugs)
- Minors who are mentally disabled

Special commitment provisions may govern requirements for admission and discharge of minors who are mentally disabled, in addition to the numerous due-process rights afforded these individuals.

Procedures and Standards

Procedures for involuntary civil commitment vary from state to state according to three principal factors:

- The nature of the commitment
- The purpose of the commitment
- The primary authority seeking the commitment

Hospitalization of patients is either voluntary or involuntary. *Voluntary hospitalization* consists of two types: informal and conditional. They are distinguished by the degree of freedom a patient is given in leaving the hospital. An *informal* voluntary admission permits a patient to leave at any time during the hospitalization, although minimal conditions may be attached (e.g., the discharge can only occur during a day shift, Monday through Friday). Only moral suasion can be used to induce the patient to stay in the hospital; no coercion is permissible. A *conditional* voluntary admission statutorily authorizes the hospital to detain a patient thought to be potentially dangerous to self or others. The patient may be held only for a specified number of days after the initial written notice of discharge is given in order to be evaluated for possible involuntary hospitalization.

Civil commitment, or involuntary hospitalization, is the hospitalization of a person against his or her will for a statutorily determined time based on the assessment that the person is mentally ill and a danger to self or others.

The last factor, *primary authority,* refers to the statutorily mandated official or body designated to decide whether an individual should be committed. Essentially, there are two commitment authorities:

- Judicial commitment
- Administrative institutionalization

Medical certification is for the purpose of obtaining an involuntary inpatient psychiatric evaluation of an individual deemed mentally ill and a danger to self or others. It is not a commitment.

Statutes Addressing the Purpose of Commitment

Generally, statutes addressing the purpose of commitment can be divided into three categories:

- Emergency detention
- Hospitalization for observation
- Extended custody

Most states provide for *emergency* hospitalization which is a brief, temporary measure implemented when it has been determined that an individual presents a clear and present risk of danger to self, others, or—in some states—property. The "hold period," until a hearing is conducted, is usually 48 to 72 hours, particularly if the state requires a "probable cause" hearing.

Observational hospitalization, or short-term commitment, is for a designated period of time in order to adequately observe and diagnose an individual's condition, followed by a limited amount of treatment. Although only approximately one-half of the states have formal observational commitment statutes, nearly every state has some functional equivalent. Short-term commitment involves a longer period of time than emergency commitment. Although greater procedural protection is required, the hospital or psychiatrist rather than the court is initially responsible for the decision to hospitalize the patient. Short-term commitments are usually not used by states that hold probable-cause hearings. Substantive standards for short-term commitment may not be as stringent as standards for long-term commitment. At the end of an observational period, either the patient must be discharged or commitment procedures must be reinstated.

The last category, *extended custody,* is procedurally the most formal and, in most states, is judicially implemented. Because the duration of the detention is generally longer, a number of due-process protections are afforded an individual to ensure that the commitment is not unduly burdensome or unnecessarily long term. Moreover, the commitment must serve an essential and continuing state purpose.

Each state has a variety of statutory procedures for voluntary and involuntary hospitalization of a person who is mentally ill. Clinicians should be familiar with the procedures and standards in their state.

Liability

The most common lawsuit involving involuntary admission is the claim of wrongful commitment of a person, which gives rise to a cause of action for false imprisonment. Other areas of liability that may arise from an alleged wrongful commitment include assault and battery, malicious prosecution, abuse of process, and intentional infliction of emotional distress. In order to have a valid cause of action for false imprisonment or for any of the other torts, a plaintiff must show that the defendant failed to exercise reasonable care. States have provisions in their commitment statutes that grant psychiatrists immunity from liability as long as they use reasonable professional judgment and act in good faith when petitioning for involuntary hospitalization. Evidence of willful, blatant, or gross failure to adhere to statutorily defined commitment procedures will not meet the good faith provision. Psychiatrists have also faced malpractice suits alleging failure to commit an individual who was subsequently involved in a tragedy. Other malpractice suits have alleged a failure to properly assess and involuntarily hospitalize patients at risk of violence and the negligent discharge of suicidal and violent inpatients.

Psychiatrists and other mental health professionals have been found liable for infringement of civil rights under Section 1983 of the Civil Rights Act (1). The patient must establish that the conduct in question was committed by an individual acting "under color of state law and the conduct deprived the patient of rights, privileges or immunities secured by the constitution or United States laws."

■ CLINICAL MANAGEMENT OF LEGAL ISSUES

Current Trends in Civil Commitment

Recent legislative changes and court decisions in most states have partially abandoned the *parens patriae* standard and have emphasized the police power criteria, using dangerousness as the standard for civil commitment. The psychiatrist's power to commit patients without court review has been markedly limited. Patients have been granted broad procedural protection similar to that granted to criminal defendants. Based primarily on the due-process and equal-protection clauses of the Fourteenth Amendment, all states now require some form of judicial hearings with notice to the patient, representation by counsel, and proof of mental disorder and dangerousness by at least clear and convincing evidence.

Currently, there appears to be a growing movement among state legislatures to revise commitment statutes in order to respond to the treatment needs of individuals who are seriously mentally ill before they become a danger to themselves or to society. An increasing effort by patient advocates, psychiatrists, and state legislators is being made to move away from the narrowly defined dangerousness standard as the primary basis for civil commitment. A middle ground is being sought between meeting the treatment needs of individuals with severe mental illness and preserving their legal rights (2).

Procedures and Types of Commitment

Mental health professionals do not make commitment decisions about patients. Commitment is a judicial decision that is made by the court or by a mental health commission. The clinician files a petition or medical certification that initiates the process of involuntary hospitalization. Carefully following the letter and spirit of the guidelines for civil commitment may preempt legal challenge or malpractice claims on procedural grounds (3).

Emergency Commitment

State laws vary substantially regarding procedures and types of commitment. Most states provide for brief, emergency hospitalization until a hearing is held. A majority of states have a short "hold period" of 48 to 72 hours, particularly those states that require probable-cause hearings. Probable-cause hearings determine whether substantial evidence exists that the patient meets the standards for involuntary hospitalization. If sufficient evidence is found, the patient may continue to be hospitalized until the formal hearing. The basis for emergency commitment is that the patient suffers from a mental illness and presents a clear danger to self or others. Dangerousness is often loosely defined. States require a recent overt act, imminent danger, or the risk of substantial harm to the patient, another person, or, in a few states, property.

Commitment statutes do not require involuntary hospitalization of persons under defined circumstances. Rather, commitment statutes are permissive (4); that is, they enable mental health professionals and others to seek involuntary hospitalization for persons who meet certain substantive criteria. The duty to seek involuntary hospitalization of a patient under the clinician's care is a standard-of-care issue. In *Schuster v. Altenberg* (5), the Wisconsin Supreme Court found an affirmative duty to commit. In most other jurisdictions, however, the law states that clinicians *may* seek commitment of patients under certain conditions.

Procedures for initiating commitment vary considerably from state to state. A report or form is usually required in which the reasons for emergency hospitalization are stated, along with a description of the statements and behaviors of the patient. Police officers, next of kin, psychiatrists, other physicians, psychologists, social workers, or even "interested parties" may file a petition for emergency hospitalization. If the psychiatrist is concerned about endangering the treatment alliance with the patient, the patient's next of kin may be asked to petition for involuntary hospitalization.

Short-Term and Long-Term Commitment

A number of states provide for short-term commitment in addition
to emergency commitment. The periods of retention specified for
emergency, short-term, and long-term commitment vary considerably from state to state. For long-term commitment, all states
require judicial or administrative determinations. Long-term
commitment procedures vary considerably among jurisdictions,
although the requirement that the substantive criteria of mental
illness and dangerousness be met is usually followed. Hospitalization for indeterminate durations has given way to periodic review for continued involuntary hospitalization. Such reviews are
usually done by the court that conducted the original hearing.
Reviews may be made every 3, 6, or 12 months.

Release of Patients

Psychiatrists must not confuse their discretionary freedom to release
civilly committed patients with requirements governing release responsibilities for patients who have been criminally committed. The
latter require an order for release from the committing court. Psychiatrists have been sued when a criminally committed patient was
released without court approval and subsequently harmed another
person (6).

Minors

Minors may be hospitalized under "voluntary" provisions, which
vary considerably from state to state. In some states, a minor is
given some discretion over the voluntary admission. If a minor
refuses to consent when his or her consent is statutorily required,
the parent may initiate involuntary hospitalization. In *Parham v.
J.R.* (7), the U.S. Supreme Court held that in addition to prescribed
state law procedures, the federal due-process clause required review by an independent and neutral physician of a parental decision
to commit a minor child. The Court rejected the claim that the due-
process clause necessitated more rigorous procedural safeguards.

Outpatient Commitment

Outpatient civil commitment is one alternative for the pressing problem of the individual who is mentally ill, homeless, but non-dangerous and who may be in dire need of treatment and care. The revolving-door patient, regardless of residence, is the person for whom outpatient commitment may be most beneficial. Approximately one-quarter of violent patients who are involuntarily hospitalized subsequently experience another violent episode that requires rehospitalization (8).

Standard of Proof

The minimum standard of proof required for long-term commitment was determined by the U.S. Supreme Court in *Addington v. Texas* (9). The Court held that the minimum standard of proof required, before depriving an individual of his or her liberty, was "clear and convincing evidence" that the individual meets civil commitment requirements. This decision represents a midway position between the standards of "a preponderance of the evidence" in civil cases and "beyond a reasonable doubt" in criminal cases.

Clinical Role

Proper clinical procedures for civil commitment that maintain the traditional treatment role of psychiatrists include conducting a careful examination of the patient, abiding by the requirements of the law, and ensuring that sound reasoning motivates the certification of those who are mentally ill. *The Principles of Medical Ethics With Annotations Especially Applicable to Psychiatry* provides, in part, that "the psychiatrist may permit his/her certification to be used for the involuntary treatment of any person only following his/her personal examination of that person" (10, Section 7, Annotation 4).

Substantive Standards for Long-Term Commitment

Involuntary hospitalization represents, to varying degrees, the exercise of the state's *parens patriae* and police powers. Mental illness is a fundamental requirement for civil commitment, although state statutes define mental illness differently. For example, some states list specific psychiatric disorders, whereas others apply an impairment requirement that leaves the diagnosis to the professional judgment of the certifying clinician.

In addition to mental illness, all state statutes require a finding of dangerousness. The dangerousness standard refers to "dangerous to self or others" as the most common basis for long-term commitment, but definitions of dangerousness also vary considerably. In many states, "inability to provide for basic needs" has replaced the old criterion of "in need of treatment."

Another criterion that may justify involuntary hospitalization of an individual is being gravely disabled. The definition of *gravely disabled* varies from state to state but generally encompasses life-threatening self-neglect or the inability to provide for such basic needs as food, clothing, or shelter. A smattering of states have additional criteria allowing involuntary hospitalization for patients who refuse voluntary admission, patients who are expected to benefit from treatment, and patients who are unable to make rational decisions about treatment, as well as requirements that involuntary hospitalization practices follow the principle of the least-restrictive alternative.

Maintaining Clinical Roles

Psychiatrists must not certify persons solely on the basis of dangerousness. The person must have a mental illness that relates to his or her potential for violence. The world is full of violent individuals who would not be considered mentally ill. Persons who are deemed "dangerous" but who are not mentally ill according to current diagnostic criteria are the responsibility of the police, not the psychiatrist. The main clinical tasks confronting the psychiatrist participating in the commitment process are as follows:

- Assessing the patient's suitability for involuntary hospitalization
- Minimizing the threat to the therapist-patient relationship

- Managing tensions between legal requirements and professional duties owed to the patient

Assessing a person's suitability for involuntary hospitalization requires careful diagnosis and violence risk assessment. Minimizing the potential adverse consequences of involuntary hospitalization depends on the patient's ability to understand an empathic explanation of the commitment process as an emergency intervention. Maintaining even the semblance of a therapeutic alliance during involuntary hospitalization can be a daunting task with those who are severely ill. Psychiatrists may experience role conflict when involuntary hospitalization is sought for an individual who is dangerous but who does not have treatable mental disorders (e.g., sociopathic personality disorder). Psychiatrists should not be placed in the position of being society's police. Involuntary hospitalization should be a clinical intervention.

Stone's (11) proposed "thank you theory" of civil commitment captures the essence of the clinical approach. It asks the psychiatrist to focus inquiry on illness and treatment while asking the law to guarantee treatment before intervening in the name of *parens patriae*. Stone feels that moral and legal justification for the doctrine of *parens patriae* can be achieved if the three essential ingredients of reliable criteria are present: diagnosis of illness, incompetent refusal, and a decent institution. Stone's "thank you theory" divests civil commitment of a police function. Dangerousness is returned to the province of criminal law. Only the mentally ill, treatable, and incidentally dangerous patient would be confined in mental health systems, prompting a thank you from an ultimately grateful patient.

Dangerousness

The statutory definitions of the dangerousness requirement are often vague and reflective of the value judgments of the statute's authors. The term *dangerousness* ordinarily refers to legal status rather than psychiatric disposition. Instead of dangerousness, the term *risk of violence* is preferable. The validity of violence risk assessments performed by the clinician is only modestly greater than chance. Furthermore, violence is multifactorial (social, clinical, personality, situation). Violence is also the product of the unique interaction between the individual and the environment and, as such, often defies predictability. Therefore, psychiatrists and other mental health practitioners should refrain from making predictions of violence and instead limit themselves to short-term assessments of the risk of violence (see Chapter 9, The Potentially Violent Patient).

Grave Disability

Assessment difficulties arise from the almost universal requirement that a prediction of dangerousness to self or others be made prior to commitment. The assessment of grave disability has received much less attention in the literature than has that of overt dangerousness. The psychiatrist is on firmer ground when assessing a patient's ability to properly care for him- or herself during an acute psychotic episode or if he or she has an advanced form of dementia. In reality, there may be a disjunction between the presence of certain severe mental disorders and the ability to take day-to-day care of oneself. Some patients with chronic schizophrenia manage their lives reasonably well in the presence of hallucinations, delusions, and a thought disorder. Assessment of functional ability for this group should focus on survival tasks. Can the patient manage food, finances, clothing, and shelter requirements? Is a support system in place? Are any changes occurring in the environment that may be destabilizing?

Therapeutic Alliance

Involuntarily hospitalization may severely strain the psychiatrist-patient relationship. Once a treatment relationship is damaged or destroyed, the patient's subsequent relationships with mental health caregivers may be adversely affected. Therefore, a psychiatrist should strive to keep the patient informed of, or even involved with, the decision-making process concerning involuntary hospitalization.

Family involvement, if available and supportive of the patient's welfare, can often help mitigate the potential trauma of involuntary hospitalization. As a result, the therapeutic alliance may be preserved.

Questionable Commitments

Even though patients who do not meet commitment criteria might benefit from hospitalization, they should not be involuntarily hospitalized. Doubtful situations arise in which the psychiatrist has reason to believe that a patient is at significant risk for violence but remains uncertain about this conclusion. Erring on the side of involuntary hospitalization may be justified when it appears likely that the patient who may be potentially violent can benefit from hospitalization. In these situations, psychiatrists should rely on their training and clinical experience to determine which course is in the patient's best interest, while allowing the courts to temper clinical biases through legal scrutiny. For example, a patient in dire need of hospitalization was seen in the hospital emergency room. When told that involuntary hospitalization was being considered, the patient agreed to a voluntary admission, only to sign out shortly thereafter. To avoid a destructive revolving-door process, patients who are likely to sign out of the hospital prematurely should be considered for involuntary hospitalization at the outset, even though this course may not be technically consistent with a policy of least-restrictive treatment.

Psychiatrists must not use the threat of involuntary hospitalization to coerce patients into accepting treatments or procedures when they have no real intention of petitioning for commitment. If a psychiatrist expects to seek involuntary hospitalization for a patient, the patient should be informed of this action. Failing to inform the patient may deal a severe blow to the patient's trust and may adversely affect future treatment efforts. Malcolm (12) has noted the subtle differences in the concepts of coercion and persuasion. *Persuasion* is defined as the physician's aim "to utilize the patient's reasoning ability to arrive at a desired result" (p. 125). On the other hand, *coercion* occurs "when the doctor aims to manipulate the patient by introducing extraneous elements which have the effect of undermining the patient's ability to reason" (p. 125). Lidz et al. (13) have demonstrated that patients' feelings of being coerced into mental hospital admissions appear to be closely related to their sense of procedural justice. *Procedural justice* was defined as the patient's perception of being treated with concern, respect, and fairness and being taken seriously. Even among patients legally committed, Lidz et al. advised that patients' experiences of coercion can be minimized by the clinician's paying closer attention to procedural-justice issues.

Using the Diagnostic and Statistical Manual of Mental Disorders

One of the two essential prongs of all commitment statutes is the presence of mental illness in the person being considered for involuntary hospitalization. Persons who are dangerous but not mentally ill do not qualify. To ensure adequacy of diagnosis, psychiatrists should consider using the diagnostic criteria contained in the fourth edition of the *Diagnostic and Statistical Manual of Mental Disorders* (14). Following officially approved diagnostic criteria may help preclude allegations of caprice or malice in diagnosing mental illness for the purpose of involuntary hospitalization. Such a practice is also an effective antidote to the temptation to finesse the mental-illness requirement in order to circumvent a perceived legal impediment to involuntary hospitalization (15).

Avoiding Quasi-Legal Roles

Dangerousness, the second prong of commitment statutes, is loosely defined in state statutes and often is shaped by the societal and political issues that influence legislators. Psychiatrists should not be distracted or deterred from their traditional diagnostic and treatment functions by assuming quasi-legal roles as interpreters of statutory meanings. Although statutory definitions need to be understood and followed as a guide to the commitment of patients, the minute scrutiny of these definitions is not an appropriate role for the psychiatrist. Statutory interpretation should be left to lawyers and judges.

Controlled studies have found that involuntary hospitalization is a valid intervention for appropriate patients. In retrospect, patients involuntarily hospitalized have mostly been appreciative for the care they were given (16, 17).

Managed Care and Involuntary Hospitalization

In managed care settings, only suicidal, homicidal, or gravely disabled patients with major psychiatric disorders pass strict precertification review for hospitalization. Usually, in order to gain precertification for admission in managed care settings, patients must meet "medically necessary" criteria, the stringency of which often equals or exceeds that of the substantive criteria for involuntary civil commitment. If a patient cannot be managed on a psychiatric unit and continues to pose a danger to self or others, involuntary hospitalization should be considered only when the patient meets civil-commitment criteria for mental illness and dangerousness. In a large majority of states, involuntary hospitalization is permissible only when a less restrictive, clinically appropriate setting is not available. Patients should never be involuntarily hospitalized solely because a managed care organization (MCO) denies insurance coverage for continued hospitalization. The usual candidate for involuntary hospitalization is a patient with psychosis who poses a significant risk of violence to self or others, who refuses treatment, or who signs a formal request for discharge against medical advice.

Involuntary hospitalization is always a clinical intervention. It must never be used as a defensive tactic to avoid malpractice liability or to provide a legal defense against a malpractice claim. Most clinicians would choose to err on the side of safeguarding the lives of their severely ill patients or endangered others by seeking continued hospitalization rather than giving precedence to preserving the patient's civil liberties.

■ **REFERENCES**

1. 42 U.S.C. §1983 (1982)

2. Appelbaum PS: Almost a Revolution: Mental Health Law and the Limits of Change. New York, Oxford University Press, 1994, pp 17–70

3. Levin RB, Hill EH: Recent trends in psychiatric liability, in American Psychiatric Press Review of Clinical Psychiatry and the Law, Vol 3. Edited by Simon RI. Washington, DC, American Psychiatric Press, 1992, pp 129–150

4. Appelbaum PS, Zonana H, Bonnie R, et al: Statutory approaches to limiting psychiatrists' liability for their patients' violent acts. Am J Psychiatry 146:821–828, 1989

5. 144 Wis 2d 223, 424 NW 2d 159 (1988)

6. Semler v Psychiatric Institute of Washington, DC, 538 F2d 121 (4th Cir 1976), cert denied, 429 US 827 (1976)

7. Parham v JR, 442 US 584 (1979)

8. Miller RD: Involuntary civil commitment, in American Psychiatric Press Review of Clinical Psychiatry and the Law, Vol 2. Edited by Simon RI. Washington, DC, American Psychiatric Press, 1991, pp 95–172

9. 441 US 418 (1979), on remand, State v Addington, 588 SW 2d 569 (Tex 1979)

10. American Psychiatric Association: The Principles of Medical Ethics With Annotations Especially Applicable to Psychiatry. Washington, DC, American Psychiatric Association, 1998

11. Stone AA: Mental health and law: a system in transition (Publ no ADM-76–176). Rockville, MD, National Institute of Mental Health, 1976

12. Malcolm JG: Informed consent in the practice of psychiatry, in American Psychiatric Press Review of Clinical Psychiatry and the Law, Vol 3. Edited by Simon RI. Washington, DC, American Psychiatric Press, 1992

13. Lidz CW, Hoge SKI, Gardner W, et al: Perceived coercion in mental hospital admission: pressures and process. Arch Gen Psychiatry 52:1034–1039, 1995

14. American Psychiatric Association: Diagnostic and Statistical Manual of Mental Disorders, 4th Edition, Text Revision. Washington, DC, American Psychiatric Association, 2000

15. Simon RI: Clinical Psychiatry and the Law, 2nd Edition. Washington, DC, American Psychiatric Press, 1992, p 167

16. Spensley J, Edwards DW, White E: Patient satisfaction and involuntary treatment. Am J Orthopsychiatry 50:725–727, 1980

17. Gove WR, Fain T: A comparison of voluntary and committed psychiatric patients. Arch Gen Psychiatry 34:669–676, 1977

8

THE SUICIDAL PATIENT

■ OVERVIEW OF THE LAW

The most frequent legal action involving psychiatric care is the failure to reasonably protect patients from harming themselves. An overview of the most common areas of negligence for which an inpatient provider (psychiatrist or hospital) and an outpatient therapist may be held liable, if death or injury results from a patient's suicide or suicide attempt, is given in Table 8–1.

In essence, theories of negligence regarding suicide can be grouped into two broad categories:

- Failure to properly diagnose (assess suicide risk)
- Failure to implement an appropriate treatment plan (use reasonable treatment interventions and precautions)

These theories, each of which applies to inpatient and outpatient settings, are based on the practitioner's failure to act reasonably in exercising the appropriate duty of care owed to the patient. Patient suicides leading to wrongful death suits are based on the legal concepts of foreseeability and causation. A typical lawsuit will argue that the patient's suicide risk was not assessed and treated properly, resulting in the patient's death.

As a general rule, a psychiatrist who exercises reasonable care in compliance with accepted medical practice will not be held liable for any resulting injury. Normally, if a patient's suicide was not reasonably foreseeable or if the suicide occurred as a result of superceding intervening factors, no liability will be found.

144

TABLE 8–1. **Civil liability for the suicide of a psychiatric patient: causes of action and defenses**

Inpatient liability

Diagnosis
1. Unforeseeable suicide: failure to properly assess
2. Foreseeable suicide:
   a. failure to properly document
   b. improper diagnosis or assessment

Treatment (foreseeable suicide)
1. Failure to supervise properly
2. Failure to restrain (high-risk patient)
3. Premature release (e.g., pass)
4. Negligent discharge
5. Unjustified freedom of movement

Defenses
1. Compliance with accepted medical practice
2. Lack of reasonable knowledge of suicidality
3. Justifiable allowance of freedom of movement (e.g., "open ward")
4. Reasonable physician's decision regarding diagnosis or course of treatment
5. Intervening acts or factors (e.g., third parties)
6. Extraordinary circumstances precluding or circumventing reasonable precautions or restraint

Outpatient liability

Diagnosis
1. Unforeseeable suicide: failure to properly assess
2. Foreseeable suicide: improper diagnosis or assessment

Treatment
1. Negligent treatment (e.g., supervision, abandonment, referral)
2. Failure to control (e.g., hospitalize)

Defenses
1. Compliance with standard of care
2. Diagnosis of suicidality not reasonable
3. Intervening acts
4. Extraordinary circumstances

Source. Adapted from Smith J, Bisbing S: *Suicide: Caselaw Summary and Analysis.* Potomac, MD, Legal Medicine Press, 1988.

Foreseeable Suicide

As an accepted standard of care, an evaluation of suicide risk should be done with all patients regardless of whether they present overt suicidal complaints. A review of case law shows that reasonable care requires that a patient who is either suspected or confirmed to be at risk for suicide must be the subject of certain affirmative precautions. A failure to either reasonably assess a patient's suicidality or implement an appropriate precautionary plan once the suicide risk becomes recognized is likely to render a practitioner liable, if the patient is harmed because of a suicide attempt.

States differ in their definitions of the standard of care required of a mental health professional. The standard of care should not be statistically determined. The duty to exercise that degree of skill and care ordinarily employed in similar circumstances by other psychiatrists that was affirmed in *Stepakoff v. Kantar* (1) appears to come close to, if not actually be, a statistical standard of care. To illustrate by using an extreme example, suppose that 99,999 practitioners are having sex with their patients. It would be pure folly to conclude, on a statistical basis, that the one practitioner who abstains from having sex with patients is violating the standard of care. Similarly, if a majority of clinicians are not performing and recording suicide risk assessments, does this practice (or lack thereof) become the standard of care? Although it may be possible to find an expert who would testify to that proposition, credible testimony would state that a reasonable, prudent practitioner performs and records suicide risk assessments that drive appropriate treatment and management decisions of patients at suicide risk. The standard of care in most states must be measured by the practice of the reasonable, prudent practitioner.

The law judges psychiatrists not on the absolute accuracy of their determinations but rather on the clinical reasonableness of their suicide risk assessment process. Courts also closely scrutinize a suicide case to determine if the patient's suicide was foreseeable. Foreseeability is a legal term of art that has no clinical equivalent. It is a commonsense, probabilistic concept rather than a scientific construct. Foreseeability is the reasonable anticipation that harm or injury is a likely result from certain acts or omissions (2). Recording competent suicide risk assessments that direct clinical interventions should more than adequately meet a fair legal interpretation of foreseeability. For example, when a psychiatrist determines that a patient is at significant risk for suicide, it is reasonable to expect that self-harm will likely occur unless preventive measures are undertaken. Moreover, it is a mistake to equate the legal concept of foreseeability with predictability, because no professional standards exist for predicting who will commit suicide. Foreseeability must also be distinguished from preventability. A suicide that may not have been foreseeable may, in hindsight, have been preventable.

Inpatients

Intervention in an inpatient setting usually requires the following:

- Screening evaluations
- Case review by clinical staff
- Development of an appropriate treatment plan
- Implementation of that plan

Careful documentation of suicide risk assessments and management interventions with responsive changes to the patient's clinical situation should be considered clinically and legally sufficient psychiatric care. Psychiatrists are more likely to be sued when a psychiatric inpatient commits suicide. The law presumes that the opportunities to foresee (anticipate) and control (treat and manage) suicidal patients are greater in the hospital.

Outpatients

Outpatient therapists face a somewhat different situation. Psychiatrists are expected to assess a patient's level of suicide risk. The result of the assessment dictates the nature of the duty-of-care options. Courts have reasoned that when an outpatient commits suicide, the therapist will not necessarily be held to have breached a duty to safeguard the patient from self-harm because of the difficulty in controlling the patient (3). Instead, the reasonableness of the psychiatrist's efforts will be the determining factor.

Legal Defenses

One legal defense that has created a split in the courts is the use of an "open-door" policy in which hospitalized patients are allowed freedom of movement for therapeutic purposes. In these cases, the individual facts and reasonableness of the staff's application of the open-door policy appear to be paramount. Nevertheless, courts have difficulty with abstract treatment notions such as personal growth when faced with a suicide.

Another defense, the doctrine of sovereign or governmental immunity, may be used to statutorily bar a finding of liability against a state or federal facility. Intervening causes of suicide over which the clinician has no control may also provide a valid legal defense. For example, a father and son go hunting. The father accidentally shoots and kills his son. In his despair, he turns the gun on himself and dies. The father was being treated for depression. A suit is filed against the psychiatrist alleging negligent treatment of the father that led to his suicide. The claim alleges, among other things, that the father should have been warned about going hunting while he was depressed. The court finds that the cause of the father's death was the accidental shooting, not the psychiatrist's negligence. Finally, the best-judgment defense has been used successfully when the patient was properly assessed and treated for suicide risk but committed suicide anyway (4).

■ CLINICAL MANAGEMENT OF LEGAL ISSUES

Assessment

The evaluation of suicide risk by the practitioner is one of the most complex, difficult, and challenging tasks in psychiatry. The psychiatrist's ability to perform an adequate suicide risk assessment is basic to clinical practice (5). Clinical standards do not exist for the prediction of suicide (6). Psychiatrists have not been held legally liable for inaccurate assessments of suicide risk per se. Lawsuits against psychiatrists have succeeded because of failure to properly collect and logically evaluate necessary data in making an assessment of suicide risk. All suicide risk assessments should be recorded in the patient's chart at the time of evaluation. For the outpatient at suicide risk, an assessment should be made at each session. The hospitalized patient should also have frequent assessments, particularly when a change in status is considered, such as room or ward change, pass, or discharge. When a suicide risk assessment is noticeably absent, the court is less able to evaluate the appropriateness of the decision-making process in assessing the risk of suicide. Suicide risk assessment is a continuing process, not an event.

Assessing the risk of suicide involves three separate steps:

1. Identifying patients with individual, clinical, interpersonal, situational, and epidemiologic risk factors associated with suicide
2. Assessing the overall risk of suicide based on the rating of specific risk factors
3. Implementing treatment and preventive interventions that bear a logical nexus to the overall suicide risk assessment

Risk-Benefit Analysis

In the treatment and management of the suicidal patient, assessing suicide risk alone is usually insufficient. The benefits of treatment and management interventions must also be considered. Risk-benefit analysis provides a systematic assessment of the balance of clinical factors favoring or opposing the treatment intervention under consideration. A risk-benefit evaluation allows the psychiatrist more therapeutic latitude with the suicidal patient in situations where fears of malpractice may inhibit appropriate therapeutic interventions. When treating a suicidal patient, psychiatrists must not be so fearful of legal liability that they overly restrict patients to the latter's therapeutic detriment. If, after reasonable clinical examination and evaluation, the clinician feels that the potential benefits to the patient of a given psychiatric intervention outweigh the specific risks of that intervention, then these judgments should be recorded in a risk-benefit note in the patient's chart. The record should reflect what sources of information were consulted, what factors went into the clinical decision, and how the factors were balanced by the use of risk-benefit assessment.

Risk-benefit notes are decisional road marks. When in doubt about a particular intervention, a risk-benefit analysis should be conducted and recorded. For example, when considering a hospital pass or discharge, both the risks and the benefits of going out on a pass or being discharged, as well as the risks and benefits of remaining in the hospital, should be considered.

Passes and Discharges

Discharging a patient from the hospital is often a more difficult decision than admission. Although keeping the patient hospitalized may reduce the chance of suicide and also diminish the psychiatrist's anxiety, resumption of the patient's usual lifestyle as soon as it is clinically feasible can be very therapeutic. For suicidal patients requiring greater restrictions, the situation is complicated by court directives that require such patients to be treated by the least restrictive means. The tension between promoting individual freedom and protecting a patient from self-injury is often encountered in the clinical management of suicidal patients (7). The psychiatrist can feel caught on the horns of this dilemma. Nevertheless, clinical judgment based on the treatment needs of the patient takes precedence. An open-door policy cannot be applied in stock fashion to all psychiatric patients. Autonomy in the hospital setting must bear a rational nexus to the patient's diagnosis, clinical condition, and level of functional mental capacity. Before the patient who has seriously contemplated or attempted suicide in the past is allowed out on a pass or is discharged, the psychiatrist needs to consider many factors (see Table 8–2).

The therapeutic alliance is usually a solid indicator of a patient's subsequent adjustment outside of the hospital. The patient who does not have a working relationship with the psychiatrist or the treatment team or have a supportive relationship with others is often at increased risk for self-destructive behavior on discharge. In managed care settings, sufficient time may not be available for the psychiatrist or treatment team to develop an alliance with the patient. Moreover, only the sickest patients are admitted who may not have the capacity to establish a working alliance. Discharge of

---

TABLE 8–2. **Suicidal patients: pass and discharge considerations**

Benefits of release versus risk: analysis

    Determined by direct evaluation

    Consultation with all appropriate staff

    Review of patient's current and past course of hospitalization

Evidence of posthospitalization self-care ability

    Can patient function without significant affective and cognitive impairment?

Capability of and accessibility to obtaining assistance

    Is patient physically and emotionally able to employ others for support?

Remission of illness

    What remains unchanged and can be dealt with as an outpatient?

Control by medication

    Can side effects be tolerated and managed outside the hospital and will patient comply with treatment?

Support system

    Does family or do significant others exist and, if so, are they stabilizing or destabilizing?

Timing of proposed release

    Does staff adequately know the patient?

    Has the patient been acclimated adequately to the therapeutic milieu, with sufficient time allowed to develop meaningful relationships?

    Has sufficient time elapsed to evaluate the effectiveness of treatment (e.g., medication)?

Therapeutic alliance

    Will the patient continue to work with the psychiatrist or other mental health professionals?

---

these patients should be carefully planned, structured, and followed up for compliance.

In reviewing the records of patients who have successfully committed suicide, one invariably finds frequent notations of seclusive behavior, lack of involvement in ward activities, and the avoidance of meaningful personal relationships with other patients and staff. Therapists must also be careful to recognize that, in patients with serious depression, the therapeutic alliance present during the therapy hour may dissipate between treatment sessions.

The 3 months following hospitalization is a time of significantly increased suicide risk. In one diagnostically heterogeneous sample of 94 patients, 65% of suicides occurred within 3 months of discharge from the hospital (8). A Veterans Administration study of outpatient referrals found that of 47 inpatients referred to a Veterans Administration mental health clinic, 21 did not keep their first appointments (9). Follow-up by the clinician is important.

The patient's willingness to cooperate is crucial to appropriate follow-up. The clinician's obligation is to structure the follow-up to encourage compliance (e.g., scheduling an initial appointment prior to releasing the patient, using reminder letters or phone calls, recruiting family members to ensure that the patient comes to appointments and takes medications). If the patient does not keep the follow-up appointment, the psychiatrist must weigh confidentiality concerns against the dangers posed by the patient's nonadherence to aftercare before considering any additional interventions. However, once a patient is discharged from the hospital, the psychiatrist's intervention options may be limited or nonexistent (10). The limits to psychiatrists' powers to ensure adequate follow-up must be acknowledged by both the psychiatric and the legal communities.

Patients who are no longer at acute risk of violence toward self or others may nevertheless remain at long-term, chronic risk of manifesting destructive behaviors. All the psychiatrist can do is carefully note that the patient is not at acute risk at the time of discharge. Once the patient is discharged, the potential for violence will depend on the patient's mental disorder, compliance with treatment and course of the concurrent situational factors. Violent behavior is the result of dynamic, complex interaction among a variety of clinical, personality, social, and environmental factors whose relative importance varies across time and situations (11).

Suicide Risk Factors

There are no pathognomonic predictors of suicide. Some of the major clinical indicators of suicide risk reported in the psychiatric literature are shown in Table 8–3. This list of suicide risk factors,

TABLE 8–3. **Assessment of suicide risk factors**

Risk factor	Facilitating suicide	Inhibiting suicide
Individual		
Unique, characteristic patient factors		
Clinical		
Current attempt (lethality)		
Panic attacks[a]		
Psychic anxiety[a]		
Loss of pleasure and interest[a]		
Alcohol abuse[a]		
Depressive turmoil[a]		
Diminished concentration[a]		
Global insomnia[a]		
Suicide plan		
Suicidal ideation[b]		
Suicide intent[b]		
Hopelessness[b]		
Prior attempts (lethality)[b]		
Psychiatric diagnoses (Axes I and II)—symptom severity		
Recent discharge from psychiatric hospital (within 3 months)		
Drug abuse		
Impulsivity		
Physical illness		
Family history of suicide		
Mental competency		
Recent humiliation		
Interpersonal		
Therapeutic alliance		
Work relations		
Family relations		
Spousal or partner relations		
Children		
Situational		
Living circumstances		
Employment status		

TABLE 8–3. **Assessment of suicide risk factors (*continued*)**		
Financial status		
Availability of lethal means (e.g., guns)		
Managed care setting		
Statistical		
Age		
Sex		
Marital status		
Race		
Overall Risk Rating		

Instructions:
1. Rate risk factors present as low (L), moderate (M), high (H), nonfactor (0).
2. Judge overall suicide risk as low, moderate, or high.

[a] Risk factors statistically significant within 1 year of assessment.
[b] Associated with suicide 2–10 years following assessment.

by no means exhaustive, separates risk indicators into individual, clinical, interpersonal, situational, and statistical categories. The table also distinguishes short-term and long-term risk factors for suicide. In their prospective study of suicide among 954 persons with major affective disorders, Fawcett et al. (12) found the following short-term suicide indicators to be statistically significant within 1 year of assessment: panic attacks, psychic anxiety, loss of pleasure or interest, alcohol abuse, depressive turmoil, diminished concentration, and global insomnia. They demonstrated in their prospective study that the suicide risk factors for individuals with major affective disorders who committed suicide within 1 year of assessment were different from the suicide risk factors found among individuals who committed suicide within 2 to 10 years of assessment. In the former group, the anxiety-related symptoms of panic attacks, psychic anxiety, global insomnia, diminished concentration, alcohol abuse, and loss of interest and pleasure were significantly more severe. Clinical interventions directed at treating anxiety-related symptoms (treatable risk factors) in patients with major affective disorders may significantly diminish a number of short-term suicide risk factors.

The more traditional suicide risk factors, including hopelessness, suicidal ideation, suicidal intent, and a history of previous suicide attempts, were not associated with short-term suicide but were significantly associated with long-term suicide. Long-term suicide risk factors are derived from community-based psychological autopsies and the retrospective study of completed suicide by psychiatric patients (13). Long-term suicide risk factors are primarily severe depression-driven symptoms traditionally assessed by clinicians that are significantly associated with completed suicides 2 to 10 years following assessment. The National Comorbidity Survey demonstrated that the transition probabilities from suicide ideation to suicide plan were 34% and from plan to attempt were 72% (14). Approximately 90% of unplanned and 60% of planned first attempts happened within 1 year of suicide ideation onset.

The short-term and long-term distinctions among suicide risk factors have important clinical implications. For instance, the reliability of short-term risk factors may be greater than that for long-term risk factors. Additional prospective studies are needed to confirm the findings that distinguish short-term from long-term suicide risk factors.

Some patients exhibit suicide risk factors that are uniquely individual. For example, one patient who had a severe stutter would begin to speak clearly as he became suicidal. A clinician's awareness of such an individually unique suicide risk factor can come only from knowing the patient well. In the managed care era, this degree of knowledge about patients is usually difficult or impossible to obtain. A managed care setting can become a suicide risk factor if the clinician allows the managed care organization (MCO) to dictate treatment.

Suicide is a multidetermined act that results from a complex interplay of a number of factors. Clinicians rely on a number of clinical risk variables in assessing the suicide potential of a patient. Suicide is a rare event with low specificity (high false-positive rates). Some of the suicide risk variables are vague and difficult to interpret. Furthermore, it is extremely difficult for the practitioner to assign accurate clinical weight to the various factors that might signal suicide risk. Risk variables identify too many false-positive situations to be useful in long-range suicide prediction. The clinical usefulness of these risk variables is much greater, however, for short-range assessment of suicide risk in the patient undergoing an acute suicidal crisis.

Suicide Risk Assessment

A method of assessing suicide risk as a low, moderate, or high potential for suicide is given in Tables 8–3 and 8–4. In Table 8–3, suicide risk factors are not listed in order of clinical importance; that determination depends on the patient's clinical presentation. These tables may be used for comprehensive assessment of suicide risk when time does not allow for consultation. Some psychiatrists use a method like the one presented in Table 8–3 for patient self-assessment of suicide risk. This should be done only in conjunction with the psychiatrist's own assessment. The clinician cannot rely solely on the patient's assessment of suicide risk. The clinician must remember that the systematic assessment of suicide risk is

TABLE 8–4. **Assessment of suicide risk and examples of outpatient psychiatric intervention options**

Suicide risk	Psychiatric interventions
HIGH	Immediate hospitalization
MODERATE	*Consider* Hospitalization Frequent outpatient visits Reevaluate treatment plan frequently Remain available to patient
LOW	Continue with current treatment plan

Note. Tables 8–3 and 8–4 represent only one method of suicide risk assessment and intervention. The purpose of these tables is heuristic, encouraging a systematic approach to risk assessment. The practitioner's clinical judgment concerning the patient remains paramount. Because suicide risk variables will be assigned different weights according to the clinical presentation of the patient, the method presented in these tables cannot be followed rigidly.

good clinical practice and only secondarily a risk-management technique. Risk assessment is a continuing clinical process rather than a singular event.

Practice parameters for the assessment of suicide risk have been formulated by professional organizations such as the American Academy of Child and Adolescent Psychiatry. The Academy's recommendations in official practice guidelines generally indicate the degree of importance or certainty of each recommendation (15). For example, *minimal standards* recommendations are based on substantial empirical evidence (such as well-controlled, double-blind studies), or overwhelming clinical consensus, or legal and regulatory requirements, or all of the above. Minimal standards are expected to apply greater than 95% of the time, for instance, in almost all cases. If the clinician does not follow this standard in a particular case, the rationale should be documented in the medical record.

Clinical guidelines are recommendations that are based on empirical evidence such as open trials and clinical studies or on strong clinical consensus or both. Clinical guidelines pertain approximately 75% of the time. The clinician should always consider these recommendations but there are exceptions to their applicability.

Options are pragmatic recommendations that are acceptable but not required. Insufficient empirical evidence is available to support recommending such practices as minimal standards or clinical guidelines. In some cases, the practice may be entirely appropriate, whereas in other situations it should be avoided.

The category of *not endorsed* applies to practices that are known to be useless or contraindicated.

By these definitions, the recommendation that clinicians perform formal (systematic) suicide risk assessments on patients who are at suicide risk is supported by overwhelming clinical consensus, thus meeting the criteria for minimal standards of practice.

Weather forecasting is an apt metaphor for the process of suicide risk assessment. Astronomical events such as eclipses can be predicted with 100% accuracy. Weather forecasts, however, are made within certain probabilities. Like weather forecasting, the suicide risk assessment is a time-driven method of evaluation. Because time attenuates assessment accuracy, the weather forecast model has a certain applicability to the evaluation of patients at suicidal risk. Short-term assessments of suicide risk (24–48 hours) are much more accurate than long-term assessments, because the parameters that influence future occurrences can be specified with greater precision in the short term. The assessment of suicide risk is a here-and-now determination whose accuracy is eroded by time. For assessments of suicide risk made at a greater temporal distance, the clinician loses the ability to specify both psychological and environmental determinants of behavior and, thus, to assess with any precision the likelihood of particular outcomes. Accordingly, a patient undergoing a suicidal crisis should be seen frequently and the suicide risk assessed from session to session. Like a weather forecast, suicide risk assessments need to be updated frequently.

Overall suicide risk assessments of low, moderate, or high risk are based on reasonable clinical judgment (see Table 8–4). There are no clinical standards for predicting the *occurrence* of a suicidal act, only for the assessment of suicide risk. Once an assessment is made, however, appropriate clinical interventions must be initiated (e.g., hospitalization, more frequent patient visits, or medication adjustments) (see Table 8–4).

Risk factors may be also evaluated along a variety of parameters that enhance suicide risk assessment (see Table 8–5). For example, a suicide risk factor can be rated as acute or chronic. Demographic or statistical suicide risk factors such as age, gender, and race are generally considered to be relatively fixed. Acute risk factors are the focus of current clinical evaluation. Chronic risk factors have been present for a year or longer before assessment. Patients with

TABLE 8–5.	**Risk factor parameters**
	Short-term–long-term
	Acute–chronic
	Necessary–sufficient
	Facilitating–inhibiting
	Individual–situational

Axis I disorders, especially schizophrenic, anxiety, and major affective disorders, generally present with acute (state) suicide risk factors. Patients with Axis II disorder, frequently display chronic (trait) suicide risk factors. Patients with comorbid Axis I and II disorders often have both acute and chronic risk factors present. Comorbidity is an important "predictor" of suicide attempts above and beyond the presence of a single psychiatric disorder (14). A suicide risk factor may also be both acute and chronic, as with recurrent depression. Other risk factor parameters include short-term and long-term (discussed above), facilitating and inhibiting, individual (unique, characteristic) and situational (usually loss), and necessary and sufficient.

Most depressed patients do not kill themselves. For instance, the suicide rate in the general population is 10 to 15 per 100,000 per year. The suicide rate for individuals having affective disorders is 180 per 100,000 per year. Turning this statistic on its head, 99,820 patients with depression will not commit suicide in a single year (6). Thus, on a statistical basis alone, the vast majority of patients with depression will not commit suicide. The clinical challenge is to identify those patients with depression at significant risk for suicide (16).

Suicides usually occur when both necessary (depression) and sufficient (perturbation) factors are present (17, 18). For instance, the patient with a major depression who is also experiencing an interpersonal or occupational crisis may have both necessary and sufficient suicide risk factors operating. Many suicide risk factors listed in Table 8–3 can be evaluated on necessary-sufficient parameters. The individual (state or trait)-situational (loss) parameter can be also applied to the above example and the suicide risk factors in Table 8–3. Generally, however, a number of risk factor parameters are considered simultaneously.

The risk factors listed in Table 8–3 can also be evaluated along facilitating-inhibiting (protective) parameters. For example, a depressed patient who is assessed for hopelessness may actually express hope about the future. Hopelessness is not a presenting symptom. Thus, hopefulness, the obverse of hopelessness, may be considered a factor that inhibits or lowers suicide risk. Also, if no suicide plan is present, then that risk factor can also be considered to inhibit or lower suicide risk. However, as previously noted, 26% of patients with suicidal ideation transition to an unplanned attempt. Supportive relationships, responsibility for children, religious beliefs, and gratifying work may act as inhibiting or protective factors. Each suicide risk factor in Table 8–3 can be assessed as an inhibitor or facilitator in the assessment of a patient's overall suicide risk. Suicide risk increases with the total number of risk factors, also giving a quasi-quantitative dimension to suicide risk assessment (19).

The method of suicide risk assessment presented here is highly schematic. Tables 8–3 and 8–4 need not be reproduced in the patient's chart. A standard note containing an adequate suicide risk assessment is all that is necessary (see Table 8–5). This model of suicide-violence risk assessment is derived from the author's clinical experience and the psychiatric literature but has not been empirically tested for reliability and validity. Other approaches to suicide risk assessment are also available to the clinician (20–22). Regardless of which method is used, however, the important point is that in the management of suicidal patients, suicide risk assessments must be made and contemporaneously recorded in the medical chart. The competent clinician must be able to perform an adequate suicide risk assessment. Simply asking a patient if he or she is suicidal and obtaining a "no-harm" contract is insufficient. A layperson could just as easily ask these simple questions. Especially with new patients, there is no credible basis for relying on such reassurances. Moreover, approximately 25% of suicidal patients do not admit to being suicidal (12). The clinician should be able to identify suicide risk factors and perform suicide risk assessments that inform appropriate clinical interventions. Suicide prevention contracts, either oral or written, should not be used as a substitute for adequate suicide risk assessments.

It is a serious clinical mistake to equate the absence of suicide risk with a patient's denial of suicidal ideation, even if the patient is telling the truth. A patient may be at increased risk for suicide because of the heightened presence of other significant suicide risk factors, particularly impulsivity. Fawcett (23) has noted impulsivity as a high risk "pathway" for suicide. Impulsivity, usually a chronic trait factor, may be acutely exacerbated by stressful events (e.g., loss of a relationship, substance abuse). In patients with suicidal ideation, the probability of transition from suicidal thoughts to unplanned attempt is 26% (14). Observational data obtained from the general psychiatric examination and the mental status examination can provide objective information about the patient's clinical status that does not depend strictly on the patient's subjective reporting (e.g., depressive turmoil, diminished concentration, drug or alcohol withdrawal, little or no relatedness, impulsivity, bizarre [psychotic] behaviors, and other observable risk data).

The clinician should not rely on the single scores of suicide risk assessment scales and inventories (24–26). Structured or semistructured suicide scale questionnaires may complement but should not take the place of a thorough clinical assessment of suicide risk. Self-administered suicide scales have the disadvantage of being oversensitive and underspecific. The reliance on clinical checklists alone creates the danger that the practitioner will reflexively suspend clinical skills and judgment in assessing suicide risk. No checklist can encompass all pertinent suicide risk factors. Plaintiffs' attorneys are quick to point out omissions on checklists that were used to assess the patient who committed suicide. Furthermore, a checklist can neither replace a psychodynamic understanding of the patient, nor assess suicide risk factors unique to the individual patient.

The Therapeutic Alliance

No one suicide risk variable can be counted on exclusively in the assessment of suicide risk. Nonetheless, one of the most significant suicide risk factors is the lack of a therapeutic alliance with the patient. The therapeutic alliance is defined as the conscious and unconscious working relationship between therapist and patient in which each implicitly agrees to collaborate in the process of treatment. The presence of a therapeutic alliance is a solid indicator of the patient's willingness to seek help and sustenance during serious emotional crises. The presence or absence of the therapeutic alliance can be used by clinicians as a here-and-now indicator of the patient's suicidal vulnerability. For new patients or for patients seen in emergencies, sufficient time may not have elapsed for a therapeutic alliance to be established and evaluated. In addition, for a variety of clinical reasons, the therapist may not be able to develop a working alliance with the patient.

An important clinical caveat against excessive dependence on the therapeutic alliance in assessing suicide risk is evident when working with certain depressed patients. During the treatment session, a depressed patient may manifest a working therapeutic alliance. After leaving the therapist, however, the patient may not be able to internalize or maintain the alliance because the depression worsens. An intercurrent impulsive act may momentarily overcome the alliance. The therapist needs to assess with the patient the status of the therapeutic alliance outside of the sessions. The therapist may falsely assume that a viable, ongoing therapeutic alliance exists with the patient that minimizes suicide risk. This clinical phenomenon often accounts for the bewilderment of therapists after a patient, with whom a working therapeutic alliance was thought to exist, commits suicide.

Prior Suicide Attempts

Studies show that between 9% and 33% of individuals with previous suicide attempts eventually go on to completed suicide (27). Placing significant clinical weight on the distinction between a suicide gesture and a suicide attempt can be perilous, particularly if the act occurred some time ago. Without question, some suicide attempts can be identified as gestures because the patient does not have the slightest intention of self-destruction. Unconscious distortion or retrospective falsification by the patient, however, may disguise a genuine attempt as a gesture.

Upon proper authorization, medical and psychiatric records should be obtained regarding previous diagnoses, treatments, or suicidal acts. Ignoring records of previous treatments is a serious error. Vital information pertinent to the current treatment and management of the patient may be contained in prior medical records.

If there is a history of prior psychiatric treatment, the psychiatrist should attempt to call the patient's previous therapist. Summaries of prior treatments and hospitalizations may be obtained quickly via fax. With the patient's permission, family members should be contacted or interviewed to obtain additional history. Questions concerning past suicidal attempts should include the following: Did the patient intend to die? What was the lethality of the method used? Did the patient expect to be found in time? Was there some obvious manipulation or secondary gain? Was the patient overtly depressed?

Weisman and Worden (28) devised a risk-rescue rating utilizing a descriptive and quantitative method for assessing the lethality of suicide attempts. For example, a patient who takes a few minor tranquilizers and immediately calls the physician is at low risk and high rescue. The patient who makes superficial slashes with a razor while in the psychiatric unit but remains alone is at low risk and low rescue. A high-risk, high-rescue patient attempts hanging in the presence of a friend. The high-risk, low-rescue situation occurs, for example, when the patient buys a hose to fit a car exhaust and waits for everyone to leave the house. The hypothesis underlying the suicide risk rating is that the lethality of the method of suicide, defined as the probability of inflicting irreversible damage, may be expressed as a ratio of factors influencing risk and rescue. The risk-rescue rating correlates well with the level of treatment recommended, the subject's sex, and whether the subject lived or died. Alone, the risk-rescue rating is not a predictive instrument. When considered along with other factors, such as explicit intention to die, prior history of mental illness, and availability of family and community support, the risk-rescue rating can assist the clinician in making an individualized suicide assessment.

Demonstration of Suicide Risk Assessment

After doing a complete psychiatric examination, the clinician should be able to perform and record a competent suicide risk assessment within a few minutes. Another method of documenting the suicide risk assessment is to construct a simple table and label it as demonstrated in Table 8–6. The patient's risk factors should be rated as low (L), moderate (M), high (H), or nonfactor (0). After weighing all of the risk factors, the overall assessment of suicide risk should be rated as low, moderate, or high.

The following clinical vignette illustrates the importance of assessing a patient's suicide risk at the time of a contemplated discharge. After reviewing the vignette, the reader is encouraged to do an independent suicide risk assessment before considering the psychiatrist's assessment.

A 36-year-old woman is transferred from the obstetrical service to the psychiatric unit of a general hospital with a diagnosis of major depressive episode following the delivery of her first son. She was discovered trying to climb onto the fifth floor windowsill in order to jump.

After 10 days in the psychiatric unit, the patient's depression improves with psychotherapy and the administration of an antidepressant. In particular, she sleeps and eats better and has more energy. However, she continues to display a lack of pleasure and interest in her newborn child. Occasionally, she experiences brief episodes of intense anger followed by anxiety and depression amidst moderate agitation. She denies suicidal impulses but occasionally has unbidden ruminations about "what it would be like to be dead." She also denies having a suicide plan. Her initial suicide attempt arose from a momentary impulse that now is frightening and unacceptable to her. Cognitive mental capacity is intact.

The patient develops a working alliance with her psychiatrist. She is cooperative and agrees to a "contract" to inform him if suicidal impulses reoccur. She also has a good marital relationship. Her husband, an engineer, is very supportive but is not psychologically minded. He feels very threatened by his wife's depression. Her husband is extremely happy about "finally having a son."

After her first child was born, the patient willingly gave up a position as a certified public accountant. She enjoys staying home to raise her two daughters, ages two and three, whom she loves.

The patient's past history reveals no psychiatric disorders. There is no history of alcohol or drug abuse. Her mother had a successful course of electroconvulsive therapy for recurrent depression. Her father is a recovered alcoholic who was quite abusive toward the patient throughout her childhood. Ten years ago, the father stopped drinking. A paternal uncle had manic-depressive illness. During a depressive episode, this uncle committed suicide with a handgun.

The patient has been a devout Catholic from her early teen years. Her religion is an important source of solace during periods of crisis. A downturn in her husband's business during this last pregnancy has caused considerable emotional distress. The patient always has worried about money matters. Financial prospects are not favorable for the coming year. However, the couple's comfortable home is not in jeopardy.

While a patient in the psychiatric unit, she is accompanied by a staff member when visiting her baby in the maternity ward. These visits usually are productive but are preceded by a moderate amount of anxiety. Occasionally, the visits end with an increase in her feelings of depression. While in the psychiatric ward, she tends to be seclusive. She avoids other patients and staff, preferring to stay in her room. A loss of interest and pleasure in reading and in her longstanding hobby of needlepoint are evident. She complains of mild difficulty concentrating. No evidence of an Axis II personality disorder is present. No prior history of impulsive behavior is obtained.

After 10 days of hospitalization, the MCO authorizes two additional hospital days following a doctor-to-doctor appeal. The MCO will not provide further coverage for continued hospital treatment. The patient also requests discharge. The patient wants to resume full care of her baby. She misses her daughters and feels guilt about "not being able to take care of my children." The patient's parents will be staying with the patient after she is discharged. The husband is a sportsman who has a collection of guns at home that he keeps locked away. The key to the gun cabinet is kept at his office outside the home. The psy-

chiatrist tells the husband to remove the guns from the home.
The psychiatrist conducts a suicide risk assessment, judging
the patient's overall risk to be in the moderate to high range
(see Table 8–6). The suicide risk assessment is included in the
risk-benefit evaluation for both continued hospitalization and

TABLE 8–6. **Demonstration of a rapid, competent suicide risk assessment**

Risk factor	Facilitating suicide	Inhibiting suicide
Anxiety	M	
Loss of pleasure and interest in child	H	
Depressive turmoil	M	
Diminished concentration	L	
Therapeutic alliance		H
Family relations		M
Hopelessness	L	
Psychiatric diagnosis	M	
Prior attempts	0	0
Current attempt (lethality)	H	
Specific plan	0	0
Living situation		H
Employment		L
Availability of gun	M	
Suicidal ideation/intent	L (passive)	
Family history	H	
Impulsivity	M–H	
Drug/alcohol	0	
Depression/postpartum	M	
Religion		L–M
Insomnia	L	
Other children		H
Physical condition		M
Cognition/competence		M–H
Marital relationship		M–H
Overall Risk Rating: moderate-high (at discharge)		

discharge. The psychiatrist concludes that the patient can be discharged but must attend a partial hospitalization program. An appointment is arranged with the psychiatrist for the day following discharge.

This vignette has been presented at clinical conferences where clinicians were asked to assess the patient's suicidal risk and appropriateness for discharge. Most of the practitioners rated the patient's suicide risk as moderate to high. Suicide risk assessments varied substantially among clinicians because of differences in training, experience, and whether the clinician had lost a patient to suicide. However, a number of practitioners would not discharge the patient until her suicide risk diminished in response to antidepressant medication. Others felt that it would be impractical to continue hospital treatment without insurance coverage. Moreover, the patient was worried about money matters. Incurring a substantial debt for uninsured hospitalization could exacerbate the patient's depression and suicidality. They felt that many patients at moderate to high suicide risk are currently managed as outpatients. However, close, continuing follow-up would be necessary immediately after discharge.

This situation arises frequently and poses a difficult problem for clinicians who do not receive authorization from the MCO for additional hospital days for patients who require continuing treatment. A managed care setting must not be allowed to become a suicide risk factor. In a crisis, the practitioner may need to continue treatment until the patient is clinically stabilized.

Suicide Prevention Contracts

Some therapists attempt to formalize the alliance with the patient by a verbal or even a written contract stating that the patient will call on the psychiatrist if serious doubts about control of suicidal intentions arise. These contracts have no legal force (29). Although a patient may agree to such a contract, some patients simply state that they cannot be sure that they can or will want to call the therapist if self-destructive impulses occur. The patient who refuses a no harm contract gets the attention of the clinician and staff as an important indicator of significant suicide risk. Thus, a patient's contract refusal is of greater clinical value than a *pro forma* agreement. Unfortunately, the latter is all too frequently the situation. The problem with a suicide prevention contract is that it can falsely reassure the therapist and lower vigilance without having any appreciable effect on the patient's suicidal intent. Frequently, such contracts reflect the therapist's attempt to control the inevitable anxiety associated with treating suicidal patients. Contracts against suicide may be of therapeutic value when used to affirm the therapeutic alliance, but their limitations should be understood by the therapist. Finally, contracts must never be used as a substitute for the adequate assessment of suicide risk (30).

Treatment

It is important for clinicians to distinguish between acute suicidal states related to Axis I clinical syndromes and chronic suicidal behavior associated with an Axis II personality disorder, the so-called "state" vs. "trait" distinction. Treatment and management of the two differ considerably. Suicidal patients with personality disorders may also develop Axis I disorders. An awareness of the presence of comorbid Axis I and Axis II disorders may help clarify the clinical situation when a depressed suicidal patient with a personality disorder does not respond fully to an appropriate course of treatment.

Inpatient and Outpatient Settings

It is more difficult for the psychiatrist to supervise a patient outside than inside the hospital. The opportunities to monitor the patient and to anticipate suicide are greater in the hospital setting, although hospitalization does not guarantee that suicide will not be attempted. Often, the hospitalized patient will put the psychiatrist "on notice" by a prior attempt or by exhibiting suicidal behavior on the ward. For a variety of reasons, a patient at suicide risk may not exhibit any signs or symptoms of self-destructive behavior after hospital admission. Because a patient can be placed on suicide precautions (e.g., constant one-on-one supervision or 15-minute observations) in the hospital, one would expect a higher level of awareness and diligence in reducing the likelihood that the patient will commit suicide. Suicide precautions should be tailored to the clinical needs of the patient. Patients can and do commit suicide in the interval between 15-minute checks. Some patients may require safety checks at 5- or 10-minute intervals. Definitions of suicide precautions and observation usually vary from hospital to hospital. The clinician should have a clear understanding of how these terms are being used. A consistently heightened awareness that patients can, and do, commit suicide as inpatients is critical to ensure safety. Nevertheless, there is no such thing as a suicide-proof psychiatric unit (31).

The courts tend to be less stringent in evaluating outpatient suicide in the absence of clear signs of suicidal intent because of the difficulty in controlling the patient. The courts assess whether suicide risk was recognized and whether the psychiatrist adequately balanced the risk of suicide against the benefit of greater control. Asking a patient specifically about suicide should be part of every psychiatric evaluation.

For the outpatient at risk for suicide, an important treatment option is seeing the patient more frequently. Time attenuates assessments of suicide risk. Daily or even more frequent visits with a patient at risk for suicide diminish the reliance of the clinician on long-term probability determinations of suicide. The therapist needs to be readily available to the patient and monitor closely any medications that are administered. Ultimately, the patient may require hospitalization.

Involuntary hospitalization may be a final option for the high-risk suicidal patient who refuses treatment and for whom no less restrictive treatment option exists. Accordingly, liability may be incurred for the suicide of an outpatient if a gross error is made in deciding not to seek commitment of the patient.

Informing Third Parties of a Patient's Suicidal Intent

The competent patient's request for the maintenance of confidentiality must be honored unless the patient is a clear danger to self or to others. *The Principles of Medical Ethics* (32) states: "Psychiatrists at times may find it necessary, in order to protect the patient or the community from imminent danger, to reveal confidential information disclosed by the patient" (Section 4, Annotation 8).

The duty to warn or to inform third parties exists only if the danger of physical harm is threatened toward others, not toward patients themselves. Nevertheless, psychiatrists have a professional duty to take appropriate preventive measures to keep patients from harming themselves. This duty may necessitate communicating with family members about specific aspects of the patient's care, attempting to ameliorate pathological family interactions with the patient, or mobilizing family support.

Suicide as a Function of Psychiatric Illness

Suicide is the result of dynamically interactive, complex factors including diagnostic (psychiatric and medical), constitutional, occupational, environmental, social, cultural, existential, situational, and chance factors. Although there is a loose fit between diagnosis and suicide, suicide rarely occurs in the absence of psychiatric illness. Individuals who make serious suicide attempts have high rates of mental disorders and of comorbid conditions (33). Chance or opportunity may be an unanticipated factor in suicide. For example, a patient may become determined to attempt suicide for just a few seconds, minutes, or hours during the course of a psychiatric hospitalization. If the patient then discovers an unlocked window, an area under construction, or a lethal instrument carelessly left about, she or he may take advantage of the opportunity to commit suicide.

Acute and chronic suicidal states bear some relation to psychiatric diagnoses. Acutely suicidal patients often have Axis I disorders, such as major affective or schizophrenic illnesses requiring immediate hospitalization and treatment. The risk of suicide usually passes with the remission of the acute episode of illness. In these situations, the clinician is on notice to act quickly and affirmatively to hospitalize and supervise these patients appropriately. Patients with chronic waxing and waning suicidal ideation are usually treated as outpatients. The most frequent diagnoses are Axis II personality disorders, especially borderline personality disorder. These patients may require psychiatric hospitalization if their suicidal impulses are exacerbated because of some life crisis or if they develop an inter-current Axis I clinical disorder (usually a major depression).

Exacerbations in the chronic suicidal state of patients with per-sonality disorders is often the result of intense rage dyscontrol and unstable self-esteem regulation, triggered by some interpersonal crisis. The possibility of suicide is seized on as a comforting means of escape and control. At times of crisis, real suicide risk may exist. If not hospitalized, these patients should be seen frequently and reevaluated for suicide risk from session to session. Their medication should be monitored very closely. The patient's support system should be mobilized. The psychiatrist needs to be readily available. Both the patient and the psychiatrist must be able to tolerate recur-rently heightened levels of chronic suicidal ideation in order to con-tinue the work of therapy (34).

Psychiatric Residents and Training Program Orientation

Psychiatric residents treating patients at acute risk of suicide should consider increasing the frequency of supervision with their attend-ing psychiatrists. Not only is this policy clinically prudent, but it will help establish that the patient was provided a reasonable stan-dard of care.

Psychiatric residents also need to maintain perspective on the theoretical orientation and treatment biases of their training pro-gram and supervisors. Psychodynamic approaches to treatment may tend to de-emphasize strategies such as discussion of the sui-cidal patient's condition with family members or use of organic therapies such as psychopharmacotherapy or electroconvulsive therapy. As a result, vital information about the patient may be overlooked. Organic therapies that may be the treatment of choice for certain psychiatric disorders may be given insufficient consid-eration. Conversely, biologically oriented training programs and supervisors may not place enough emphasis on the need for an ongoing treatment relationship with the patient as the essential context for psychopharmacological interventions. Also, too many medications may be prescribed in place of seeing the patient more frequently. Psychiatrists are most effective when they can provide balanced treatment approaches tailored to the clinical needs of patients.

Managed Care and the Suicidal Patient

The treatment of psychiatric inpatients has changed dramatically in the managed care era. The number of reimbursed outpatient visits has been severely curtailed. Most psychiatric units, particularly those in general hospitals, are now short-stay, acute care psychiatric facilities. Usually, only suicidal, homicidal, or gravely disabled patients with major psychiatric disorders pass strict precertification review for hospitalization. Approximately half of these patients have comorbid substance-related disorders.

The goal of hospitalization is crisis intervention and management to stabilize severely ill patients and to ensure their safety. However, close scrutiny by utilization reviewers generally allows only brief hospitalization for these patients. In addition, the hospital administration may exert pressure for early discharge in order to maintain length-of-stay statistics within predetermined limits. Treatment of acutely and chronically ill patients is provided by a variety of mental health professionals. With reduced provider reimbursement for inpatient treatment, the psychiatrist may be tempted to turn over more of the patient's care to the multidisciplinary team. Irrespective of payment, the psychiatrist is responsible for the care of the patient (25).

The psychiatrist must bear the ultimate burden of liability for treatments gone awry. Limited opportunity exists during the hospital stay to develop a therapeutic alliance with patients. The ability to communicate with patients, the psychiatrist's stock-in-trade, is usually severely curtailed. Usually, in order to gain precertification for admission in managed care settings, patients must meet "medically necessary" criteria, the stringency of which often equals or exceeds that of the substantive criteria for involuntary civil commitment. All of these factors contribute to the greatly increased risk of malpractice suits against psychiatrists, especially suits alleging premature or negligent discharge of suicidal patients due to cost-containment policies (35).

In both the outpatient and inpatient managed care settings, psychiatrists continue to be responsible for the care of acutely suicidal patients, even if further insurance benefits are denied by the MCO. The psychiatrist's professional, ethical and legal duty to provide care to the patient is not dependent on payment. MCOs can limit or deny payment for services but not the actual services themselves. After the emergency is over, the psychiatrist may refer the patient to other appropriate health care providers, see the patient at a reduced fee, or discharge the patient if no further treatment is deemed necessary.

The psychiatrist should record in the discharge note that the suicide risk assessment is a "here and now" evaluation. The discharge note should detail the acute suicide risk factors that have abated along with chronic suicide risk factors that persist. The note should also state that patients at chronic suicide risk can become acutely suicidal, depending on the nature and course of their mental illness, the adequacy of future treatment, adherence to treatment recommendations, and exposure to life's unpredictable vicissitudes. Suicidal behaviors are the result of a dynamic, complex interaction among a variety of clinical, personality, social, and environmental factors that vary across time and situations.

Supervision by Family or Friends

In outpatient practice, the practitioner has no legal duty to inform others that the patient is at risk for suicide (36). However, good clinical practice frequently requires that family members or other persons to be apprised of the patient's risk of suicide or be included in the treatment, provided the patient competently agrees to such interventions. If an outpatient at suicide risk requires constant family supervision, then psychiatric hospitalization is likely indicated.

Because of MCO limitations on inpatient length of stay, family supervision is frequently relied on. Patients requiring some level of psychiatric unit supervision for suicide risk should not be given unaccompanied passes. It is usually not possible to wait for patients to become totally free of suicide ideation before issuing a pass or before discharge. In fact, most patients at moderate levels of suicide risk are treated as outpatients or may not seek treatment. The decision to send an outpatient at low to moderate suicide risk on a family-accompanied pass depends on the stability of the patient, the stability of the family, the nature of the interaction between patient and family, and the purpose, risks, and benefits of the pass.

There are potentially two basic problems with families. First, the interaction between the patient and the family is likely to be impaired. Seriously mentally ill patients rarely come from families whose members are without substantial psychological impairment. Moreover, some members of the patient's family may be more disturbed than the patient. Releasing a patient at suicide risk to a troubled family could cause the patient to regress and be at increased risk of suicide. Family members have been known to dissuade the patient from taking necessary medication because of their denial of mental illness.

The second problem is that family members are not trained to diagnose and manage suicidal patients. Asking family members to supervise the patient places on them a burden that they often cannot manage. Specifically, asking family members to keep constant watch on the patient will likely fail. Family members usually will not follow the patient into the bathroom or stay up all night to observe the patient. Moreover, family members usually make exceptions, either due to denial, fatigue, or the pressing need to attend to other matters. For example, one family that was told to keep the patient under constant watch allowed the patient to drive alone.

There is an important role for the family, but it is not as a substitute for the care provided by trained mental health professionals. Family support and feedback about the patient's thoughts and behaviors is an appropriate, helpful role. Family members that have a reasonably sound relationship with the patient are usually sensitive to reportable changes in the patient's mental condition.

Physician-Assisted Suicide

With increasing legal recognition of physician-assisted suicide (PAS), psychiatrists are likely to be called on to act as gatekeepers. Such a role represents a radical departure from the physician's code of ethics, which prohibits an ethical doctor's participation in any intervention that hastens death. In the 1990 case of *Cruzan v. Director, Missouri Department of Health* (35), the United States Supreme Court ruled that terminally ill persons could refuse life-supporting medical treatment. Courts and legislatures will have to determine whether the hastening of death is an unwarranted extension of the right to refuse treatment. Every proposal for PAS requires a psychiatric screening or consultation to determine the terminally ill person's competency to choose suicide. The presence of psychiatric disorders associated with suicide, particularly depression, will have to be ruled out as the driving factor behind the request for PAS (37). Much controversy rages over the ethics of this gatekeeping function (38).

■ REFERENCES

1. Stepakoff v Kantar, 473 NE 2d 1131, 1134 (Mass 1985)
2. Black HC: Black's Law Dictionary, 6th Edition. St. Paul, MN, West Publishing, 1990, p 649
3. Speer v United States, 512 F Supp 670 (ND Tex 1981), aff'd, Speer v United States, 675 F2d 100 (5th Cir 1982)
4. Robertson JD: The trial of a suicide case, in American Psychiatric Press Review of Clinical Psychiatry and the Law, Vol 2. Edited by Simon RI. Washington, DC, American Psychiatric Press, 1991, pp 423–441
5. Simon RI: Psychiatrists awake! suicide risk assessments are all about a good night's sleep. Psychiatric Annals 28:479–485, 1998
6. Simon RI: Clinical risk management of suicidal patients: Assessing the unpredictable, in American Psychiatric Press Review of Psychiatry and the Law, Vol 3. Edited by Simon RI. Washington, DC, American Psychiatric Press, 1992, pp 3–66

7. Amchin J, Wettstein RM, Roth LH: Suicide, ethics, and the law, in Suicide Over the Life Cycle. Edited by Blumenthal SJ, Kupfer DJ. Washington, DC, American Psychiatric Press, 1990, pp 637–663

8. Roy A (ed): Suicide. Baltimore, MD, Williams and Wilkins, 1986

9. Zeldow PB, Taub HA: Evaluating psychiatric discharge and aftercare in a VA medical center. Hospital and Community Psychiatry 32:57–58, 1981

10. Simon RI: Discharging sicker, potentially violent psychiatric inpatients in the managed care era: standard of care and risk management. Psychiatric Annals 27:726–733, 1997

11. Widiger TA, Trull TJ: Personality disorders and violence, in Violence and Mental Disorder: Developments in Risk Assessment. Edited by Monahan J, Steadman HJ. Chicago, IL, University of Chicago Press, 1994, pp 203–226

12. Fawcett J, Scheptner WA, Fogg L, et al: Time-related predictors of suicide in major affective disorder. Am J Psychiatry 147:1189–1194, 1990

13. Fawcett J, Clark DC, Busch KA: Assessing and treating the patient at risk for suicide. Psychiatric Annals 23:244–255, 1993

14. Kessler RC, Borges G, Walters EE: Prevalence of and risk factors for lifetime suicide attempts in the national comorbidity survey. Arch Gen Psychiatry 55:617–626, 1999

15. Shaffer DA, Pfeffer CR, Bernet W, et al: Practice parameters for the assessment and treatment of children and adolescents with suicidal behavior. J Am Acad Child Adolesc Psychiatry 36(10), 1997 (supplement)

16. Jacobs DG, Brewer M, Klein-Benheim M: Suicide assessment: an overview and recommended protocol, in Guide to Suicide Assessment and Intervention. Edited by Jacobs JG. San Francisco, CA, Jossey-Bass, 1999, pp 3–39

17. Schneidman ES: Definition of Suicide. New York, Wiley, 1985

18. Goodwin FK, Runck BL: Suicide intervention: integration of psychosocial, clinical, and biomedical traditions, in Suicide

and Clinical Practice. Edited by Jacobs DG. Washington DC, American Psychiatric Press, 1992, pp 1–22

19. Murphy GE, Wetzel RD, Robins E, et al: Multiple risk factors predict suicide in alcoholism. Arch Gen Psychiatry 49:459–463, 1992

20. Maris RW, Berman AL, Maltsberger JT, et al: Assessment and Prediction of Suicide. New York, Guilford, 1992

21. Chiles JH, Strohsall K: The Suicidal Patient: Principles of Assessment, Treatment, and Case Management. Washington, DC, American Psychiatric Press, 1995

22. Clark DC, Fawcett J: An empirically based model of suicide risk assessment for patients with affective disorders, in Suicide and Clinical Practice. Edited by Jacobs D. Washington, DC, American Psychiatric Press, 1992, pp 55–73

23. Fawcett J: Profiles in completed suicides, in Guide to Suicide Assessment and Intervention. Edited by Jacobs JG. San Francisco, Jossey-Bass, 1999, pp 115–124

24. Beck AT, Brown GK, Steer RA, et al: Suicide ideation at its worst point: a predictor of eventual suicide in psychiatric outpatients. Suicide Life-Threat Behav 29:1–9, 1999

25. Simon RI: Psychiatrists' duties in discharging sicker and potentially violent inpatients in the managed care era. Psychiatr Serv 49:62–67, 1998

26. Busch KA, Clark DC, Fawcett J, et al: Clinical features of inpatient suicide. Psychiatric Annals 23:256–262, 1993

27. Perr IN: Suicide liability: a clinical perspective. Legal Aspects of Psychiatric Practice 1:5–8, 1984

28. Weisman AD, Worden JW: Risk-rescue rating in suicide assessment. Arch Gen Psychiatry 26:553–560, 1972

29. Simon RI: The suicide prevention contract: clinical, legal, and risk management issues. J Am Acad Psychiatry Law 27:445–450, 1999

30. Simon RI: The suicide prevention pact: clinical and legal considerations, in American Psychiatric Press Review of Clinical Psychiatry and the Law, Vol 2. Edited by Simon RI. Washington, DC, American Psychiatric Press, 1991, pp 441–451

31. Benesohn H, Resnik HLP: Guidelines for "suicide-proofing" a psychiatric unit. Am J Psychother 26:204–211, 1973

32. American Psychiatric Association: The Principles of Medical Ethics With Annotations Especially Applicable to Psychiatry. Washington, DC, American Psychiatric Association, 1998

33. Beautrais AL, Joyce PR, Mulder RT, et al: Prevalence and comorbidity of mental disorders in persons making serious suicide attempts: a case-control study. Am J Psychiatry 153: 1009–1014, 1996

34. Simon RI: Clinical Psychiatry and the Law, 2nd Edition. Washington, DC, American Psychiatric Press, 1992 pp 283–284

35. Cruzan v Director, Missouri Department of Health, 497 US 261 (1990)

36. Bellah v Greenson, 81 Cal App 3d 614, 146 Cal Rptr 535 (Cal Ct App 1978)

37. Simon RI: Silent suicide in the elderly. Bulletin of the American Academy of Psychiatry and the Law 17:83–95, 1989

38. Physician-Assisted Suicide: Code of Medical Ethics Reports. Chicago, IL, American Medical Association, Vol 5, No 2, July 1994, pp 269–275

9

THE POTENTIALLY VILENT PATIENT

■ OVERVIEW OF THE LAW

As a general rule, one person has no duty to control the conduct of a second person in order to prevent that person from physically harming a third person (1). Applying this rule to psychiatric care, psychiatrists traditionally have had only a limited duty to control hospitalized patients and to exercise due care upon discharge. After the 1976 *Tarasoff v. Board of Regents* case (2), the therapist's legal duty and potential liability significantly expanded. In *Tarasoff,* the California Supreme Court first recognized that a duty to protect third parties was normally imposed only when a special relationship existed between the victim, the individual whose conduct created the danger, and the defendant. The court held that "the single relationship of a doctor to his [or her] patient is sufficient to support the duty to exercise reasonable care to protect others" from the violent acts of patients.

In some jurisdictions, courts have held that the need to safeguard the public well-being overrides all other considerations, including confidentiality. In the majority of states, a psychotherapist has a duty, established by case law or statute, to act affirmatively to protect an endangered third party from a patient's violent or dangerous acts. Although some courts have declined to find a *Tarasoff* duty in a specific case, a number of courts have recognized some variation of the original *Tarasoff* duty. Very few courts have limited or outright rejected the *Tarasoff* doctrine (3, 4). In *Thapar v. Zezulka* (5), the Texas Supreme Court ruled that the state statute *permits* but does not *require* disclosures by therapists of threats of harm by patients against others.

When Does the Duty to Protect Arise?

Some courts and state legislatures have determined that a duty to exercise reasonable care to protect others arises when a psychotherapist determines, or should have determined, based on the standards of the profession, that a patient poses an imminent threat of serious harm to an identifiable third party. The duty to protect has been acknowledged by legal commentators as vague and open to interpretation. For example, determining what the "standards of the profession" are in evaluating an imminent threat (i.e., predicting dangerousness) and how the duty should be carried out is unsettled. As a result, this area of mental health law is one of the most controversial and vexing. Clinicians have found that the revised duty to protect provides more latitude for treatment interventions than the original duty-to-warn doctrine. Except in states with immunity statutes limiting the responsibility of therapists for their patients' violent acts, no hard-and-fast rules have been applied. In jurisdictions where no duty to warn or protect currently exists, case law from other states may be applied in deciding suits alleging such a duty.

As Beck (6) has pointed out, if professionals fail to exercise their clinical judgment and think they are excused from doing so by a statute, serious risks may be incurred. If a patient seriously injures another person and the therapist failed to exercise due care, the courts will find a way to hold the therapist liable, even in the presence of an immunity statute.

Discharging the Duty

A number of courts and state statutes have addressed the duty-to-protect doctrine. The statutes usually require that an identifiable victim be warned and/or the police notified (7). Courts typically focus on whether the violence was foreseeable and whether a sufficient element of control was present. Three threshold factors need to be addressed by the psychiatrist in a potential duty-to-protect situation:

1. Assess the threat of violence to another
2. Identify the potential object of that threat
3. Implement some affirmative, preventive act

Foreseeability is much more difficult when a class of persons or society in general is threatened. In discussing the duty to protect, courts have been divided on the issue of control of outpatients.

The law tends to assume that violence is preventable if it is foreseeable. However, foreseeability is a legal term of art. It does not and should not imply an ability of clinicians to predict violent behavior. Nor should foreseeability be confused with preventability. In hindsight, some violent acts seem preventable that were clearly not foreseeable.

Assessing the Threat

Despite psychiatrists' inability to predict the occurrence of violence reliably, the law requires that therapists exercise reasonable care in making such assessments. This type of evaluation requires compliance only with ordinary violence assessment procedures used in the profession. Steps such as a thorough pretreatment history, asking about and exploring past or present violence, and attention to factors reasonably thought to contribute to violent behavior are likely to satisfy a reasonable standard of care (see Tables 9–1 and 9–2 later in this chapter).

Identifying the Intended Victim

If the psychiatrist determines that a threat of violence exists, it is clinically and legally necessary to follow up that assessment with a determination of the person(s) who might be the object of the threat. Early cases and a growing number of recent court decisions have held that the duty to protect applies only when there is a "specific or identifiable threat to a specific or identifiable victim"

(8). A few courts have broadened this finding by requiring the duty to protect whenever there is a "foreseeable risk of harm" to the public at large (9). Whether a specific victim is identified or not, it is essential for the psychiatrist to act in some affirmative way to safeguard others against a potential risk of harm.

Exercising an Affirmative Act

The broad language used in the current case decisions involving the duty to warn and protect affords a therapist certain latitude in determining "whatever steps are reasonably necessary" to discharge that duty. A conceptual model for assessing violence and implementing suggested psychiatric interventions is provided (see Tables 9–1 and 9–2 later in this chapter). The legal reasoning applied in cases involving the duty to warn and protect suggests a number of factors to consider in order to reduce the risk of potential liability, if a patient threatens harm to others (see Tables 9–3 and 9–4 later in this chapter).

Special Considerations

Time Limitations

The courts have not specifically addressed the time limits of a therapist's duty to protect. Instead, it appears that the reasonableness of a therapist's evaluation of a patient's potential for violence plays a more important role in a court's finding of liability than the amount of time elapsing between the last therapy contact and the injury of a third party. For example, in *Naidu v. Laird* (10), the Delaware Supreme Court found that an inpatient psychiatrist was negligent in failing to foresee a former patient's potential to commit a violent act five-and-one-half months after discharge. The court stated that the lapse of time, by itself, was not a bar to recovery, but one factor to be weighed by the jury.

Confidentiality and Liability

Even in jurisdictions affirmatively endorsing the duty to warn, the therapist might be sued for breach of confidentiality. The disclosure must be made with discretion and in a manner that will preserve the patient's privacy while preventing potential harm. Moreover, the disclosure must be based on a reasonable risk of violence. Those courts not recognizing the duty to warn, and thus adhering to the common-law recognition of doctor-patient confidentiality, will likely favor a reasonable clinical alternative to breaching patient confidentiality (e.g., hospitalization).

Unforeseeable Violence

Liability will not be imposed if the evaluation that a patient is at low risk for violence is based on acceptable and reasonable clinical considerations and judgment. When liability is found despite a clinical judgment of a low risk of violence, the evidence generally shows that the therapist's evaluation and treatment procedures were substandard or that the therapist substantially departed from acceptable clinical practice.

Risk of Patient Self-Harm: Duty to Inform Third Party?

The danger of physical harm must be to others, not to the patient. Therefore, a psychotherapist does not have a duty to inform another party (e.g., a parent) if a patient is going to harm himself or herself. Sound clinical practice, however, may require that the family be brought into the treatment of the suicidal patient.

Unreachable Identified Victims

In situations in which the patient is judged to be a threat to a third party, but the third party cannot be reached in order to be warned, the therapist must consider notifying the police or contacting someone in close relationship with the potential victim. If clinically indicated, the patient may require hospitalization. Documenting that the therapist was unable to reach the identified victim and that alternative approaches were used may prevent liability.

Evolving Trends

An important, evolving trend is the application of the *Tarasoff* duty to sexual abuse cases by an alleged pedophile. A psychiatrist was successfully sued for not reporting to the medical school that his patient was a pedophile (11). The patient, a psychiatric resident, molested a child at a hospital crisis center. However, the defendant psychiatrist's control over the psychiatric resident was far greater than the typical psychiatrist-patient relationship. A *Tarasoff* duty was also found where a spouse had knowledge of her husband's sexually abusive behavior against children in the neighborhood (12, 13). In another case, the court found that a *Tarasoff* duty could exist but declined to find the parents of a babysitter liable for his dangerous sexual behavior (14). The court determined that no evidence existed that the parents knew of their son's proclivity to commit a sexual assault.

Summary

Although potential liability for violence has expanded significantly, a relatively small number of psychiatrists and other mental health professionals have been found guilty of negligence. The *Tarasoff* decision should be considered, however, as a national standard for clinical practice affecting psychiatrists and other mental health professionals in every jurisdiction (15). Monahan (16) provided guidelines for limiting therapist exposure to lawsuits in *Tarasoff* cases.

Since *Tarasoff,* a number of psychiatrists, psychotherapists, and hospitals and other health care facilities have been sued for allegedly breaching the duty to protect (17). In 1990, Beck (18) estimated that approximately 50 psychiatrists were sued each year for breach of the duty to protect. Of these cases, roughly two-thirds settled before trial. Of the 17 trials, approximately two-thirds resulted in defendant verdicts. Thus, six psychiatrists a year were found liable. For a psychiatrist who is a member of the American Psychiatric Association (APA) (total membership of approximately 35,000), Beck estimated that the odds of being sued for breach of the duty to protect, going to trial, and being found liable are 5,800 to 1 in any one year.

■ CLINICAL MANAGEMENT OF LEGAL ISSUES

Predicting Violent Behavior

The term *dangerousness* ordinarily refers to legal status rather than to a psychiatric disposition. The concept of dangerousness has never been adequately explained by the courts. Courts tend to avoid precise meanings in defining dangerousness, preferring to keep its meaning vague in the common law tradition of preserving applicability to specific situations. Instead of dangerousness, the term *risk of violence* is used in this book. A robust pattern of findings across studies supports a causal connection only between some mental disorders and violence (19). The National Institute of Mental Health Epidemiological Catchment Area Study estimated that 90% of persons with current mental illnesses are not violent (20). If a person was not having an acute psychotic episode or if psychotic symptoms were not part of the psychiatric problems, the individual was no more likely to be involved in violent behavior than the average person. Even when psychotic symptoms were present, there was only a modest increase in risk of violence above the norm. The persons with the highest risk of violence were young, substance-using males from lower socioeconomic classes. Seriously mentally ill patients with schizophrenia, major depression, mania, or bipolar disorder had an incidence of violence 5 times higher than that of persons with no diagnosed mental illness. The incidence of violence was 12 to 16 times higher among persons who were alcohol and substance abusers.

Violent behavior is a function of the dynamic interaction between social, clinical, personality, and environmental factors over situations and time (21). "Second generation" research on violence prediction shows that certain elements of the clinical situation contribute to imminent violence of the patient, thereby allowing appropriate interventions to be made. Violence is a function of the dynamic interaction between a specific individual and a specific situation for a given period of time. Nevertheless, because of the lack of clinical standards for the prediction of violence in any context or time frame, the prediction of violence becomes an unreliable exercise.

Stone (22), however, contended that psychiatrists do have some expertise in determining whether a patient manifests violent tendencies from the mental status evaluation. Therapists' predictions of the actual *occurrence* of violent acts by patients, however, cannot be made with any degree of professional skill. Nevertheless, Tardiff (23) maintained that well-trained psychiatrists should be able to predict a patient's short-term *potential* for violence by using evaluation techniques similar to those used in the short-term assessment of suicide risk. Binder (24) posed the question, "Which mentally ill, under what circumstances, are dangerous?" Her research data shows that short-term predictions of violence can be relatively accurate, that clinicians are better at predicting violence for certain patients, and that specific acute symptom patterns are related to violent acts.

The notion that therapists have no more skill than laypersons in predicting imminent violence was derived from "first generation" research studies on the long-term clinical prediction of violent behavior in populations of people convicted of criminal offenses (25). It should be noted, however, that a number of these studies were methodologically flawed. Nevertheless, according to these studies, the accuracy level has been roughly one correct prediction out of every three predictions made. These predictions have been limited by emphasis on certain traits of those guilty of criminal offenses, without the benefit of any situational analysis.

Because of psychiatrists' high false-positive prediction rate combined with a low base-rate occurrence of violence in outpatient psychiatric populations, accurate prediction of long-term violence to endangered third parties remains highly problematic. The MacArthur Violence Risk Assessment Study was established to help rectify this situation. Its purpose was to improve clinical risk assessment validity, to enhance effective clinical risk management, and to provide data on mental disorders and violence for informing mental health law and policy (26). In this study, violence risk assessments were found to have a validity that was modestly better than chance. Until more studies are available, sound clinical practice requires that thorough violence risk assessments be routinely performed on potentially violent patients based on our current knowledge of violence risk factors.

An accurate assessment of a high risk of violence may be more likely for some patients when violence seems imminent, especially when the unique interplay of patient and situational factors is psychodynamically understood. Assessment accuracy can also be improved when dealing with defined homogeneous populations having high base rates of violence. For example, a closed psychiatric unit containing very disturbed patients may have a violence base rate of 25% to 35%. Epidemiologic data containing known base rates for specific groups are an important assessment variable. In fact, more recent studies that focus on inpatient populations have demonstrated significantly improved predictability (27).

The best protection against allegations of negligence when assessing the risk of violence is to evaluate the patient according to methods and procedures that take into account known violence risk factors (see Tables 9–1 and 9–2). Because the psychiatrist is likely to be wrong more often than not, humility and sound clinical judgment dictate careful documentation of how the assessment of violence is conducted.

In *Barefoot v. Estelle* (28), a capital punishment case, the U.S. Supreme Court held that if jurors are authorized to bear responsibility for a death penalty based on predictions of future behavior, then psychiatrists are justified in testifying about dangerousness despite the low predictive ratio of one out of three. If an accuracy of one out of three predictions of dangerousness is sufficient to justify execution, an even lower level of predictive accuracy should be acceptable in litigation involving the duty to warn and protect. The Court's support for the validity of psychiatric predictions of dangerousness in capital cases tends to give impetus to judicial expectations of psychiatric prediction in *Tarasoff*-type cases (29).

TABLE 9–1.   Assessment of violence risk factors

Risk factor	Facilitating violence	Inhibiting violence
Specific person threatened[a]		
Past violent acts[a]		
Accessible victim		
Motive		
Therapeutic alliance (ongoing patient)		
Other relationships		
Psychiatric diagnosis (Axis I and II)		
Thought insertion or control		
Command hallucinations		
Fear of control		
Control of anger		
Situational status		
Employment status		
Epidemiological data (age, sex, race, socioeconomic group, marital status, violence base rates)		
Availability of lethal means (e.g., guns)		
Syntonic or dystonic violence		
Specific plan		
Childhood abuse (or witnessing parental spouse abuse)		
Alcohol abuse		
Substance abuse		
Mental competency		
History of impulsive behavior		
Central nervous system disorder		
Low intelligence		
Overall Risk Rating		

Instructions:
1. Rate risk factors present as low (L), moderate (M), high (H), nonfactor (0).
2. Judge overall violence risk as low, moderate, or high.

[a]When a specific person is threatened and past violence has occurred, a high risk rating for violence exists.

TABLE 9–2. **Assessment of violence risk and examples of outpatient psychiatric intervention options**

Violence risk	Psychiatric interventions
HIGH	Immediate hospitalization if mentally ill and likely to benefit from hospitalization
MODERATE	Hospitalization Frequent outpatient visits Consider warning endangered person(s) and calling the police Reevaluate patient and treatment plan frequently Remain available to the patient
LOW	Continue with current treatment plan

Note. Tables 9–1 and 9–2 represent only one method of violence risk assessment and intervention. The purpose of these tables is heuristic, encouraging a systematic approach to risk assessment. The therapist's clinical judgment concerning the patient remains paramount. Because violence risk factors will be assigned different weights according to the clinical presentation of the patient, the method represented in these tables should not be followed rigidly.

Violence Risk Factors

Certain personal, socioeconomic, situational, and clinical risk factors are associated with violence. Monahan (30) demonstrated a statistical association between violence and epidemiologic data:

- Sex (males 10 to 1 over females in the United States)
- Race (controversial)
- Younger age
- Employment and residential instability
- History of alcohol abuse
- History of drug abuse
- Previous violence

According to Monahan (31), the current violent crime rate in the United States is considerably higher among blacks than whites. This, however, refers to the prevalence of violence but not to the incidence of violence in persons once they become violent. In other words, once individuals become involved in crime, racial differences disappear. Tardiff (23), however, disputes race as a factor in violence. Studies of patients with and without criminal convictions do not uniformly find a correlation in the incidence of violence with race (32).

Situational factors associated with violence include the following:

- An unstable family
- A violent environment
- A violent peer group
- Availability of weapons (e.g., handguns)

Some of the risk factors reported to be associated with violence in the general psychiatric literature are listed in Table 9–3.

Every study on the assessment of violence risk factors has found that the single factor most highly correlated with the potential for future violence is a history of violence. Violent patients should be asked how they feel about having committed or threatened to commit violent acts. Determining whether violent behavior is syntonic or dystonic for the patient is an essential element of violence risk assessment.

TABLE 9–3.   **Clinical risk factors associated with violence**

The stated desire to hurt or kill another

History of violence

Alcohol and substance abuse

Inability to control anger

Impulsivity (e.g., previous violence toward others or self, reckless driving, unrestrained spending, sexual promiscuity)

Paranoid ideation, thought insertion or control, fear of harm

Command hallucinations

Psychosis

Personality disorders: antisocial, borderline, and organic personality disorder (explosive type)

"Soft" neurological signs

Substance abuse

Low intelligence

The therapeutic alliance can be a very effective deterrent to violence. With new patients or patients seen in an emergency, sufficient time may not have elapsed for an alliance to form. Link and Stueve (33) found a relationship between a subset of psychotic symptoms and violence, specifically thought insertion, thought control, and the fear of being harmed by others. The index of suspicion for potential violence should be high in patients with acute psychosis who are substance abusing, angry, fearful of being harmed, and experiencing delusions of being controlled or influenced. Substance abuse significantly raises the rate of violence in both patient and comparison groups (26).

A number of factors have been identified in young persons that should alert mental health professionals to an increased potential for future violence (34) (see Table 9–4).

Motive is a very important clinical variable in the assessment of violence (15). When the patient responds affirmatively to the question about wanting to hurt someone, the questions Who? When? Where? Why? and For how long? must be asked by the therapist. Information gleaned from these inquiries is critical to the evaluation of the following:

- How imminent is the threat of violence?
- Who is the object of potential violence?
- What can be done to treat the patient and protect potential victims?

TABLE 9–4. **Major risk factors in young persons associated with increased potential for violence**

Serious violence as a juvenile
Psychotic symptoms
Major neurological impairment or head injury
Childhood abuse
Witnessing parental spouse abuse
Psychiatric hospitalization
Relatives with psychosis

Careful assessment and documentation of pertinent risk factors used in assessing the potentially violent patient may prevent allegations of negligence. Even if the therapist is tragically wrong in the assessment of the risk of violence, a mistake is not malpractice if a reasonable standard of care was used. Nevertheless, the clinician must remember that the systematic assessment of the risk of violence is good clinical practice and only secondarily a risk management technique.

The "weather forecast" model of violence assessment and intervention is shown in Tables 9–1 and 9–2. Because time attenuates assessment accuracy, a time-driven assessment method, such as the weather forecast model, is applicable to the assessment of violence. Assessments of the risk of violence are here-and-now determinations. Probability assessments of the risk of violence, like weather forecasting, become progressively less accurate beyond the immediate short term (e.g., 24–48 hours). The model presented in Tables 9–1 and 9–2 is suggested only as a guide. Professional judgment concerning the clinical facts about the patient and the associated situational factors should dictate appropriate decision making. Accordingly, with the exception of *specific person threatened* and *past violent acts,* violence risk factors in Table 9–1 are not listed in order of clinical importance. That determination depends on the patient's clinical presentation.

The method of violence risk assessment presented here is highly schematic. Tables 9–1 and 9–2 need not be reproduced in the patient's chart. A standard note containing an adequate violence risk assessment is all that is necessary. The weather forecast model provides one way of thinking about violence risk assessment. This model of suicide-violence risk assessment is derived from the author's clinical experience and the psychiatric literature. No model has been empirically tested for reliability and validity. Other approaches to violence risk assessment exist (35). Regardless of which method is used, the important point is that in the management of violent patients, violence risk assessments need to be made and recorded in the medical chart as required.

Demonstration of Violence Risk Assessment

After doing a complete psychiatric examination, the clinician should be able to perform and record a competent violence risk assessment within a few minutes. One method of documenting the violence risk assessment is to construct a simple table and label it as demonstrated in Table 9–5. The patient's risk factors should be rated as low (L), moderate (M), high (H), or nonfactor (0). After weighing all of the risk factors, the overall assessment of violence risk should be rated as low, moderate, or high. The following clini-

TABLE 9–5. **Demonstration of a rapid, competent violence risk assessment**

Risk factor	Facilitating violence	Inhibiting violence
Specific person threatened	0 (in hospital)	0
Past violence	H (stabbed cousin)	
Accessible victim	H (mother)	
Therapeutic alliance		L–M (with staff)
Psychiatric diagnosis	H	
Command hallucinations	0 (in hospital)	0
Employment		L
Specific plan	0	0
Treatment response		H
Medication compliance		H (in hospital)
Structured environment		H
Alcohol dependence	H	
Substance abuse	0	0
History of impulsivity	H	
Guns		L (none at home)
Compliance with aftercare	H	
Relationships	M–H (loner)	
Overall Risk Rating: low (at discharge)		

cal vignette illustrates the importance of assessing a patient's violence risk at the time of a contemplated discharge. After reviewing
the vignette, the reader is encouraged to do an independent violence
risk assessment before considering the psychiatrist's assessment.

A 35-year-old patient with chronic schizophrenia is admitted to
the psychiatric unit of a general hospital because of auditory
hallucinations commanding him to kill his mother. He also expresses the delusion that his mother is poisoning him. The patient has not lived apart from his mother. He works sporadically
as a laborer. His only income is from Social Security Disability
Insurance. The patient is treated with antipsychotic medication
and individual and group therapies. Because the patient speaks
only broken English, verbal interaction between the psychiatrist
and the patient is minimal. The psychiatrist relies heavily on
observation of the patient's behavior on the ward and the input
from the treatment team.

The psychiatrist learns from the patient's mother that the
patient has been involuntarily hospitalized three times in the
past 10 years. An assault preceded each of the previous hospitalizations. Prior to the second hospitalization, the patient
stabbed a cousin. He was criminally charged but found not
guilty by reason of insanity. The psychiatrist feels that he needs
more information. He asks the unit secretary to call and request
fax copies of the patient's previous hospital summaries.

After 10 days of hospitalization, the psychiatrist reviews the
clinical course of the patient with the staff. The patient stays to
himself most of the time. There is no evidence of any violent
behavior. The patient is described in the nursing notes as "very
cooperative." He complies with ward routine and regulations.
Medication is not refused. After the fourth day of hospitalization, the patient denies any hallucinations or delusions. The staff
informs the psychiatrist that the patient becomes sullen and
withdrawn when his mother visits. No passes are requested by
the patient.

A discharge conference is held with the treatment team. The
conference participants conclude that the patient is ready for

discharge. The patient denies any intent to harm his mother or anyone else. At the discharge conference, the just-received fax summaries of the previous hospitalizations are reviewed. The summaries reveal that the patient was diagnosed with paranoid schizophrenia on each admission. The history is also consistent for each hospitalization. The patient fails to keep his outpatient visits, stops taking his medication, and begins drinking. After some variable period of time, he becomes delusional, begins to hear voices, and then becomes assaultive. The psychiatrist and the treatment team are concerned about the patient's revolving-door history of paranoid schizophrenia, alcohol dependence, noncompliance with treatment, decompensation, violence, and rehospitalization. The patient's history is similar to that of a number of other patients with schizophrenia admitted to the unit. Psychiatric facilities for long-term hospitalization are not available. The treatment team concludes that the patient has received maximal therapeutic benefit from inpatient treatment. The patient has one more hospital day authorized by the managed care organization. The psychiatrist performs a violence risk assessment, judging that the patient's overall lifetime risk of violence is very high but is low *at the time of discharge* (see Table 9–5). The violence risk assessment is included in a risk-benefit assessment that weighs the risks and benefits for both continued hospitalization and discharge. The risk-benefit assessment favors discharge.

The psychiatrist is careful to note that the violence assessment is a here-and-now evaluation. At the time of discharge, the patient's risk of violence is assessed as low. However, the patient may be at a high risk for violence in the future based on exacerbation of his psychiatric disorder, noncompliance with treatment, alcohol abuse, an altercation with his mother, and other, unforeseen, situational stress factors.

Because the patient has progressed so well, the psychiatrist decides to discharge the patient. The psychiatrist discusses the discharge with the patient's mother. She expresses some trepidation but agrees to have her son live at home. She hopes her son will be able to go back to his job as a laborer. The patient rejects referrals to Alcoholics Anonymous and the hospital's day treatment program. The social worker arranges an appointment for the patient at the community outpatient center for the first available session. His appointment is scheduled for 1 week after discharge. The patient is seen on the day of discharge and appears eager to leave.

This vignette has been presented at clinical conferences where clinicians were asked to assess the patient's risk of violence and appropriateness for discharge. The clinicians were clustered into two groups on the violence risk rating. All agreed that the patient had a high lifetime risk of violence. However, disagreement arose about the psychiatrist's low violence risk rating at the time of discharge. Some clinicians (group A) felt that the distinction between the low risk of violence at the time of discharge versus the patient's high lifetime risk was a distinction without a difference. This group explained that the patient was at just as high a risk of violence at discharge.

Group A clinicians felt that, as expected, the patient functioned quite well in a structured hospital environment where he was monitored for medication compliance. However, it was entirely foreseeable that the patient would repeat the prior cycles that led to violence and rehospitalization. These clinicians recommended that the patient be involuntarily hospitalized and then transitioned to outpatient commitment status to ensure follow-up and compliance.

Another group of clinicians (group B) felt that these recommendations were impractical. The purpose of hospitalizing a patient in the managed care era was rapid stabilization and referral to outpatient treatment. Inpatient psychiatrists provide acute care for very sick patients, similar to the intensive care unit for medical-surgical patients. Involuntary hospitalization would be inappropriate because the patient would not meet substantive standards for involuntary commitment, especially the usual requirement of imminent danger to self and others. Moreover, hospitals receiving involuntary patients discharge them rapidly if the patients are stable.

Long-term private psychiatric hospitalization was not an option for this patient who, except for receiving Social Security disability benefits, was impecunious. Group B felt that the best course of action was to carefully structure outpatient follow-up for compliance with treatment. Because the potential for violence toward the mother exists, referral of the patient should be made to a supervised residential setting where his condition and medication could be monitored. The conferees were in agreement that managed care pressures should not lead to a premature discharge. However, a lively debate invariably occurred about clinicians' responsibility for continuing care of an unstable inpatient after a managed care organization (MCO) refuses to authorize payment for additional stay. Younger clinicians with families had greater difficulty in assuming the financial loss of caring for acutely ill patients until they were stabilized and discharged.

Tarasoff and Psychiatric Practice

The *Tarasoff* duty applies to outpatient cases. The majority of courts have held that the therapist's control over the outpatient is not sufficient to establish a duty to protect without a foreseeable victim. In treating an outpatient, the *Tarasoff* duty generally applies when there is evidence, through either expressed or implied threats or acts, that the patient is dangerous to a specific, foreseeable victim. The danger must be substantial, involving serious bodily harm or death. If no threats or violent acts are uncovered after careful clinical evaluation, liability is unlikely even if violence occurs (see Table 9–6).

In inpatient release cases, the courts have held that there is a duty to control with or without a foreseeable victim if there is reasonable evidence that the patient may be dangerous. Evaluation of the patient for potential violence would obviate a *Tarasoff* duty, if imminent violence required continued hospitalization. If the court should release a patient deemed dangerous by the psychiatrist, the psychiatrist should go on record with his or her concern about the patient's potential for violence. Psychiatrists are successfully sued much more often for negligent release of violent patients than for a failure to warn and protect endangered third persons in outpatient cases.

As always, the therapist should attempt to integrate the *Tarasoff* duty into the clinical work with the patient. Thus, in some states, statutory provisions limiting the *Tarasoff* duty to that of warning an endangered, identifiable victim may distract psychiatrists from providing the full spectrum of clinical interventions (36). Warning, by itself, is often insufficient as a clinical intervention. Usually, more needs to be done clinically.

Beck (37) notes that once the clinical assessment is made that a patient is potentially violent, three basic options are open to the clinician:

- Deal with the violence in the therapy
- Warn the victim and/or the police
- Hospitalize the patient voluntarily or involuntarily

TABLE 9–6. **Managing potentially violent inpatients: clinical approaches**

Inpatient perceived as "minimally dangerous"

1. Perform and record a violence risk assessment prior to releasing the patient in order to substantiate this clinical decision.
2. Review the patient's chart, including nursing and all other allied professional notes, to ascertain any incidence of assaultiveness.
3. Confer with other staff regarding their observations and assessments of the patient's status with regard to violence.
4. Inquire into the patient's plans while on pass or following discharge.
5. Schedule aftercare appointments prior to discharge.

Inpatient perceived as "dangerous"

1. Steps 1–4 above.
2. Inquire about feelings of hurting oneself or someone else.
3. Explore the patient's feelings and fantasies for specific intent.
4. If there is still doubt about the patient's intent or condition, consult with another psychiatrist.
5. If the doubt persists after careful evaluation and consultation, detain the patient until the potential for violence diminishes or transfer to an appropriate facility for further treatment.

If, after conducting a careful assessment, the therapist is satisfied that the patient will not commit violence before the next scheduled appointment, then the therapist can continue to treat the potential violence as a purely therapeutic issue. If the therapist believes that the patient will become violent within 24 to 48 hours, hospitalization is generally the treatment of choice. If an intermediate position exists in which the therapist believes that violence is a distinct possibility but is not imminent, then the best course is usually to warn the victim. Warning may also be the intervention of choice if it appears that a patient will become violent before the next session but is not committable. In addition to warning, a full spectrum of clinical interventions should be considered.

Short-term assessments of the risk of violence are more accurate because the parameters that influence future occurrences can be specified with greater precision. For assessments made at a greater distance, the clinician loses the ability to specify both psychological and environmental determinants of behavior and thus to assess with reasonable accuracy the likelihood of particular outcomes. Accordingly, potentially violent patients should be seen face to face frequently and their risks for violence reassessed at each of these visits.

Documentation that a violence risk assessment was conducted demonstrates that the clinician was careful and thorough in the evaluation of the patient and adhered to the standard of care. Violence risk assessment is an ongoing process, not merely a onetime event. In treating the potentially violent patient, clinicians cannot ensure the outcome of their assessments, only the process of assessment.

Assessment is not an academic exercise. Its sole purpose is to guide patient management. As Appelbaum aptly stated, "Clinicians have learned to live with *Tarasoff*, recognizing that good common sense, sound clinical practice, careful documentation, and a genuine concern for their patients are almost always sufficient to fulfill their legal obligations" (36).

Clinical Considerations

Long before *Tarasoff*, therapists warned endangered third persons as part of their professional and ethical duty. The duty arose when the therapist possessed "insider information" from the treatment about potential risk of violence posed by a patient to others. The problem for therapists is not to become mesmerized by the duty to warn at the expense of implementing other clinical interventions that may be more effective. The great majority of potentially violent patients can be managed through good clinical practice. Although it is important to seek consultation with an attorney in certain cases, the clinician should be aware of the tendency of some attorneys to rapidly adhere to the full letter of the law and recommend a warning by registered mail. If followed blindly, this course could be an invitation to practice the worst form of defensive psychiatry. In addition, the patient's rights may be abused and the potential victim unduly traumatized. Lawyers tend to be risk averse. Psychiatrists must not abandon their clinical judgment in dealing with potentially violent patients. The duty to warn, however, should not be ignored if required or appropriate, but it should be only one of many clinical interventions to be used after consideration of the patient's needs and circumstances.

Warning Endangered Third Parties

Simply issuing a warning as a legal formalism is not an acceptable approach to managing the violent patient. Although a number of states have defined the *Tarasoff* duty in statutes and have narrowed the potential liability, the therapist who does not exercise reasonable professional judgment in managing the violent patient may still be vulnerable to a suit. Therapists must be reasonably certain that the threat of harm to others is imminent. Moreover, clinical efforts to manage and control the patient should be attempted before issuing a warning to the intended victim. Frequently, the patient's treatment ends when a warning is made to an endangered third party. At this point, the therapist's intervention options are severely limited or nonexistent. Involuntary hospitalization may be an appropriate, last resort intervention for selected patients who meet the substantive criteria (mentally ill and dangerous) for civil commitment.

Whether the law mandates it or not, therapists have a moral, ethical, and professional duty to protect patients and their potential victims. From a treatment perspective, the legal imposition of this duty is incidental to the therapist's professional duty. When the duty to warn is implemented, every effort should be made to include the patient in the warning process.

Warning endangered third parties is not without peril. Even if the victim is able to escape or evade the violent patient, the predictability of violence is inaccurate to the extent that many individuals will be falsely warned. For example, receiving a letter or a phone call from a therapist warning of serious violence will likely be extremely frightening. Warned individuals can themselves become so severely distressed that they become unwitting victims who are psychologically harmed by the duty to warn. Furthermore, warning often becomes an empty gesture when police are reluctant to act before a crime is committed. Preventive detention is not constitutionally permitted. What if the endangered individual is out of town? Should a letter be sent? Should it be sent by certified mail or by special delivery? How long will it take to be delivered? Locating potential victims may be an impossible task.

In general, if the therapist decides to warn, a phone call is appropriate. A phone call allows the potential victim to ask questions. Nuances and difficulties in communication can also be appreciated by both parties. Telephoning in the patient's presence helps to temper exaggerated remarks by the therapist, who may be overreacting to the threat of violence. In addition, the patient's presence tends to head off suspicions or outright paranoid ideas that the psychiatrist is acting duplicitously. Sometimes, a trusted third party may act as a go-between. The warning should be made clearly. The clarity of the warning has been open to second-guessing by some courts. Successful malpractice suits are unlikely when good faith warning and reporting are based on reasonable medical judgment.

The psychology of victimization is pertinent to the decision to warn (38). For example, the psychodynamics of victim-victimizer, husband-wife, or partner relationships in which one party is being abused may dictate attempting to move the victim toward a sheltered environment rather than warning the abuser that the abused partner is considering retaliatory violence. To do otherwise might seriously endanger the patient or precipitate mutual violence.

How the warning is given, not whether one is given, is sometimes the more critical factor. When the clinician discusses the warning with the patient before giving it, generally the clinical result is positive. Failing to discuss the warning with the patient often harms the therapeutic alliance and the therapy. Potential victims should be warned in a clinically supportive manner. If they feel that evasive action can be taken and that the therapist is acting in a responsible, genuinely concerned manner, the warnings are likely to be received positively.

Generally, courts have refused to impose a duty on psychiatrists to warn the foreseeable victim when the latter knew of the potential for violence from a patient (39). In *In re: Estate of Heltsley v. Votteler* (40), the plaintiff had knowledge of the patient's previous aggressive behavior but contended that a warning from the psychiatrist would have made her appreciate the significance of the threat. The Iowa Supreme Court rejected this argument. On the other hand, in *Jablonski v. United States* (41), the defendant's wife, who was killed by the patient, had received warnings about the patient from her priest, her mother, her attorney, and a hot-line service. She had even voiced her fears to the psychiatrist, but nonetheless, the court imposed liability.

The therapist should not assume that an endangered person who has been previously threatened or harmed by the patient fully appreciates the current danger of his or her situation. Denial may cause the person to minimize or ignore the threat. Depending on the nature of the case and of the relationship between the patient and the potential victim, the therapist may nonetheless decide to warn the endangered person of the specific threats made by the patient, despite his or her prior knowledge.

Confidentiality Concerns

Trust is the cornerstone of psychiatric treatment. Without trust, no therapeutic alliance can develop, damaging the patient's chances of receiving psychotherapeutic help. In the real world, confidentiality, like trust, cannot be absolute. Exceptions to the maintenance of confidentiality exist for the protection of both the patient and society.

In *Tarasoff,* the court was mindful of the importance of maintaining as much confidentiality as possible in the therapist-patient relationship. The court stated that warning of a victim should be done in such a way as to preserve confidentiality consonant with the prevention of threatened danger. Confidentiality should not be breached by warning a third party unless the threat is serious and imminent, and an identifiable victim is endangered. Nevertheless, a plaintiff may allege breach of confidentiality.

The Principles of Medical Ethics With Annotations Especially Applicable to Psychiatry states, "When in the clinical judgment of the treating psychiatrist the risk of danger is deemed to be significant, the psychiatrist may reveal confidential information disclosed by the patient" (42, Section 4, Annotation 8). The *Tarasoff* exception to confidentiality is part of the same public policy exception requiring the reporting of contagious diseases, suspected child abuse, and gunshot wounds for the welfare of the patient and society. The duty to maintain confidentiality versus the duty to protect may also arise concerning the capacity of some patients' ability to drive an automobile. A *Tarasoff* duty has been found in cases where patients have injured third parties with their vehicles (43). Generally, courts do not impose liability unless the physician had significant control over the patient (e.g., outpatient vs. inpatient) (44). In *Lester v. Hall* (45), the New Mexico Supreme Court held that a physician did not owe a duty to the driver of a car who was injured in a collision with a car driven by the physician's patient. The patient was prescribed lithium. The court stated that in an outpatient setting, a physician may advise a patient about taking medication, but the patient must also assume some responsibility.

Mental health professionals should know the law governing confidentiality in their jurisdiction. Although the *Tarasoff* duty arises only occasionally, the maintenance of confidentiality is a constant duty in clinical practice because the breach of confidentiality occurs much more frequently. In 1996, the U.S. Supreme

Court ruled in *Jaffe v. Redmond* (46) that communications between psychotherapist and patient are confidential in federal cases under the Federal Rules of Evidence. Perlin (47) pointed out that a footnote in *Jaffe* states an exception to the privilege where a serious threat of harm exists to the patient or others that "can be averted only by means of a disclosure by the therapist" (pp. 20–21). He comments that "the relationship of this footnote to the *Tarasoff* doctrine has not yet been fully explored" (pp. 20–21).

Some therapists give *Miranda*-type warnings to new patients about the therapist's duty to warn or protect third parties against harm from violent patients. Starting a treatment on this note usually casts a pall over the fledgling therapeutic process. Patients already frightened of their own aggression may find such a warning confirmatory of their worst fears. Secretive patients may seize upon such a warning to withhold verbal expression of violent feelings. When the protection of others from patient violence is necessary, clinical interventions will often allow for the preservation of confidentiality, making *Miranda*-type warnings to patients a gratuitous gesture.

If a patient gives the therapist good reason to believe that a warning should be issued to an endangered third party, the confidentiality of the communication that gave rise to the warning may be lost. The warning of endangered third parties has resulted in psychiatrists being compelled to testify in criminal cases (48).

Protecting Endangered Third Parties

The therapist should proceed clinically in the management of the violent patient. There is no inherent conflict between the duty to treat the patient and the duty to protect third parties. Above all, therapists must not be so worried about legal issues that they become distracted from providing good clinical care. Although therapists must practice within the law, they need not become lawyers.

Whereas *Tarasoff I* emphasized the duty to warn exclusively, *Tarasoff II* stated that the psychiatrist must exercise his or her own best judgment consistent with that reasonable degree of skill, knowledge, and care ordinarily exercised by psychiatrists under similar circumstances to *protect* the victim from the foreseeable violence of dangerous patients. The court does not require perfect skill but only the skill exercised by psychiatrists in similar circumstances. The duty to protect does permit a more broad and meaningful clinical approach to the management of violent patients. Although warning may be part of a therapist's intervention strategy, it rarely should be relied on initially or exclusively.

The Patient With HIV

With the universal fear concerning the spread of acquired immunodeficiency syndrome (AIDS), psychiatrists who treat patients testing positive for the human immunodeficiency virus (HIV) face special ethical and legal dilemmas. For example, how should the psychiatrist manage the patient who is HIV-positive and who continues to have multiple sexual relationships, yet refuses to inform his or her partners? Consent between adults is a sham under this circumstance. Unlike other potentially dangerous patients, the patient who is promiscuous and has concealed HIV infection constantly carries a potentially lethal weapon where the occasion for harm commonly occurs within the unguarded embrace of a sexual relationship. Eth (49) noted four clinical situations in which violating confidentiality to protect life is ethically indicated: 1) communicable disease, 2) child abuse, 3) threat of violence, and 4) HIV seropositivity.

Psychiatrists treating patients with diagnosed HIV infections who pose a continuing danger of infection to others should evaluate these patients in the same manner as other potentially dangerous patients. It is the patient's behavior, and not the HIV status per se, that represents the immediate danger. The psychiatrist should focus the evaluation particularly on the following questions:

- What is the patient's diagnosis (Axis I and Axis II)?
- Is the patient treatable by available psychiatric therapies?
- What is the motivation of the patient for not informing sexual partners of HIV-positive status while displaying an apparent indifference to the welfare of the sexual partners?
- Can the endangering behavior be contained by and within the treatment?

- Can support groups and organizations be mobilized to help the unemployed, isolated HIV patient?

Often, patients who are HIV-positive are unemployable, shunned by society, alone, and terrified. Sexual contact with others may be motivated not so much by sexual interest as by the need for human contact, affection, and support. To expect these patients to be sexually abstinent without providing other sources of emotional sustenance is naive and insensitive. Support groups and organizations are critically important for these individuals.

On the other hand, the patient who is antisocial or has borderline personality disorder may be motivated to infect others out of malice or may display a callous indifference to the welfare of others. If this behavior cannot be managed clinically, serious consideration must be given to telling the patient that a warning will be issued if the identity of the endangered parties is known. A report to the health department should also be considered, if the authorities will conduct tracing and notification. A full notation of all measures taken should be recorded in the patient's chart. Consultation with a colleague should also be considered. As in other *Tarasoff*-type situations, warnings must be discreet, balancing the right of society to be protected from disease against the psychiatrist's duty to maintain patient confidentiality.

Successful malpractice suits for breach of confidentiality are possible, even when good-faith warning and reporting are based on reasonable medical judgment. Clinicians should become familiar with health regulations and laws governing the reporting of HIV positivity. Immunity from liability for health care providers may be available, similar to that found in mandatory reporting requirements currently applicable for other contagious diseases.

In 1993, the APA's Commission on AIDS revised its confidentiality and disclosure guidelines to permit psychiatrists to notify an endangered identifiable third party at risk from a patient who is unable or unwilling to take precautions, including abstinence (50). Other important issues covered in the APA guidelines include 1) the use of involuntary hospitalization when an HIV-positive patient's endangering behaviors are the result of mental illness that can be treated by hospitalization, and 2) the permissibility of notifying public health authorities of previously exposed individuals who are no longer in contact with and at risk of exposure to the HIV-positive patient, if the patient is unable or unwilling to cooperate. However, as with all warnings given to endangered third parties, the psychiatrist must consider the serious emotional impact and adverse consequences that notification may have on the person warned. Appelbaum and Appelbaum (51) have provided an indepth analysis of confidentiality versus the duty to protect in the management of the patient with HIV.

The Risk-Benefit Assessment

With any treatment intervention undertaken with a potentially violent patient, a risk-benefit assessment should be conducted and recorded in the patient's chart immediately. In the event of a violent outcome, a documented risk-benefit analysis that considers clinically relevant interventions with potentially violent patients will be useful in demonstrating that reasonable care was taken with the patient. Absolute statements that a patient is no longer at risk of violence are not clinically defensible. Considering risks alone leads to unduly defensive practices. Risk-benefit assessments bring a balanced perspective to clinical decision making.

Risk-benefit assessments should evaluate the risks and benefits both for and against the intervention under consideration. For example, in considering a hospital discharge for a patient who has displayed a potential for violence, both the risks and the benefits of the discharge must be considered against the risks and the benefits of continued hospitalization. A note should include a statement about the likelihood of violence, a proposed course of action, and the reasoning behind the chosen interventions, citing the clinical data relied on.

Consultation with a colleague may be reassuring to both the patient and the therapist. The consultant should document her or his findings. If time does not allow for the patient to be seen, an informal consultation can take place over the phone. Although not ideal, such a consultation is better than none at all. The psychiatrist should summarize the consultant's opinion in the patient's record. If legal questions arise later, consultation may help establish that a reasonable standard of care was provided to the patient.

Psychiatric residents should consider increasing the frequency of their supervision when a dangerous patient is undergoing a crisis. Decisions regarding management of the potentially violent patient should be endorsed by the supervisor's signature.

Assessing and Managing the Risk of Violence

Assessing and managing the risk of violence involves three basic steps (see Tables 9–1 and 9–2):

1. Identifying patients with risk factors associated with violence
2. Assessing the overall risk of violence based on the rating of specific risk factors
3. Implementing treatment and preventive interventions that bear a logical nexus to the overall violence risk assessment

Therapists are on sounder clinical footing when clinically assessing the potential risk of violence than when trying to predict violent acts. Assessing violence according to a reasonable standard of care can be undertaken in the emergency room, outpatient clinic, or office, or at the time of the patient's discharge from the hospital. Based on the assessment of violence risk factors, a probability determination of low, moderate, or high potential for violence can be made according to a tabulation of clinical factors that increase or decrease the risk of violence (see Tables 9–1 and 9–2). The assessment of the patient's overall risk of violence is based on clinical judgment. No clinical standards exist for predicting the occurrence of a violent act.

Psychiatrists have not been held legally liable for inaccurate assessments of the risk of violence per se. Lawsuits have been successful against them when psychiatrists have failed to properly collect necessary data and to logically assess the risk of violence. The method illustrated in Tables 9–1 and 9–2 also may be used when time and circumstances do not permit obtaining a consultation (52).

Approaching potential violence clinically allows consideration of the possible connection between violence and mental disorders. Thus, the psychiatrist stays within a familiar province of clinical practice. Psychiatrists certainly possess the ability to treat and manage most patients who are currently violent. On the other hand, legal definitions of dangerousness tend to be arbitrary and abstract concepts, not readily translatable into the diagnostic and treatment models used by psychiatrists.

The assessment of potential violence contains two major prongs: 1) gathering information and 2) assessing the risk of violence. Appelbaum (36) suggested that clinicians routinely ask patients two questions: "Have you ever seriously injured another person?" and "Do you ever think about harming someone else?" These two questions often yield surprising information that is not usually made available in a general psychiatric history. Areas that deserve particularly close assessment include the individual, social, situational, and clinical variables related to violence discussed earlier. The most common mistake made by clinicians is to base a violence risk assessment on insufficient information.

When treating or evaluating the violent patient, the clinician should assess the status of psychological defenses, intensity of conflicts, and other psychodynamic issues. In ongoing therapy, interventions must be revised if they fail to alter the patient's tendency toward violence. Although a standard of care does not exist for predicting violent acts, clear standards do exist for gathering sufficient information to satisfy a reasonable standard of care in the assessment of the *risk* of violence. Because prediction is so problematic, careful documentation from visit to visit of the clinical reasoning behind the overall assessment of the risk of violence is essential.

Treatment Refusal

If a potentially violent patient stops taking medication or drops out of treatment, the patient's continued need for treatment should be addressed aggressively. Voluntary or involuntary hospitalization may need to be pursued, depending on the clinical condition of the patient and the assessed risk of violence. The involvement of family members may also be necessary. If the potential for violence is high, endangered third parties and law enforcement agencies may need to be informed. A telephone call or letter (if time permits and if the patient can be located) to determine the patient's treatment intentions may be necessary. If the patient terminates treatment but is not an immediate threat to others, a letter should be sent confirming that the patient has terminated treatment unilaterally. The letter may also recommend continued treatment and state the psychiatrist's willingness to provide referral sources and the patient's records to other treaters, on proper authorization (see Chapter 2, The Doctor-Patient Relationship). If the patient is transferred to another facility, the assessment of potential violence needs to be communicated to the new treaters. Reassessment of the risk of violence should be made before discharge (see Table 9–5).

When involuntary hospitalization is sought, responsibility passes to the judicial system if the patient is not deemed committable by the court and ultimately harms someone. Nevertheless, the therapist should go on record as opposing dismissal of a violent mentally ill patient. Involuntary hospitalization should be considered only if it is in the best interests of the patient (e.g., if the patient is likely to receive benefit from hospitalization) or for the immediate safety of the patient or others. Clinicians should not shrink from seeking involuntary hospitalization as an important clinical intervention for patients when a less restrictive alternative is unavailable (see Chapter 7, Involuntary Hospitalization). Involuntary hospitalization should not be implemented defensively by the psychiatrist in an attempt to avoid liability. Seeking involuntary hospitalization solely as a risk management technique will likely destroy the treatment relationship. It will also adversely affect future treatment endeavors with the patient, paradoxically increasing the risk of the practitioner being sued.

Release of Hospitalized Patients

Discharge decisions must be carefully documented. Notes should be recorded contemporaneously with decision making. After-the-fact notes are of little value and are legally precarious.

Voluntary patients who are at risk for violence may not meet the criteria for involuntary hospitalization. If the patient will be discharged, a careful note explaining the decision-making process is essential. Individuals who were threatened or harmed by the patient before hospitalization should be given advance notice of the patient's impending discharge if the patient is still considered to be at significant risk of violence. Appointments should be scheduled for as soon after discharge as possible. A significant number of violent patients are noncompliant with treatment recommendations. A Veterans Administration study of outpatient referral found that of 47 inpatients referred to a Veterans Administration mental health clinic, 21 did not keep their first appointments (53).

Every discharge is a complex process that must be tailored to the patient's individual treatment needs and circumstances. A risk-benefit assessment should be recorded that evaluates the risks and benefits of continued hospitalization versus the risks and benefits of discharge. Factors to be considered and weighed in the risk-benefit assessment include the risk of violence (against self or others), the severity of illness, the likely compliance with follow-up care, the availability of family or other support, the presence of substance abuse and/or of other comorbid conditions, the need for safety, the importance of resuming life outside the hospital, and other significant individual factors. The absence of violent thoughts, feelings, or impulses is not as important at the time of discharge as an assessment of the patient's ability to control such impulses and the sufficiency of the environment to support the patient's self-control mechanisms. The majority of patients manifesting violent ideation are treated as outpatients. Clinicians can avoid "doomed to fail" discharges by asking themselves what is different about the patient's condition and life situation at discharge as compared with those aspects at admission.

A well-reasoned, clearly documented risk-benefit annotation that reveals the psychiatrist's clinical thinking at the time of discharge will help preempt second-guessing by a court, if a lawsuit is later filed. Assessing the risk of violence toward self or others is a here-and-now determination performed at the time of discharge. Once the patient is discharged, the potential for violence will depend on the patient's mental state at any given time, as well as on concurrent situational factors. As previously noted, violent behaviors are the result of dynamic, complex interaction among a variety of clinical, personality, social, and environmental factors whose relative importance varies across time and situations.

The clinician's obligation is to structure the follow-up so as to encourage compliance. There are limits to psychiatrists' powers to ensure adequate patient follow-up. These limitations must be acknowledged by the psychiatric and the legal communities. Most discharged patients retain the right to refuse further treatment. The American Medical Association Council on Scientific Affairs has developed evidence-based discharge criteria for safe discharge from the hospital (54).

Managed Care and Premature Release

The treatment of psychiatric inpatients has changed dramatically in the managed care era. Most psychiatric units, particularly in general hospitals, have become short-stay, acute care psychiatric facilities. Generally, only suicidal, homicidal, or gravely disabled patients with major psychiatric disorders pass strict precertification review for hospitalization. Approximately half of these patients have comorbid substance-related disorders. Usually, in order to gain precertification for admission in managed care settings, patients must meet "medically necessary" criteria whose stringency often equals or exceeds that of the substantive criteria for involuntary civil commitment.

The purpose of hospitalization is to provide crisis intervention and management to stabilize severely ill patients and to ensure their safety. However, close scrutiny by utilization reviewers permits only brief hospitalization for these patients. In addition, the hospital administration may exert pressure on the psychiatrist for early discharge to maintain length-of-stay statistics within predetermined limits. The treatment of these patients is increasingly being provided by a variety of mental health professionals. Yet, the psychiatrist must often bear the ultimate burden of liability for treatments gone awry. Limited opportunity usually exists during the hospital stay for psychiatrists to develop a therapeutic alliance with their patients. The ability to communicate with patients, the psychiatrist's stock-in-trade, is often severely curtailed. All of these factors contribute to a greatly increased risk of malpractice suits against psychiatrists that allege premature or negligent discharge of patients due to cost-containment policies (55).

Psychiatrists have certain responsibilities as well as legal duties to patients treated in managed care settings. These include disclosure of all treatment options, exercise of appeal rights, continuance of emergency treatment, and reasonable cooperation with utilization reviewers, each of which is important in the management of the potentially violent inpatient. The duty to warn and to protect endangered third parties will likely arise with increased frequency as cost-containment measures tighten to curtail the lengths of hospitalization.

Managed care organizations generally limit or deny payment for services but not the actual services themselves. How a patient is treated is strictly the physician's decision. Although the *quality of care* may be adversely affected by MCO restrictions, the *standard of care* for treating self-destructive or potentially violent psychiatric inpatients has not changed. As a result, psychiatrists may appear to be practicing under conflicting standards (56). As in the past, psychiatrists will be judged by whether they fulfill their professional, ethical, and clinical duties to the patient.

Psychiatrists are being held to a new standard of efficiency by third-party payers. They are expected to rapidly gather patient information, to quickly determine a diagnosis, and to expeditiously develop a multidisciplinary treatment plan. Psychiatrists must acquire new treatment skills for the rapid management and discharge of potentially violent patients. In addition, they need to have the personal and professional skills necessary to collaborate effectively with the multidisciplinary team in managing violent patients. Psychiatrists practicing in the managed care era are expected to be knowledgeable in the uses and limitations of group modalities and behavioral techniques and in the effective use of medications to achieve quick improvement. In addition, psychiatrists are expected to provide competent, efficient clinical care despite stringent MCO restrictions on insurance coverage for psychiatric treatment.

■ REFERENCES

1. Restatement (Second) of Torts §315(a) (1965)
2. Tarasoff v Regents of the University of California, 17 Cal 3d 425, 551 P2d 334, 131 Cal Rptr 14 (1976)
3. Evans v United States, 883 F Supp 124 (5D Miss 1995)
4. Green v Ross, 691 502d 542 (FLA App 1997)
5. Thapar v Zezulka, 944 SW 2d 635 (TX 1999)
6. Beck JC: Current status of the duty to protect, in Confidentiality Versus the Duty to Protect: Foreseeable Harm in the Practice of Psychiatry. Edited by Beck JC. Washington, DC, American Psychiatric Press, 1990, p 19
7. Appelbaum PS, Zonana H, Bonnie R, et al: Statutory approaches to limiting psychiatrists' liability for their patients' violent acts. Am J Psychiatry 146:821–828, 1989
8. Thompson v County of Alameda, 27 Cal 3d 741, 614 P2d 728, 167 Cal Rptr 70 (1980); Brady v Hopper, 751 F2d 329 (10th Cir 1984); White v United States, 780 F2d 97 (DC Cir 1986)
9. Lipari v Sears, Roebuck and Co, 497 F Supp 185 (D Neb 1980); Schuster v Altenberg, 144 Wis 2d 223, 424 NW2d 159 (1988)
10. Naidu v Laird, 539 A2d 1064 (Del Super Ct 1988)
11. Garamella for Estate of Almonte v New York Medical College, 23 F Supp 2d 167 (D Conn 1998)
12. JS v RTH, 714 A2d 924 (NJ 1998)

13. Touchette v Ganal, 922 P2d 347 (Haw 1996)
14. People v Rose, 573 NW 2d 765 (Neb 1998)
15. Beck JC: The psychotherapist's duty to protect third parties from harm. Mental Phys Disabil Law Rep 11:141–148, 1987
16. Monahan J: Limiting therapist exposure to Tarasoff liability. Am Psychol 48:242–250, 1993
17. Beck JC: Current status of the duty to protect, in Confidentiality Versus the Duty to Protect: Foreseeable Harm in the Practice of Psychiatry. Edited by Beck JC. Washington, DC, American Psychiatric Press, 1990, p 4
18. Ibid, pp 9–10
19. Monahan JP: Mental disorder and violent behavior: perceptions and evidence. Am Psychol 47:511–521, 1992
20. Swanson JW, Holzer CE, Ganju UK, et al: Violence and psychiatric disorder in the community: evidence from the epidemiology catchment area surveys. Hospital and Community Psychiatry 41:761–770, 1990
21. Widiger TA, Trull TJ: Personality disorders and violence, in Violence and Mental Disorder. Edited by Monahan J, Steadman HJ. Chicago, IL, University of Chicago Press, 1994, pp 203–226
22. Stone AA: Law, Psychiatry, and Morality. Washington, DC, American Psychiatric Press, 1984, pp 161–190
23. Tardiff K: A model for the short-term prediction of violence potential, in Current Approaches to the Prediction of Violence. Edited by Brizer DA, Crowner ML. Washington, DC, American Psychiatric Press, 1988, pp 1–12; see also Tardiff K: Violence by psychiatric patients, in American Psychiatric Press Review of Clinical Psychiatry and the Law, Vol 2. Edited by Simon RI. Washington, DC, American Psychiatric Press, 1991, pp 175–236
24. Binder RL: Are the mentally ill dangerous? J Am Acad Psychiatry Law 27:189–201, 1999
25. Dix GE: Clinical evaluation of the "dangerous" or "normal" criminal defendants. Virginia Law Review 66:523, 1980
26. Steadman HJ, Mulvey EP, Monahan J et al: Violence by people discharged from acute psychiatric inpatient facilities and by

others in the same neighborhoods. Arch Gen Psychiatry 55:393–401, 1998

27. McNeil DE, Binder RL: Clinical assessment of the risk of violence among psychiatric inpatients. Am J Psychiatry 148:1317–1321, 1991; Janofsky JS, Spears S, Neubauer DN: Psychiatrists' accuracy in predicting violent behavior on an inpatient unit. Hospital and Community Psychiatry 39:1090–1094, 1988

28. Barefoot v Estelle 459 -LTS 1169 (1983)

29. Beigler JS: Tarasoff v confidentiality. Behav Sci Law 2:273–290, 1984

30. Monahan J: The Clinical Prediction of Violent Behavior. Rockville, MD, National Institute of Mental Health, 1981, pp 63–90

31. Monahan J: The clinical prediction of dangerousness. Currents in Affective Illness 10 (June):5–12, 1991

32. Klassen D, O'Connor WA: Demographic and case history variables in risk assessment, in Violence and Mental Disorder. Edited by Monahan J, Steadman HJ. Chicago, IL, University of Chicago Press, 1994, pp 203–226

33. Link BG, Stueve A: Psychotic symptoms and the violent/illegal behavior of mental patients compared to community controls, in Violence and Mental Disorder. Edited by Monahan J, Steadman HJ. Chicago, IL, University of Chicago Press, 1994, pp 137–159

34. Lewis DO, Pincus JHJ, Bard B, et al: Neuropsychiatric, psychoeducational, and family characteristics of 14 juveniles condemned to death in the United States. Am J Psychiatry 145:584–589, 1988

35. Tardiff K: Assessment and Management of Violent Patients, 2nd Edition. Washington, DC, American Psychiatric Press, 1996

36. Appelbaum PS: Implications of Tarasoff for clinical practice, in The Potentially Violent Patient and the Tarasoff Decision in Psychiatric Practice. Edited by Beck JC. Washington, DC, American Psychiatric Press, 1985, pp 98–108

37. Beck JC: The psychotherapist and the violent patient: recent case law, in The Potentially Violent Patient and the Tarasoff Decision in Psychiatric Practice. Edited by Beck JC. Washington, DC, American Psychiatric Press, 1985, pp 10–34

38. Levin RB, Hill EH: Recent trends in psychiatric liability, in American Psychiatric Press Review of Clinical Psychiatry and the Law, Vol 3. Edited by Simon RI. Washington, DC, American Psychiatric Press, 1992, pp 129–150

39. Simon RI: Clinical Psychiatry and the Law, 2nd Edition. Washington, DC, American Psychiatric Press, 1992, p 302

40. In re: Estate of Heltsley v Votteler, 327 NW2d 759 Iowa 1982

41. Jablonski v United States 712 F2d 391 (9th Cir 1983) overruled, In re: complaint of McLinn 739 F2d 1395 (9th Cir 1984)

42. American Psychiatric Association: The Principles of Medical Ethics With Annotations Especially Applicable to Psychiatry. Washington, DC, American Psychiatric Association, 1998

43. Pettis RW: Tarasoff and the dangerous driver: a look at driving cases. Bulletin of the American Academy of Psychiatry and the Law 20:427–437, 1992

44. Foreman T: Physicians do not have duty to third-party drivers. J Am Acad Psychiatry Law 27 (4):637–639, 1999

45. Lester v Hall, 970 P 2d 590 (NM 1998)

46. Jaffe v Redmond, 1165 Ct 1923 (1996)

47. Perlin ML: Tarasoff at the millennium: new directions, new defendants, new dangers, new dilemmas. Psychiatric Times, November 1999, pp 20–21

48. Leong GB, Eth S, Silva JA: The psychotherapist as witness for the prosecution: the criminalization of Tarasoff. Am J Psychiatry 149:1011–1015, 1992

49. Eth S: The sexually active, HIV-infected patient: confidentiality versus the duty to protect. Psychiatric Annals 18:571–576, 1988

50. APA Official Actions: AIDS Policy: Position Statement on Confidentiality, Disclosure, and Protection of Others. Am J Psychiatry 150:852, 1993

51. Appelbaum K, Appelbaum PS: The HIV antibody-positive patient, in Confidentiality Versus the Duty to Protect: Foreseeable

Harm in the Practice of Psychiatry. Edited by Beck JC. Washington, DC, American Psychiatric Press, 1990, pp 121–140

52. Simon RI: The duty to protect in private practice, in Confidentiality Versus the Duty to Protect: Foreseeable Harm in the Practice of Psychiatry. Edited by Beck JC. Washington, DC, American Psychiatric Press, 1990, pp 23–54

53. Zeldow PB, Taub HA: Evaluating psychiatric discharge and aftercare in a VA medical center. Hospital and Community Psychiatry 32:57–58, 1981

54. Report of The Council on Scientific Affairs: Evidence-based Principles of Discharge and Discharge Criteria (CSA Report 4-A-96). Chicago, IL, American Medical Association, 1996

55. Simon RI: Discharging sicker, potentially violent psychiatric inpatients in the managed care era: standard of care and risk management. Psychiatric Annals 27:726–733, 1997

56. Simon RI: Psychiatrists' duties in discharging sicker and potentially violent inpatients in the managed care era. Psychiatr Serv 49:62–67, 1998

10

THERAPIST-PATIENT SEX
Maintaining Treatment Boundaries

■ OVERVIEW OF THE LAW

Civil Liability

Psychiatrists who sexually exploit their patients are subject to civil and criminal actions as well as ethical and professional licensure revocation proceedings. Malpractice is the most common area of liability. The patient-plaintiff must establish the four requisite elements of a malpractice claim:

- Duty (of care)
- Deviation (breach of that duty)
- Damages
- Direct causation (deviation caused damage)

In a sexual exploitation case, the patient will have the burden of proving, by a preponderance of the evidence (i.e., more than a 50% chance), that the exploitation actually took place. This burden can be met with corroborating evidence such as testimony from other abused (former) patients, letters, pictures, and hotel or motel receipts. If the defendant practitioner admits to the exploitation, the plaintiff is left with the responsibility of showing that she or he sustained injuries as a result of the sexual activity. Typically, patient injury occurs in the form of emotional injury (e.g., worsened psychiatric condition). Expert psychiatric testimony usually is required to establish the type and extent of psychological damages, as well as to establish whether a breach of the standard of care occurred.

An increasing number of states have statutorily made sexual activity both civilly and criminally actionable. For instance, Minnesota has enacted legislation that states

> A cause of action against a psychotherapist for sexual exploitation exists for a patient or former patient for injury caused by sexual contact with the psychotherapist if the sexual contact occurred: 1) during the period the patient was receiving psychotherapy . . . or 2) after the period the patient received psychotherapy . . . if a) the former patient was emotionally dependent on the psychotherapist; or b) the sexual contact occurred by means of therapeutic deception. (1)

The number of states that have enacted civil statutes proscribing sexual misconduct is constantly increasing (2). Some states make therapist sexual misconduct a crime (3). A number of states can and do prosecute sexual exploitation suits under their sexual assault statutes. More state legislatures are considering enacting statutes that will provide civil or criminal remedies to patients who are sexually abused by their therapists (4).

Three types of statutory remedies have resulted:

- Reporting statutes requiring disclosure to state authorities by a therapist who learns of any past or current therapist-patient sex
- Civil statutes proscribing sexual misconduct (California, Florida, Illinois, Minnesota, and Wisconsin) (5)
- Civil statutes incorporating a standard of care that makes malpractice suits easier to pursue

For example, Minnesota has enacted a statute that provides a specific cause of action against psychiatrists and other psychotherapists for injury caused by sexual contact with a patient (1). Some of these statutes also restrict unfettered discovery of the plaintiff's past sexual history. Criminal sanctions may be the only remedy for exploitative therapists without malpractice insurance who are unlicensed or do not belong to professional organizations.

Other Civil Theories and Defenses

A plaintiff who has been sexually exploited by a psychotherapist may assert a variety of causes of action (see Table 10–1). In a minority of states, the spouse of the injured patient also has legal standing to initiate his or her own cause of action against an exploitative practitioner on the grounds of loss of consortium (interference with the marital relationship).

Although a variety of defenses have been raised to diminish or protect against liability, to date, few have been legally successful. For instance, contentions that the patient "consented" to the sexual contact, that the patient was aware that sex was not a part of treatment, that the sexual contact occurred outside the treatment setting, or that treatment ended before the sexual relationship began have all been rejected by the courts. Other defenses used in sexual misconduct cases are listed in Table 10–2.

There is no "respected minority" in the mental health profession that claims that sexual relations with patients is therapeutic. This position had a few adherents at one time but is no longer publicly or privately advocated by mental health professionals.

Criminal Sanctions

Under certain circumstances, sexual exploitation of a patient may be considered rape or some analogous sexual offense and therefore

---

TABLE 10–1. **Legal and ethical consequences of sexual exploitation**

Civil lawsuit
  Negligence
  Loss of consortium
Breach of contract action
Criminal sanctions (e.g., adultery, sexual assault, rape)
Civil action for intentional tort (e.g., battery, fraud)
License revocation
Ethical sanctions
Dismissal from professional organizations

222

TABLE 10–2.	Legal defenses asserted by defendants in sexual misconduct cases

Denial of plaintiff's allegations of sexual misconduct

Suit barred by statute of limitations

No doctor-patient relationship

Terminated treatment of patient (no legal fault under immunity statute)

No causation of harm (inherent course of mental disorder)

No damages (no psychological harm caused by sex with patient)

Superseding intervening variable causing harm (not caused by sex with patient)

Contributory and comparative negligence (plaintiff's "contribution" to sexual misconduct)

Liability in supervision of offending therapist—sexual misconduct of supervisee beyond the scope of employment ("detour and frolic")

Marriage to patient

Improper pleading by plaintiff

Consent (in sexual assault claims)

criminally actionable. Typically, the criminality of the exploitation is determined by one of three factors: the practitioner's means of inducement, the age of the victim, or the availability of a relevant state criminal code.

Sex with a current patient may be criminally actionable under sexual assault statutes, if the state can prove beyond a reasonable doubt (e.g., with 90%–95% certainty) that the patient was coerced into engaging in the sexual act. Typically, this form of evidence is limited to the use of some type of substance (e.g., medication) to either induce compliance or reduce resistance. Anesthesia, electroconvulsive treatment, hypnosis, force, and threat of harm have been used to coerce patients into sexual submission (6). To date, claims of "psychological coercion" via the manipulation of the transference phenomenon have not been successful in establishing the coercion necessary for a criminal case. In cases involving a minor patient, the issue of consent or coercion is irrelevant, because minors and incompetent individuals (including adults) are considered unable to provide valid consent. Therefore, sex with a child or an individual who is incompetent is automatically considered a criminal act.

An increasing number of states have made sexual relations between a therapist and a patient a statutory criminal offense (3). For example, a Wisconsin statute holds that

> any person who is or who holds himself or herself out to be a therapist and who intentionally has sexual contact with a patient or client during any ongoing therapist-patient or therapist-client relationship regardless of whether it occurs during any treatment, consultation, interview, or examination is guilty of a class D felony. Consent is not an issue in an action under this subsection. (7)

A number of other states are currently considering enacting legislation that would criminally penalize a psychotherapist's sexual contact with a patient.

Professional Disciplinary Action

State statutes typically grant licensing boards certain regulatory and disciplinary authority for the purpose of adjudicating allegations of professional misconduct. As a result, state licensing organizations, unlike professional associations, may discipline an offending professional more effectively by suspending or revoking his or her license. Because licensing boards are not as constrained as civil and criminal courts by rigorous rules of evidence in trial procedures, it is generally less difficult for the patient to seek redress through this means. A review of published reports of sexual misconduct adjudicated before licensing boards revealed that in the vast majority of cases in which the evidence was reasonably sufficient to substantiate a claim of exploitation, the professional's license was revoked or suspended for varying lengths of time, including permanently.

Patients may bring ethical charges against psychiatrists before the district branches of the American Psychiatric Association (APA) (10). Ethical violators may be reprimanded, suspended, or expelled from the APA. All national organizations of mental health professionals have ethically proscribed sexual relations between therapist and patient. Ethical charges can be filed only against members of a professional group. Obviously, this option is not available against therapists who do not belong to a professional organization.

■ CLINICAL MANAGEMENT OF LEGAL ISSUES

Incidence of Therapist-Patient Sexual Contact

In a nationwide survey regarding psychiatrist-patient sex, 7.1% of male and 3.1% of female respondents acknowledged having relationships with their patients (8). Of the sexual contacts that occurred, 88% were between male psychiatrists and female patients, 7.6% were between male psychiatrists and male patients, 3.5% were between female psychiatrists and male patients, and 1.4% were between female psychiatrists and female patients. Whereas 38.4% of the male psychiatrists were recidivists, none of the female therapists had repeated sexual contacts. Interestingly, 40.7% of the offending psychiatrists sought consultation because of their sexual involvement. Of the psychiatrists responding to the survey, 98% believed that sexual relationships with patients were inappropriate and usually harmful. However, 29% reported that a sexual relationship after termination might sometimes be acceptable, and 17.4% believed that such a relationship was permitted by the APA's ethical guidelines.

Of the psychiatrists who responded, 65% reported treating patients who had been sexually abused by previous therapists: 48% of the previous therapists were psychiatrists, 27% psychologists, 9% clergymen, 7% social workers, and 6% lay therapists. Subsequent treating psychiatrists assessed that 87% of these patients were harmed. Only 8% of these psychiatrists reported the abuse to a professional association or legal authority. These figures are undoubtedly conservative estimates. The problem is likely much more pervasive, involving other professionals besides psychiatrists.

In surveys conducted after 1980, the percentage of therapists admitting sexual contact with patients has steadily declined. In

1989, a survey of 4,800 psychiatrists showed a rate of therapist-patient sex of 0.9% for male therapists and 0.2% for female therapists (9). Although no clear reasons for this decline can be given, the conclusion that actual therapist-patient sex has declined by almost 10% since 1980 appears overly optimistic. Even though respondents remain anonymous, the threat of litigation may have caused offending therapists to forgo responding, thus further skewing the notoriously unreliable data derived from surveys in the direction of underreporting therapist-patient sex.

Ethics and Malpractice

The Principles of Medical Ethics With Annotations Especially Applicable to Psychiatry unequivocally prohibits psychiatrists from engaging in sexual activity with current or former patients:

> The requirement that the physician conduct himself/herself with propriety in his/her profession and in all the actions of his/her life is especially important in the case of the psychiatrist because the patient tends to model his/her behavior after that of his/her psychiatrist by identification. Further, the necessary intensity of the treatment relationship may tend to activate sexual and other needs and fantasies on the part of both patient and psychiatrist, while weakening the objectivity necessary for control. Additionally, the inherent inequality in the doctor-patient relationship may lead to exploitation of the patient. Sexual activity with a current or former patient is unethical. (10, Section 2, Annotation 1)

This ethical position has a venerable history. One version of the Hippocratic oath that dates back at least 2,500 years sets the following standard: "In every house where I come, I will enter only for the good of my patients, keeping myself far from all intentional ill-doing and all seduction and especially from the pleasures of love of women and men."

Sexual activity between a psychiatrist and the patient constitutes negligence per se. The psychiatrist holds him- or herself out to the public as having competent professional skill and knowledge. The psychiatrist "must have and use the knowledge, skill and care ordinarily possessed and employed by members of the profession in good standing" (11, p. 187). Because a respected minority of psychiatrists do not exist who would state that sex with a patient falls within the standard skill and knowledge of psychiatrists in good standing, sex between psychiatrist and patient is an unquestioned and unchallenged deviation in the standard of care.

Illinois, Wisconsin, California, and Minnesota make therapist-patient sex negligence per se by statute, creating a nonrebuttable presumption concerning the therapist's duty of care (12). To establish liability, the plaintiff need only prove that sexual contact occurred and that it caused her or him damage.

In legislation prohibiting therapist-patient sexual exploitation, sexual behavior is defined in a variety of ways, some so vague as to invite constitutional challenges based on violation of the due-process clause in the United States Constitution and state constitutions (13). Most statutes define sexual activity as intercourse, rape, the touching of breasts and genitals, cunnilingus, fellatio, sodomy, and inappropriate or unnecessary examinations and procedures performed for sexual gratification. Obviously, statutory definitions cannot possibly encompass the wide range of sexual activities that constitute abuse of patients by therapist. Therapists who have sex with patients usually become embroiled in civil, criminal, licensure, and ethical proceedings. Therapists who sexually exploit children also violate child abuse laws.

Quite apart from the legal and professional consequences, psychiatrists more than other physicians should appreciate the emotional harm to patients who are involved in therapist-patient sex. The symptoms of a therapist-patient sex syndrome are described in Table 10–3. This syndrome likely reflects the presence of comorbid psychiatric disorders often seen in victims of therapist sexual misconduct. In forensic evaluations of these individuals, specific diagnoses made according to the APA's *Diagnostic and Statistical Manual of Mental Disorders,* Fourth Edition (DSM-IV), criteria will usually be required.

TABLE 10–3.	**Psychological consequences of sexual intimacy with patients**

Exacerbation of preexisting psychiatric disorders
Production of therapist-patient sex syndrome
   Ambivalence
   Guilt
   Feelings of isolation
   Emptiness
   Cognitive dysfunction
   Identity disturbances
   Inability to trust
   Sexual confusion
   Mood liability
   Suppressed rage
   Increased suicidal risk
Damage to personal relationships
Destructive to future treatment

Source. Adapted from Pope KS, Bouhoutsos JL: *Sexual Intimacy Between Therapists and Patients.* New York, Praeger, 1986.

Evaluation, Consultation, and Group Therapy

In an evaluation or in consultation, the usual doctor-patient relationship may not exist. Thus, whether the patient could bring a malpractice claim for sexual misconduct may be in question. However, the ethical issue remains unchanged. Sex with a patient during an evaluation or consultation is unethical and likely legally actionable. Often, the sickest patients are seen primarily for medication appointments rather than for psychotherapy. Nevertheless, because of the extent of regression, powerful transference phenomena can occur. The psychiatrist is at a disadvantage in not having an ongoing therapy situation that permits assessment of transference developments. Not surprisingly, some therapists who see patients infrequently espouse theoretical orientations that place little emphasis on recognizing or managing transference phenomena. Group therapy situations are rife with intense transference that may become focused on the therapist, but without the benefit of the closer scrutiny of transference that a one-to-one therapy can allow. Regardless of the practitioner's theoretical orientation, the clinical importance of transference and countertransference issues in any therapeutic relationship is undisputed. Therapists cannot credibly deny the existence or the importance of transference and countertransference phenomena.

Supervisors and Trainees

Trainee therapists must abide by the same ethical principles as fully trained therapists. Supervisors should be aware of sexual issues as they develop from the trainee's supervision. Failure to do so may render both the trainee and the supervisor ethically and legally liable. The possible emergence and management of sexual feelings in both the trainee and the patient need to be openly discussed. Ethical principles should be an integral part of every training program. It is rare to find a psychiatric resident who has read *The Principles of Medical Ethics With Annotations Especially Applicable to Psychiatry* (10), even when it is a basic requirement of the training program.

The issue of sexual relations between supervisors and trainees has recently received close scrutiny. *The Principles* states:

> Sexual involvement between a faculty member or supervisor and a trainee or student, in those situations in which an abuse of power can occur, often takes advantage of inequalities in the working relationship and may be unethical because: (a) any treatment of a patient being supervised may be deleteriously affected; (b) it may damage the trust relationship between teacher and student; and (c) teachers are important professional role models for their trainees and affect their trainees' future professional behavior. (10, Section 4, Annotation 14)

The "Natural History" of Therapist-Patient Sex

In psychotherapy, the potential for exploitation of psychologically needy, often regressed patients is always present. Sexual exploitation has a "natural history," or progressive scenario of personal involvement between therapist and patient, that is remarkably similar from case to case (14). The incremental steps usually occur as follows:

1. Incipient boundary violations "between the chair and the door."
2. Therapist's position of neutrality is gradually eroded.
3. Therapist and patient address each other by first names.
4. Therapy sessions become less clinical and more social.
5. Patient is treated as "special" (i.e., as confidant).
6. Therapist self-disclosures occur, usually relating to current personal problems and sexual fantasies about the patient.
7. Therapist sits closer to patient.
8. Therapist begins touching patient, progressing to hugs, embraces, and kisses.
9. Therapist gains control over patient, usually by manipulating the transference and by negligent prescribing of medications.
10. Extratherapeutic contacts occur.
11. Therapy sessions are rescheduled for the end of the day.
12. Therapy sessions become extended in time.
13. Therapist stops billing the patient.
14. Therapist and patient have drinks or dinner after sessions; dating begins.
15. Therapist-patient sex begins.

Because boundary violations leading up to sex with the patient usually occur gradually and incrementally, the therapist has time to prevent this development (15). Sharing personal information with a patient, such as current problems experienced by the therapist, is highly correlated with eventual therapist-patient sex. Particularly noxious are therapist disclosures about relationship problems, sexual frustration, sexual dreams and fantasies about the patient, and loneliness (16). Self-disclosures not only waste therapy time but also may induce a caretaking role on the part of the patient (17). Boundary violations occur in the treatment of patients when the therapist abandons a position of neutrality. Sexual misconduct rarely occurs in isolation; rather, it is usually a part of a general pattern of negligent treatment (18).

Patients with borderline, dependent, and histrionic personality disorders appear to be especially vulnerable to sexual exploitation because these patients commonly develop intense dependent and erotic transferences (see Table 10–4). Victims of incest are vulnerable to therapist-patient sexual exploitation. In one study, 23% of previously abused patients who sought psychotherapy were sexually abused by their therapist (19). An additional 23% suffered other forms of abuse by their therapist. Less than 30% of the patients received any help from the first therapist they saw, and the average incest patient saw a total of 3.5 therapists.

Maintaining Treatment Boundaries

The identification of early treatment boundary violations can be a powerful prevention tool in the hands of a competent therapist. Basic boundary guidelines exist that, with certain exceptions, would likely be endorsed by therapists from a wide spectrum of orientations (see Table 10–5) (20). The basic clinical, ethical, and legal principles that underlie boundary guidelines are listed in Table 10–6.

The number of cases where otherwise competent therapists gradually cross treatment boundaries and become sexually involved with their patients is sobering. Seasoned therapists as well as marginally competent or poorly trained therapists can benefit from learning how to identify early boundary violations. Therapists

---

TABLE 10–4.   **Some characteristics of vulnerable patients**

Previously well-functioning patients with current depression and loss of an important relationship

Dependent and other-directed personalities

Patients sexually and physically abused as children

Patients with previous hospitalizations, major psychiatric illnesses, suicide attempts, and alcohol and drug abuse

Patients with borderline, dependent, masochistic, and histrionic personality disorders

"Attractive" patients with low self-esteem

TABLE 10–5. **Boundary guidelines for psychotherapy**

Maintain relative therapist neutrality

Foster psychological separateness of patient

Protect confidentiality

Obtain informed consent for treatments and procedures

Interact verbally with patients

Ensure no previous, current, or future personal relationship with the
   patient

Minimize physical contact

Preserve relative anonymity of therapist

Establish a stable fee policy

Provide consistent, private, and professional setting

Define time and length of session

Source. Reprinted from Simon RI: "Treatment Boundary Violations: Clinical, Ethical and Legal Considerations." *Bulletin of the American Academy of Psychiatry and
the Law* 20:269–288, 1992. Used with permission.

TABLE 10–6. **Principles underlying boundary guidelines**

Rule of abstinence

Duty to neutrality

Patient autonomy and self-determination

Fiduciary relationship

Respect for human dignity

---

who naively attempt to "re-parent" their patients invariably cross
treatment boundaries as they become overly involved in their patients' lives. Other therapists masochistically surrender to the
endless demands of some patients. They are unable to extricate
themselves over the course of progressive boundary violations. Deviant treatment boundaries harm patients in a variety of ways but
most often by leading to negligent diagnoses and treatments, even
if therapist-patient sex does not occur (see Table 10–3).

   It is always the therapist's responsibility to maintain appropriate
boundaries, no matter how difficult or boundary-testing the patient

may be. If unable to do so, the therapist should refer the patient to a competent clinician. Therapists need to be clear about establishing and maintaining appropriate treatment boundaries. The conduct of psychotherapy is an "impossible task" because there are no perfect therapists and no perfect therapies. However, knowing one's boundaries makes the "impossible task" easier. For truly incompetent or predatory therapists, boundary guidelines are meaningless. Such therapists need to be weeded out.

Freud enunciated the principle of abstinence, which stated that psychiatrists must refrain from gratifying themselves at the expense of their patients. The rule of abstinence is a fundamental principle underlying boundary guidelines. The therapist's main source of personal pleasure is the professional gratification obtained from the psychotherapeutic process and the satisfaction gained in helping the patient. The fee for professional services is the only material satisfaction the therapist is permitted to receive from the patient. The duty of neutrality is a corollary of the rule of abstinence. It dictates that therapists refrain from interfering in the personal lives of their patients, thus preserving patients' autonomy and self-determination. Quite independently, a legal duty of neutrality also exists (21). The psychotherapist-patient relationship is fiducial in nature, requiring the therapist to act in the best interests of his or her patients. Respect for human dignity underlies all boundary guidelines.

A quick spot check can help a therapist identify whether a boundary violation has been committed. The first question therapists should ask themselves is whether a treatment intervention is for the benefit of the therapist or for the sake of the patient's therapy. If it appears to be for the therapist's benefit, then a second question arises whether the "treatment intervention" may be part of a series of progressive boundary violations. If the answer to either of these questions is yes, the therapist is alerted to desist immediately and take corrective action.

Epstein and Simon (22) have devised an exploitation index that can be used by therapists as an early warning indicator of treatment boundary violations. In a survey of 532 psychiatrists who completed the Exploitation Index, 43% reported that one or more of the questions had alerted them to boundary violations, and 29% made specific changes in their treatment practices (23). Gutheil and Simon (24) have postulated that the first boundary violations occur at the end of the session "between the chair and the door." Both the patient and the therapist may feel tempted to cast off their respective burdensome roles and launch into the ease of an ordinary social relationship. This "transition space" should be carefully scrutinized for incipient boundary violations. As a rule, the therapy session ends *after* the patient leaves, not before.

Managing Transference and Countertransference in Therapy

Patients who seek psychiatric treatment are undergoing mental and emotional suffering that is painful and often debilitating. As a consequence, their decision-making capacity and judgment are usually impaired. Moreover, the therapist is viewed as a critically important source of help and hope. Under these circumstances, a transference involving the expectation of beneficent care and treatment evolves that is highly influenced by early, powerful wishes for nurture and care. The therapist is frequently idealized as the all-good, all-giving parent.

In combination with the fear of losing the newly acquired idealized parental figure, the beneficent transference leaves the patient vulnerable to exploitation by the therapist (25). The beneficent transference is a common psychological reaction, experienced to varying degrees by practically all patients. It should be distinguished from the transference neurosis that develops in a number of patients undergoing intensive, usually psychodynamic psychotherapy or psychoanalysis.

Transferences often are not what they appear to be. Transferences, like dreams, have both a manifest and a latent content. Freud emphasized that "transference love" must be understood as a specific treatment phenomenon that is not identical to the experience of "falling in love" as it occurs outside of therapy. The analyst,

Freud states, "must recognize that the patient's falling in love is induced by the analytic situation and is not to be attributed to the charms of his own person; so that he has no grounds whatever for being proud of such a 'conquest,' as it would be called outside analysis" (26, pp. 160–161). The therapist who considers only the "love," or manifest, aspect of the patient's feelings seriously misjudges the clinical situation. Many patients have felt deprived of warmth and affection in their important relationships. Feelings of rage and revenge often lurk behind powerful yearnings for "love."

When sex between therapist and patient occurs, emotional conflicts pervade the relationship. Patients are almost universally dissatisfied with their sexual relationships with therapists because, in part, transference expectations are so conflicted and unrealistic. Therapists usually experience poor sexual performance because of their own countertransference problems and because of other personal conflicts. Frieda Fromm-Reichman, a renowned psychoanalyst, reportedly remarked, perhaps facetiously: "Don't have sex with your patients; you will only disappoint them."

Although it is unethical for any physician to engage in sex with his or her patient, mental health professionals hold a special position of responsibility. Unlike the general physician, who works instinctively within the ambit of a positive transference that provides hope and support to the patient, the therapist often works directly with transference phenomena as a therapeutic tool. As a treatment strategy, the therapist may encourage development of the transference, but he or she is expected to keep any countertransference feelings in check for the benefit of the patient's therapy. The very act of intently listening and caring is itself a very seductive process for both the patient and the therapist.

Unfortunately, countertransference feelings, particularly those of the erotic variety, have become associated with mismanagement of the patients' treatment and are viewed with shame and embarrassment by some therapists. The work of Winnicott (27), Little (28), and Heimann (29) stimulated a significant literature focused on the principle that countertransference, when properly managed, can be used as a valuable therapeutic tool. The psychiatric literature on this subject emphasizes that ignorance of the countertransference may harm the therapeutic process and the patient.

Pope et al. (30) surveyed 575 psychotherapists and found that 87% (95% men, 76% women) felt sexually attracted to their clients but only 9.4% of men and 2.5% of women acted out such feelings; 63% felt guilty, anxious, or confused about the attraction. This study confirms the axiom that "bad men do what good men dream" (31). Tower (32), who termed these feelings "countertransference anxieties," believed that virtually all therapists experience erotic feelings and impulses toward their patients. The vast majority of respondents (82%) in the above study by Pope et al. never seriously considered sexual involvement with patients. Reasons given for noninvolvement included that therapist-patient sex was unethical, that it would be countertherapeutic and exploitative, that it was unprofessional, that it was against the therapist's values because of present commitment to a relationship, and that censure and loss of reputation might ensue.

The issue of patient transference and competency to consent to a sexual relationship with the therapist sometimes arises in the context of undue-familiarity litigation (25). Although a patient's transference toward the therapist does not prevent the patient from *understanding* that a sexual relationship is taking place with the therapist, transference reactions may impair the patient's ability to *appreciate* that severe psychic injury will likely result from therapist-patient sex. Patient consent, however, is not the issue. It is the breach of fiduciary trust by the therapist who engages the patient in sex that is the appropriate focus of wrongdoing.

A significant number of sexual misconduct cases are not the result of the mishandling of transference or countertransference. Psychotherapists with malignant character disorders manifesting severe narcissistic, borderline, antisocial, or deviant character traits entice patients to have sexual relations with them (see Tables 10–7 and 10–8). Analogously, patients with severe character disorders may attempt to seduce or entrap therapists into a sexual relationship. Patients who have been abused in the past will likely test treatment boundaries. Nevertheless, the therapist is expected to maintain treatment boundaries with these difficult patients. Patients who are victims of sexual exploitation are not to blame for their therapists' sexual misconduct. Patients do not enter therapy in order to have sex with their therapists.

Sexual Relationships With Patients Whose Therapy Has Been Terminated

The tenet "once a patient, always a patient," represents a prudent clinical position. When patients terminate therapy, a positive trans-

---

TABLE 10–7.   Therapists at risk for exploiting patients

Character disordered	Impaired
Borderline	Alcohol
Narcissistic	Drugs
Antisocial	Mental illness
Sexually disordered	**Situational reactors**
Frotteurism	Marital discord
Pedophilia	Loss of important relationships
Sexual sadism	Professional crisis
Incompetent	
Poorly trained	
Persistent boundary blind spots	

TABLE 10–8.   Personality profile of a "typical" sexually involved therapist

Age	40s to 50s
Sex	Male
Family constellation	Teenage children, troubled marriage
Medical symptoms	Chronic, not life-threatening
Psychological symptoms	Depression, sleep disturbances, alcohol and drug abuse
Professional practice	"Burned out," ungratifying
Nature of patient	Recent loss, dependent, "object hungry"

ference may help sustain their psychological stability for a lifetime. A posttreatment relationship with the therapist, even a social relationship, may inflame old conflicts that can destabilize the patient. Furthermore, patients may need subsequent treatment during the course of their lives. A therapists' availability during a crisis can be critically important to former patients. Therapists should consider adopting a "closed door policy" that recognizes that once a patient walks through the therapist's door, it is closed forever to a personal relationship. *The Principles of Medical Ethics With Annotations Especially Applicable to Psychiatry* states that "sexual activity with a current or former patient is unethical" (10, Section 2, Annotation 1).

Currently, a few states have enacted statutes that impose civil liability on psychotherapists who engage in sex with former patients (33). Some states statutorily limit the period of time after treatment ends (usually 1 or 2 years) for which a psychotherapist may be held legally liable for sexual involvement with a former patient. Because approximately 98% of sexual involvements with patients occur within a year of clinical contact, the prohibitionary period established by statute will likely encompass most instances of posttermination sex (8). In California, a therapist will not be subject to civil liability if he or she has a sexual relationship with a former patient 2 years after termination (34). Minnesota also has a 2-year posttermination period precluding therapist-patient sex (35). Illinois' statute (36) is identical to that of Minnesota except that the period of prohibition is 1 year. Wisconsin (37) has a civil statute making sex with a former patient legally actionable for an unlimited period of time. In Florida, it is always actionable to have sex with a patient, whether the therapy is current or terminated (38). Texas prohibits any sexual contact with a former patient for 2 years following termination of treatment (39). However, in Texas, there is no time period after which the therapist will be immune from civil liability for sex with a former patient who is emotionally dependent on the therapist.

Although it may not be illegal for the psychotherapist to have sex with a former patient after expiration of a prohibition period, it still may be unethical. For example, the patient may not have had a therapeutic termination, but rather an interrupted therapy. Ethical violations involving sex with former patients often signal the likely presence of other basic deviations in care that also may have harmed the patient while in treatment. Moreover, therapists who entertain the possibility of a posttreatment sexual relationship usually communicate this attitude.

Appelbaum and Jorgenson (40) have proposed a 1-year waiting period after termination that "should minimize problems and allow former patients and therapists to enter into intimate relationships." If adopted, this policy would likely disrupt treatment boundaries from the outset. What deviations in treatment boundaries would occur if the therapist, from the very beginning of treatment, views the patient as a potential sexual partner? Would the therapy turn into a tryst and become a courtship? Would the course of therapy be prematurely shortened in order to get to the sexual relationship? Even if therapist-patient sex does not take place, maintaining the option of having sex with the patient would likely lead to boundary violations that could harm the patient. Clinically, it is untenable for a therapist to think that he or she can maintain appropriate treatment boundaries while, at the same time, holding out the possibility of having sex with the patient in the future. From the very beginning of treatment, the most credible therapist position remains "once a patient, always a patient."

Management of the Sexually Exploited Patient

Reporting Sexual Misconduct

Reporting the alleged sexual misconduct of other therapists based on the statements of patients is fraught with complex clinical, ethical, and professional dilemmas. Requiring mandatory reporting may create serious double-agent roles for therapists that can undermine treatment interventions with an exploited patient. Some states have mandatory reporting requirements (41). In most states with reporting requirements involving therapist-patient sex, reporting may not proceed without the patient's consent.

Clinical flexibility, not rigidity, is required in the treatment and management of sexually exploited patients. When the patient is a therapist who reports that he or she is exploiting patients, does a *Tarasoff* duty arise to warn and protect the therapist's other patients from potential or actual abuse? The conflicting ethical issues surrounding breaching confidentiality as well as potential *Tarasoff* duties arising from the discovery of an offending therapist's *continuing* sexual exploitation are discussed elsewhere (2).

Ethics

The Principles of Medical Ethics advises psychiatrists to "strive to expose those physicians deficient in character or competence" (10, Section 2). In addition, reporting laws that exist in some states require physicians to report impaired colleagues. The burden of reporting information about impaired physicians is most often placed on health care institutions. However, a number of states place the duty directly on the physician, although this duty varies greatly (42). The psychiatrist is placed in a conflicting position, because he or she must also maintain patient confidentiality under moral, ethical, and legal requirements.

This conflict is heightened if a requirement to report abuse collides with a patient's desire that no such disclosure be made. Most reporting statutes require the patient's consent before a report is made to the authorities. Reporting statutes may not contain immunity provisions protecting the reporting therapist against suit. Forensic and legal consultations may be necessary in these difficult situations.

Discovery of Sexual Misconduct

The most common way a psychiatrist discovers sexual misconduct is by a patient's report of sexual involvement with the previous therapist. Less commonly, patient sexual exploitation may be reported by the offending therapist who enters treatment either because of sexual involvement with a patient or for other reasons. Not too long ago, such reports from patients were considered to be either transference distortions or outright psychotic transferences. Patients were not only disbelieved but also blamed when they became sexually involved with therapists. Today, professional concern and awareness of the problem of sexual misconduct is very high. In fact, the pendulum has swung so far in the other direction that even the denials of an innocent therapist accused of sexual misconduct tend to be disbelieved. Untruthful protestations of innocence by an offending therapist are usually belied by evidence of involvement, such as numerous boundary violations combined with letters, pictures, and telephone and motel/hotel records.

The Patient's Critical Need for Therapy

Some clinicians recommend that the psychiatrist who hears about patient-therapist sex take a strong position as an advocate for the sexually abused patient because sexually exploitative therapists tend to be repeaters. Nevertheless, a strong clinical argument can be made for the position of strict therapist neutrality (2). This position does not imply an avoidance of professional responsibility or a shunning posture toward the patient. It must be remembered that the patient has concluded a relationship with a therapist in which both the therapist and the patient acted out their problems together. The patient has been emotionally devastated and is now in even greater need of treatment.

The new focus with the subsequent therapist must be on the reestablishment of trust and the development of a therapeutic alliance; otherwise, no treatment can take place. The patient needs to understand the psychological significance of the sexual involvement with the previous therapist. When psychiatrists become advocates for their patients, they again engage these patients through action. If treatment is to succeed, the patient needs less action and more time to think, feel, and reflect. Litigation can be just another way of acting out for both patient and therapist. For example, the patient may initiate litigation as a way of maintaining contact with the previous therapist. A therapist's personal agenda may underlie his or her recommendation that the patient pursue litigation.

Avoiding Double Agentry

Whether the patient should take action against the former therapist should be first addressed as a treatment issue. Therapist neutrality should not be misconstrued as a professional conspiracy to maintain silence. The patient may justifiably fear endangering his or her marriage, profession, or children by reporting therapist sexual misconduct. The patient must also ultimately decide whether he or she is in a position to face the emotional burdens of an ethical complaint procedure or litigation. The law—with its inevitable adversarial tone, financial strain, accusations of guilt, and agonizing procedural delays—is a blunt instrument. As sometimes occurs, the patient initially may not wish to seek redress for a variety of reasons, including a sense of guilt or shame, as well as continuation of feelings of love and yearning for the previous therapist.

A double-agent role arises if the patient is burdened with an adversarial procedure because of the therapist's need to vent personal outrage or to advocate the profession's need to police its own ranks. Moreover, a patient may be unable to express hostile feelings toward the new therapist when the latter has taken on an advocacy role for the patient. Accordingly, therapy should be kept as free as possible from double-agent roles by the new therapist. The new therapist must keep in mind that it is the patient who has been victimized, not the therapist. Therefore, the therapist must be able to acknowledge and control his or her personal feelings toward the previous therapist's alleged transgressions in order not to interfere with the patient's treatment.

Abused patients have been revictimized by subsequent therapists who have attempted to undo the trauma caused by the initial sexual exploitation. A common scenario occurs when the therapist bends over backward to try to prove his or her trustworthiness to the patient. As a consequence, serious, damaging boundary violations have occurred.

Guilty or Innocent?

The therapist who acts as an advocate for the patient also needs to ponder other critical issues. In a court of law, there is a presumption of innocence that must be overcome through the adversarial process, which provides for equal representation and other procedural safeguards. Psychiatrists who abandon a position of neutrality when given information about therapist sexual misconduct may assume the role of judge or jury. Clinical experience demonstrates that some patients can develop powerful, eroticized, psychotic transferences that contain the delusion of sexual involvement with their therapists. Reports of false claims of sexual misconduct against mental health professionals are rare but are expected to increase (43). Presumably, clinical judgment will differentiate fact from fiction, but is this always possible? There are also vindictive, antisocial persons who may wish to malign a therapist with charges of sexual involvement because of actual or perceived slights or grievances.

Forensic Consultation

Stone (44) provided a useful recommendation for the new therapist faced with a patient alleging sexual exploitation by a former therapist. He advised using a forensic consultant familiar with legal and ethical issues. Such a referral may help patients who cannot resolve their difficulties solely within the therapy. Also, some patients may not be able to tolerate therapist neutrality, perceiving such a stance as condemnatory or rejecting. The consultant may wish to take a more active advocacy position if this is acceptable to the patient. The extent to which a consultant may facilitate or even hinder the patient's therapeutic progress remains problematic. If reporting requirements exist, the forensic consultant may be able to fulfill this duty, thus sparing the therapist from undertaking a double-agent role with the patient.

Therapy or Litigation?

Will the patient be additionally burdened by the kinds of feelings and conflicts that are often triggered by litigation? Will the legal process mask feelings and conflicts that can only be worked out in the peace and quiet of an unperturbed treatment situation? Litigation and psychotherapy rarely mix.

Nevertheless, some therapists believe that there is therapeutic value for a patient in pursuing a lawsuit—that is, in overcoming helplessness, expressing anger and revenge, and resolving trauma. The emotional cost, however, may be high because of the almost inevitable humiliation, scrutiny of the patient's private life by opposing counsel, and a further sense of assault and trauma inflicted by the adversarial process (45). Can the patient concentrate on the therapeutic work at hand with the new therapist, or will she or he be constantly upset and distracted by the legal storm that will inevitably develop when the claim is contested? Unfortunately, some patients may have to choose between initiating litigation and receiving treatment. In addition, the new therapist is rarely free from the conflicting agenda of treatment versus litigation.

Malpractice Insurance

Malpractice insurance coverage is defined by what *is* as well as what *is not* said in the insurance policy. Many insurance carriers will not insure for sexual misconduct, excluding it as an intentional tort or criminal action. The rationale is that such behavior is not professional practice and therefore cannot be malpractice. In some malpractice policies, the psychiatrist may be able to obtain coverage for the costs of litigation but not for damages. Other carriers will insure the therapist only if the charges of sexual misconduct are denied. The APA's position of discouraging sexual misconduct has led to dropping coverage for undue familiarity from its member malpractice insurance plan. Since May 1, 1985, the plan no longer pays claims for undue familiarity, but continues to provide a legal defense of up to $100,000. In order for legal expenses to be covered, the charge of sexual involvement with the patient must be denied. Otherwise, no basis for a defense exists.

Prevention

A number of prevention options are available to the therapist who is becoming personally involved with a patient:

1. It is critically important to recognize erosion of the therapist's treatment position. This may occur when the therapist begins to think that the patient's sexual feelings are directed toward him or her personally rather than created by the role of the therapist.

2. Therapists must be able to recognize early boundary violations through application of the principle of abstinence. The therapist's gratifications come from the enjoyment of the therapeutic process and the psychological growth of the patient rather than directly from the patient.

3. If sexual feelings are impairing the therapist's ability to properly treat the patient, or if sexual feelings threaten to be acted out, the patient must be referred immediately.

4. Therapist involvement with a patient usually occurs gradually rather than suddenly. Sufficient time is ordinarily present to obtain help. If progressive boundary violations are occurring that cannot be therapeutically rectified, the patient must be immediately referred.

5. A trusted colleague should be consulted who, perhaps acting as a mentor, can restore perspective.

6. Practitioners who prescribe psychotherapy or analysis for others should seriously consider such treatment for themselves, especially when serious personal difficulties with patients arise.

7. Therapist humility is essential. Some patients may present special difficulties and personal problems for the therapist. Limitations of the therapist's ability to treat certain patients should be forthrightly acknowledged. It is a strength rather than a weakness to admit that one has personal and psychotherapeutic limitations. These patients should be referred.

8. If the therapist is stricken by the physical beauty or attractive personal qualities of a new patient, consideration should be given to immediate referral. The initial "Where have you been all my life?" reaction to a patient is a certain sign of future trouble. Psychotherapy is difficult enough without such burdensome feelings.

9. It is essential to acknowledge that mishandling of the transference is an occupational hazard for all psychotherapists.

10. Countertransference-driven parental roles with patients are doomed to fail. Attempts at reparenting patients do not cure; they merely cast a spell. The task of therapy is not to create an illusion of well-being but to help patients mourn their losses and move on with their lives (25). Omar Khayyam's powerful passage from *The Rubaiyat* (46, stanza 71) reminds us that we cannot rewrite our histories:

> *The Moving Finger writes; and having writ*
> *Moves on: nor all your Piety nor Wit*
> *Shall lure it back to cancel half a Line,*
> *Nor all your Tears wash out a Word of it.*

11. When a therapist attempts to parent the patient, a variety of boundary violations often occur that usually damage treatment. Patient exploitation also may be an unintended consequence of the therapist's reparenting role as she or he becomes hopelessly enmeshed in the patient's life.

The specialty of psychiatry can be a lonely, difficult, isolated profession. Solo practitioners may have infrequent contact with colleagues. A full life acts as a buffer against temptations to exploit patients by providing the therapist with personal gratifications outside of therapy. Love relationships, friends, hobbies, recreation, and physical activities may help vulnerable therapists to resist the tendency to live for or with their patients.

■ REFERENCES

1. MINN STAT ANN § 148A.02 (West Supp 1989)
2. Simon RI: Clinical Psychiatry and the Law, 2nd Edition. Washington, DC, American Psychiatric Press, 1992
3. Bisbing SB, Jorgenson LM, Sutherland PK: Sexual Abuse by Professionals: A Legal Guide. Charlottesville, VA, Michie, 1995, pp 833–855

4. Appelbaum PS: Statutes regulating patient-therapist sex. Hospital and Community Psychiatry 41:15–16, 1990; see also Strasburger LH, Jorgenson L, Randles R: Criminalization of psychotherapist-patient sex. Am J Psychiatry 148:859–863, 1991

5. Bisbing SB, Jorgenson LM, Sutherland PK: Sexual Abuse by Professionals: A Legal Guide. Charlottesville, VA, Michie, 1995, pp 155–179

6. Schoener GR, Milgrom JH, Gonsiorek JC, et al: Psychotherapists' Sexual Involvement With Clients: Intervention and Prevention. Minneapolis, MN, Walk-In Counseling Center, 1989, p 331

7. WIS STAT ANN § 225(2) (Supp 1982)

8. Gartrell N, Herman J, Olarte S, et al: Psychiatrist-patient sexual contact—results of a national survey, I: prevalence. Am J Psychiatry 143:1126–1131, 1986

9. Borys DS, Pope KS: Dual relationships between therapist and client: a national study of psychologists, psychiatrists, and social workers. Professional Psychology: Research and Practice 20:283–293, 1989

10. American Psychiatric Association: The Principles of Medical Ethics With Annotations Especially Applicable to Psychiatry. Washington, DC, American Psychiatric Association, 1998

11. Keeton W, Dobbs D, Keeton R, et al: Prosser and Keeton on Torts, 5th Edition. St Paul, MN, West Publishing, 1984, § 32, p 187

12. ILL ANN STAT ch 70, para 802 (Smith-Hurd 1989); Wis STAT ANN § 895.70 (West 1989); CAL CIV CODE § 43.93(b) (West Supp 1990); MINN STAT ANN § 148 A.02 (West 1986)

13. Jorgenson L, Randles R, Strasburger LH: The furor over psychotherapist-patient sexual contact: new solutions to old problems. William and Mary Law Review 32:645–732, 1991

14. Simon RI: The natural history of therapist sexual misconduct: identification and prevention. Psychiatric Annals 25:90–94, 1995

15. Simon RI: Sexual exploitation of patients: how it begins before it happens. Psychiatric Annals 19:104–112, 1989

16. Simon RI: Psychological injury caused by boundary violation precursors to therapist-patient sex. Psychiatric Annals 21: 614–619, 1991

17. Pope KS: Sexual Involvement With Therapists: Patient Assessment, Subsequent Therapy, Forensics. Washington, DC, American Psychological Association, 1994, pp 152–153

18. Simon RI: Sexual misconduct in the therapist-patient relationship, in Forensic Psychiatry: A Comprehensive Textbook. Edited by Rosner R. New York, Chapman and Hall, 1994, pp 154–161

19. The College of Physicians and Surgeons of Ontario: The Final Report of the Task Force on Sexual Abuse of Patients: An Independent Task Force Commissioned by The College of Physicians and Surgeons of Ontario. Ontario, Canada, November 25, 1991

20. Simon RI: Treatment boundary violations: clinical, ethical, and legal considerations. Bulletin of the American Academy of Psychiatry and the Law 20:269–288, 1992

21. Furrow BR: Malpractice in Psychotherapy. Lexington, MA, Lexington Books, 1980, pp 33–36

22. Epstein RS, Simon RI: The Exploitation Index: an early warning indicator of boundary violations in psychotherapy. Bull Menninger Clin 54:450–465, 1990

23. Epstein RS, Simon RI, Kay GG: Assessing boundary violations in psychotherapy: survey results with the Exploitation Index. Bull Menninger Clin 56:1–17, 1992

24. Gutheil TG, Simon RI: Between the chair and the door: boundary issues in the therapeutic "transition zone." Harv Rev Psychiatry 2:336–340, 1995

25. Simon RI: Transference in therapist-patient sex: the illusion of patient improvement and consent, part 1. Psychiatric Annals 24:509–515, 1994; Simon RI: Transference in therapist-patient sex: the illusion of patient improvement and consent, part 2. Psychiatric Annals 24:561–565, 1994

26. Freud S: Observations on transference-love (1914), in The Standard Edition of the Complete Psychological Works of Sig-

mund Freud, Vol 12. Translated and edited by Strachey J. London, Hogarth Press, 1968, pp 159–171

27. Winnicott D: Hate in the countertransference. Int J Psychoanal 30:69–75, 1949

28. Little M: Countertransference and the patient's response to it. Int J Psychoanal 32:32–40, 1951

29. Heimann P: On countertransference. Int J Psychoanal 31: 81–84, 1950

30. Pope KS, Keith-Spiegel P, Tabachnick BG: Sexual attraction to clients. Am Psychol 41:147–158, 1986

31. Simon RI: Bad Men Do What Good Men Dream: A Forensic Psychiatrist Illuminates the Darker Side of Human Behavior. Washington DC, American Psychiatric Press, 1996

32. Tower LE: Countertransference. J Am Psychoanal Assoc 4:224–255, 1956

33. Bisbing SB, Jorgenson LM, Sutherland PK: Sexual Abuse by Professionals: A Legal Guide. Charlottesville, VA, Michie, 1995, pp 755–756

34. CAI CIV CODE §43.93 (Deering 1987)

35. MINN STAT ANN § 148A.02 (West 1989)

36. ILL STAT ANN ch 70, §801 (Smith-Hurd Supp 1989)

37. Wis STAT ANN §893.585, 895.70(2) (West 1989)

38. FLA STAT ANN §458.329, 331 (West Supp 1986)

39. Tex Penal Code Ann §21.14(d) (West 1993)

40. Appelbaum PS, Jorgenson L: Psychotherapist-patient sexual contact after termination of treatment: an analysis and a proposal. Am J Psychiatry 148:1466–1473, 1991

41. Bisbing SB, Jorgenson LM, Sutherland PK: Sexual Abuse by Professionals: A Legal Guide. Charlottesville, VA, Michie, 1995, pp 168–169

42. Petty S: The impaired physician: a failed healer. Legal Aspects of Medical Practice 12:5–8, 1984

43. Schoener GR, Milgrom JH, Gonsiorek JC, et al: Psychotherapists' Sexual Involvement With Clients: Intervention and Prevention. Minneapolis, MN, Walk-In Counseling Center, 1989, pp 147–155

44. Stone AA: Law, Psychiatry, and Morality. Washington, DC, American Psychiatric Press, 1984, pp 191–216

45. Schafran LH: Sexual harassment cases in the courts, or therapy goes to war: supporting a sexual harassment victim during litigation, in Sexual Harassment in the Workplace and Academia. Edited by Shrier DK. Washington, DC, American Psychiatric Press, 1996, pp 133–152

46. Omar Khayyam: The Rubaiyat, stanza 71

Appendix A

SUGGESTED READINGS

American Psychiatric Association: The Principles of Medical Ethics With Annotations Especially Applicable to Psychiatry. Washington, DC, American Psychiatric Association, 1998

Alexander GJ, Scheflin AW: Law and Mental Disorder. Durham, NC, Carolina Academic Press, 1998

Appelbaum PS: Almost a Revolution: Mental Health Law and the Limits of Change. New York, Oxford University Press, 1994

Appelbaum PS, Gutheil TG: Clinical Handbook of Psychiatry and the Law, 3rd Edition. Baltimore, MD, Williams and Wilkins, 2000

Beck JC (ed): Confidentiality Versus the Duty to Protect: Foreseeable Harm in the Practice of Psychiatry. Washington, DC, American Psychiatric Press, 1990

Lazarus A (ed): Controversies in Managed Mental Health Care. Washington, DC, American Psychiatric Press, 1996

Lifson LE, Simon RI (eds): The Mental Health Professional and the Law: A Comprehensive Handbook. Cambridge, MA, Harvard University Press, 1998

Monahan J, Steadman HJ (eds): Violence and Mental Disorder: Developments in Risk Assessment. Chicago, IL, University of Chicago Press, 1994

Pope KS: Sexual Involvement With Therapists: Patient Assessment, Subsequent Therapy, Forensics. Washington, DC, American Psychological Association, 1994

Rosner R (ed): Principles and Practice of Forensic Psychiatry. New York, Chapman and Hall, 1994

Schoener GR, Milgrom JH, Gonsiorek JC, et al: Psychotherapists' Sexual Involvement With Clients. Minneapolis, MN, Walk-In Counseling Center, 1989

Simon RI: Clinical Psychiatry and the Law, 2nd Edition. Washington, DC, American Psychiatric Press, 1992

Simon RI, Sadoff RL: Psychiatric Malpractice: Cases and Comments for Clinicians. Washington, DC, American Psychiatric Press, 1992

Simon RI, Shuman DW: Predicting the Past: The Retrospective Psychiatric Assessment of Mental States in Litigation. Washington, DC, American Psychiatric Press, 2001

Slovenko R: Psychotherapy and Confidentiality: Testimonial Privileged Communication, Breach of Confidentiality, and Reporting Duties. Springfield, IL, C. Thomas, 1998

Tardiff K: Concise Guide to Assessment and Management of Violent Patients, 3rd Edition. Washington, DC, American Psychiatric Press, 1996

Appendix B

GLOSSARY OF LEGAL TERMS

Action   See *civil action.*

Adjudication   The formal pronouncement of a judgment or decree in a cause of action.

Assault   Any willful attempt or threat to inflict injury.

Battery   Intentional and wrongful physical contact with an individual without consent that causes some injury or offensive touching.

Beyond a reasonable doubt   The level of proof required to convict a person in a criminal trial. This is the highest level of proof required (90%–95% range of certainty).

Breach of contract   A violation of or failure to perform any or all of the terms of an agreement.

Brief   A written statement prepared by legal counsel arguing a case.

Burden of proof   The legal obligation to prove affirmatively a disputed fact (or facts) related to an issue that is raised by the parties in a case.

Capacity   The status or attributes necessary for a person so that his or her acts may be legally allowed and recognized.

Case law   The aggregate of reported cases as forming a body of law on a particular subject.

Cause of action   The grounds of an action (those facts that, if alleged and proved in a suit, would enable the plaintiff to attain a judgment).

Civil action   A lawsuit brought by a private individual or group to recover money or property, to enforce or protect a civil right, or to prevent or redress a civil wrong.

Clear and convincing   Proof that results in reasonable certainty of the truth of an ultimate fact in controversy (75% range of certainty). For example, the minimum level of evidence necessary to involuntarily hospitalize a patient.

Common law   A system of law based on customs, traditional usage, and prior case law rather than codified written laws (statutes).

Compensatory damages   Damages awarded to a person as compensation, indemnity, or restitution for harm sustained.

Competency   Having the mental capacity to understand the nature of an act.

Consent decree   Agreement by defendant to cease activities asserted as illegal by the government.

Consortium   The right of a husband or wife to the care, affection, company, and cooperation of the other spouse in every aspect of the marital relationship.

Contract   A legally enforceable agreement between two or more parties to do or not do a particular thing upon sufficient consideration.

Criminal law   The branch of the law that defines crimes and provides for their punishment. Unlike civil law, penalties include imprisonment.

Damages   A sum of money awarded to a person injured by the unlawful act or negligence of another.

Defendant   A person or legal entity against whom a claim or charge is brought.

Due process (of law)   The constitutional guarantee protecting individuals from arbitrary and unreasonable actions by the government that would deprive them of their basic rights to life, liberty, or property.

Duress   Compulsion or constraint, as by force or threat, exercised to make a person do or say something against his or her will.

Duty   Legal obligation that one person owes another. Whenever one person has a right, another person has a corresponding duty to preserve or not interfere with that right.

False imprisonment   The unlawful restraint or detention of one person by another.

Fiduciary   A person who acts for another in a capacity that involves a confidence or trust.

Forensic psychiatry   A subspecialty of psychiatry in which scientific and clinical expertise is applied to legal issues in legal contexts embracing civil, criminal, correctional or legislative matters.

Fraud   Any act of trickery, deceit, or misrepresentation designed to deprive someone of property or to do harm.

Guardianship   A legal arrangement wherein one individual (the guardian) possesses the legal right and duty to care for another individual (the ward) and his or her property.

Immunity   Freedom from duty or penalty.

Incompetence   A lack of ability or fitness for some legal qualification necessary for the performance of an act (e.g., a minor, or mental incompetence).

Informed consent   A competent person's voluntary agreement to allow something to happen that is based upon full disclosure of facts needed to make a knowing decision.

Intentional tort   A tort in which the actor is expressly or implicitly judged to have possessed an intent or purpose to cause injury.

Judgment   The final determination or adjudication by a court of the claims of parties in an action.

Jurisdiction   Widely used to denote the legal right by which courts or judicial officers exercise their authority.

Malpractice   Any professional misconduct or unreasonable lack of skill in professional or fiduciary duties.

***Miranda* warning**   Refers to the *Miranda v. Arizona* decision that requires a four-part warning to be given prior to any custodial interrogation.

Negligence   The failure to exercise the standard of care that would be expected of a normally reasonable and prudent person in a particular set of circumstances.

Nominal damages   Generally, damages of a small monetary amount indicating a violation of a legal right without any important loss or damage to the plaintiff.

Parens patriae   The authority of the state to exercise sovereignty and guardianship of a person of legal disability so as to act on his or her behalf in protecting health, comfort, and welfare interests.

Plaintiff   The complaining party in an action; person who brings a cause of action.

Police power   The power of government to make and enforce all laws and regulations necessary for the welfare of the state and its citizens.

Preponderance of evidence   Superiority in the weight of evidence presented by one side over that of the other (51% range of certainty). The level of certainty required in order to prevail in civil trials.

Privileged communication   Those statements made by certain persons within a protected relationship (e.g., doctor-patient) that the law protects from forced disclosure.

Proximate cause   The direct, immediate cause to which an injury or loss can be attributed and without which the injury or loss would not have occurred.

Proxy   A person empowered by another to represent, act, or vote for him or her.

Punitive damages   Damages awarded over and above those to which the plaintiff is entitled, generally given to punish or make an example of the defendant.

Respondeat superior   The doctrine whereby the master (i.e., employer) is liable in certain cases for the wrongful acts of his or her servants (i.e., employees).

Right   A power, privilege, demand, or claim possessed by a particular person by virtue of law. Every legal right that one person possesses imposes corresponding legal duties on other persons.

Sovereign immunity   The immunity of a government from being sued in court except with its consent.

Standard of care (negligence law)   In the law of negligence, that degree of care which a reasonably prudent person should exercise under the same or similar circumstances.

Stare decisis   To adhere to precedents and not to unsettle principles of law that are established.

Statute An act of the legislature declaring, commanding, or prohibiting something.

Subpoena A writ commanding a person to appear in court.

Subpoena ad testificandum A writ commanding a person to appear in court to give testimony.

Subpoena duces tecum A writ commanding a person to appear in court with particular documents or other evidence.

Tort Any private or civil wrong by act or omission but not including breach of contract.

United States Code (U.S.C.) The compilation of laws derived from federal legislation.

Vicarious liability Indirect legal responsibility (e.g., the liability of an employer for the acts of an employee).

INDEX

*Page numbers printed in **boldface** refer to tables or figures.*

274